ADVANCE PRAISE

"Never say that today's young people are apathetic—as Emily Hunter makes absolutely clear in this great volume, youth are out there in force, trying every creative tactic they can think of to safeguard the planet on which they will live out their lives. The only question is if the rest of us will follow their lead. I know I'm inspired!"

—BILL MCKIBBEN, AUTHOR OF EAARTH, CREATOR OF 350.ORG

"More and more young people are having to give up 'youthful innocence' in pursuit of saving their very future from the hands and decision-makers of those who are destroying it. It is a profoundly powerful testament to these same young people that not only are they willing to do this but that they are doing so with such clarity, commitment, and creativity. This book will break your heart, then inspire you, and hopefully move you into looking at how you can use your life to make a positive difference for the planet and all the life it sustains—now and for future generations."

—JULIA BUTTERFLY HILL, TREE SITTER, ACTIVIST,
AUTHOR OF THE LEGACY OF LUNA

THE NEXT
ECO
WARRIORS

THE NEXT
ECO
WARRIORS

22 YOUNG WOMEN AND MEN WHO ARE SAVING THE PLANET

Editor **Emily Hunter**

Conari Press

First published in 2011 by Conari Press
An imprint of Red Wheel/Weiser, LLC
With offices at:
500 Third Street, Suite 230
San Francisco, CA 94107
www.redwheelweiser.com

ISBN: 978-1-57324-486-2

Library of Congress Cataloging-in-Publication Data

The next eco-warriors : 22 young women and men who are saving the planet / editor, Emily Hunter.
    p. cm.
 Includes bibliographical references and index.
 ISBN 978-1-57324-486-2 (alk. paper)
1. Environmentalists—Biography. I. Hunter, Emily.
 GE55.N49 2011
 333.72092'2—dc22
  [B]
                    2010048431

Cover design by Barb Fisher

Interior design by Maureen Forys, Happenstance Type-O-Rama

Typeset in Karmina Sans, Chalet, Chalet Comprime, and Futura Condensed

Cover photographs: Allana Beltran by Matthew Newton; Enei Begaye by Calvin Johnson; Benjamin Potts by Jo-Anne McArthur; Rob Stewart by Brennan Grange; Tanya Fields by Flonia Telegrafi.

Printed in Canada

TCP

10 9 8 7 6 5 4 3 2 1

Printed on 100% post-consumer recycled paper

To all eco-warriors—
yesterday's, today's, and tomorrow's—
you are my hope.

At its heart, this movement sought to give political form to an awareness that predates Buddhism but is at the same time as new as the science of interdisciplinary ecology. It grew out of a flickering awareness that all our relationships are political, and that the crucial political relationships with which we must concern ourselves now have almost nothing to do with the man's relation to man, but with man's relation to the Earth itself. It is our relationship to our planetary environment, which is the most important issue of all. All human structures inevitably rest upon it.

The time has arrived when we must begin to examine the underlying realities of our relationship to all life around us. . . . Otherwise, in our lifetimes, we shall suffer the enactment of the saga of Genesis: our expulsion from paradise and the fall of nature itself.

—ROBERT HUNTER, *WARRIORS OF THE RAINBOW* (1979)

CONTENTS

ACKNOWLEDGMENTS

THE WORD *ECO-WARRIOR* WAS COINED BY MY FATHER, Robert Hunter, after a Cree Indigenous prophecy called the Warriors of the Rainbow. It is because of original eco-warriors like him that this next generation could exist.

Special thanks to Olivia Scobie, my assistant editor, whose hard work, support, and friendship made this book possible. To my assistant researchers, Marco Oved, Dayna Boyer and Graham F. Scott whose talents made this book shine. To Alisha Sevigny, my literary agent, for taking a chance on a new writer when nobody else would.

To Farley Mowat, for contributing a foreword to this book and whose prose continues to inspire new generations. To my friend and personal hero Paul Watson, who taught me to push the boundaries of activism and never apologize for it. To the crew of Sea Shepherd, who showed me for the first time that the next eco-warriors do exist.

Many thanks to my mother, Bobbi Hunter, who empowers me every day and whose love made it all possible. This world would not be what it is today without you.

And thanks to all the next eco-warriors who submitted writing for this book; you are my hope!

FOREWORD

Farley Mowat

WE ARE CURRENTLY WITNESSING THE MOST SIGNIFICANT conflict ever to engage the human species. It is the conflict between those who possess the means and the will to exploit the living world to destruction and those who are banding together in a desperate and last-ditch attempt to prevent the New Juggernaut from trashing our small planet.

If the right side wins, this combat may become known to future generations as the crusade that rescued the Earth. If the wrong side wins, there will be *no* future generations of humankind, or of innumerable other animals.

> But let's make no mistake, the living world as we know it is dying in our time, and dying quickly.

The struggle is an unequal one. The Big Battalions belong to and are commanded by some of the most powerful individuals and cabals history has ever recorded. Their battle cry is "Progress!" Their arsenals are supplied by Commerce and Industry, misusing Science and Technology. Politics is their handmaiden.

They are now the effective masters of our destiny. They believe they can and will become masters of the planet, if not the universe. Since it is so dominant, this master class is all too well-known to us. However, we know all too little about the forces that oppose it. These are so new, so diverse in character and composition, and present such a confused and kaleidoscopic set of images that we bemusedly lump them into one amorphous aggregation, which we vaguely refer to as the environmental movement.

These opposing forces are in fact the leaders and the rank and file of an army of eco-warriors who are taking it upon themselves to defend our world from despoliation, destruction, and dissolution. Unfortunately, they are almost invisible to the generality of humankind because of the overwhelming communication control exercised by the vested interests, which have the power to literally destroy our living world.

So it is vitally imperative that we become acquainted with the 21st-century eco-activists who are devoting themselves to winning the struggle. We need to sing their praises, celebrate their courage and dedication, make them the icons of our age . . . and support and follow where they lead.

My own hopes for a revival and continuance of life on Earth now turn to this newfound resolution to reassert our indivisibility with life, recognize the obligations incumbent upon us as the most powerful and deadly species ever to exist, and begin making amends for the havoc we have wrought. If we preserve in this new way, we may succeed in making humans humane . . . at last.

This book introduces us to some of these new crusaders, young men and women risking it all for seals, whales, you, and even invisible particles in the atmosphere. Transcending the boundaries of a world conceived as only resources and exploitation to a world streaming with life and vulnerability. They fight for nonhuman animals and elements as if life depended on it—because, in truth, it does. And in the age of despair and apathy, they shake the ground beneath the dominant class, flaunting glimmers of hope to the masses of another world possible.

But let's make no mistake, the living world as we know it is dying in our time, and dying quickly. From my Nova Scotian home, I look over the convergence of sea and land where the North Atlantic heaves against the eastern seaboard of the continent, and in my mind's eye I see it as it was before the arrival of Western humanity:

Pod after pod of spouting whales, the great ones together with the lesser kinds, surge through waters aripple with living tides of fishes. Wheeling multitudes of gannets, kittiwakes, and others such becloud the sky. The stony finger marking the end of the long beach is clustered with resting seals. The beach itself flickers with a restless drift of shorebirds as thick as blowing sand. In the bight of the bay, whose bottom is a metropolis of clams, mussels, and lobsters, a concourse of massive heads emerges among floating islands of eider ducks. The walrus tusks gleam like lambent flames . . .

And then the vision fails, and I behold the world as it is now. In all the vast expanse of sea and sky and fringing land, one gull soars in lonely flight—a single, drifting mote of life upon an enormous and empty stage.

When our forebears commenced their exploitation of this continent, they believed its animate resources were infinite and inexhaustible. The vulnerability of the living fabric that clothes the world—the intricacy and fragility of its all-too-finite parts—was beyond their comprehension. So it can at least be said in their defense that they were mostly ignorant of the inevitable results of their dreadful depredations.

We who are alive today can claim no such exculpation for our biocidal actions and their dire consequences. Modern humanity now has every opportunity to be aware of the complexity and interrelationships of the living world. If ignorance is to serve now as an excuse, then it can only be willful, murderous ignorance.

The hideous results of five centuries of death dealing on this content are not to be gainsaid, but there are at least some indications that we at last are developing the will, and the conscience, to look beyond our own immediate gratification and desires. Belatedly, some part of humankind is trying to rejoin the community of living beings from which we have for so long been alienating ourselves—and of which we have for so long been the mortal enemy.

Evidence of such a return to sanity is not yet to be looked for in attitudes and actions of exploiters who dominate the human world. Rather, the emerging signs of sanity are seen in individuals who, revolted by the frightful excesses to which we have subjected animate creation, are beginning to reject the killer beast that humanity has become.

Banding together with ever-increasing potency, they are challenging the vested interests' self-granted license to continue plundering and savaging the living world for policy, profit, and pleasure. Although they are being furiously opposed by the old order, they may be slowly gaining ground.

Farley Mowat (left) with Emily Hunter.
PHOTO BY BOBBI HUNTER

My own hopes for a revival and continuance of life on Earth now turn to this newfound resolution to reassert our indivisibility with life, recognize the obligations incumbent upon us as the most powerful and deadly species ever to exist, and begin making amends for the havoc we have wrought. If we preserve in this new way, we may succeed in making humans humane ... at last.

INTRODUCTION

IT'S AS IF WE'RE IN A CAR THAT IS BLAZING ALONG. We are on cruise control as we hit a crossroads. We desperately need to make a turn. But instead of slowing down or turning the wheel, we're going full-speed ahead. The passengers are a diverse and knowledgeable bunch, but all we're doing is talking, arguing, and fighting amongst ourselves—no one is making the turn. As we barrel straight forward, what lies ahead of us is the edge of a cliff.

Those of us not in the driver's seat yet bear the most responsibility, for we are the last generations to make any significant change in the direction we take. It's a crippling feeling for many of us. Just as we become conscious of the state of our world, that world is stampeding toward a demise of our own making. It's not that we're apathetic, despite being told that we are. Rather, it's simply that we do not know what to do.

Many believe they don't even exist. Al Gore said to The New York Times *in 2007, "I can't understand why there aren't rings of young people blocking bulldozers and preventing them from constructing coal-fired power plants."*

Our parents before us tried to steer humanity away from the edge decades ago, but here we are ever closer to it. It's certainly not for a lack of trying on their part. They did, after all, create an environmental revolution in the 20th century, full of civil disobedience and consciousness changing that shifted Westerners' relationship to the planet.

But their movement dwindled and grew old as they did. Their tactics rarely work anymore; their faces and voices rarely connect with us; and their stories, though still inspiring, are not our own.

We need revolutionaries now more desperately than ever. With the tipping point we face from climate change, as well as an assortment of global issues, the world is calling out for the next eco-warriors.

Many believe they don't even exist. Al Gore said to *The New York Times* in 2007, "I can't understand why there aren't rings of young people blocking bulldozers and preventing them from constructing coal-fired power plants."

It's a disappointing sentiment, shared by many. Yet it's also the inspiration for this book: because I know the doubters are wrong. For at the same time when Gore made that comment, a group of young people had already started blocking bulldozers, and many more would follow. The next eco-warriors are here. They are alive and kicking.

This war is being fought against the misinformers, denialists, and old guard of the fossil fuel regime that care only about profit, even at the expense of shortening our time here on Earth.

There is little dialogue about them, however, so it's no surprise few seem to know of their existence. This must change. For as a collective, they represent a new movement in the 21st century. It's a global movement, not just a Western green movement. It is a movement that is evolving beyond banner waving into a colorful mosaic of change. And it is a movement that is redefining the word *activism*.

The word activist is no longer held hostage to mean only a protester or an "eco-terrorist" (though these forms of activism still have their place). Instead, the next eco-warriors embrace a technicolor rainbow of strategic tactics. They use an assortment of their own talents, skills, and abilities (in some cases, paid work) to stimulate the engines of social change.

Furthermore, instead of adopting the limited notion that only those on top of the power pyramid can change the world—leaders such as president

Barack Obama—this new movement reminds us that the world of revolution is open to anyone and everyone who wants to make a substantial difference. After all, it's usually people at the bottom who make the greatest change.

It is also a movement that is as diverse as nature itself. It is people from around the world who are shifting minds, policies, and the axes of old tyrannies. No longer is this movement owned and operated by the global North. Instead, it's pushing boundaries, becoming a movement for all of us, managed by multifaceted cultures and peoples from the farthest corners of the Earth.

The faces of this movement include people like Enei Begaye, a Diné woman who is changing what is possible for her Navajo community in Arizona, from coal jobs to green jobs; Wen Bo, a Chinese student who dared to become an eco-activist just after the Tiananmen Square massacre; American Elizabeth Redmond, who is reinventing renewable technology by using our feet to generate power; Kevin Ochieng, a Kenyan youth who is leading a climate movement with underprivileged youth across Africa; and New York City native Tanya Fields, who resists oppression through guerilla gardening.

Together they fight an eco-war. But let's not be shy about it—it is a war.

But it doesn't have to be this way. We can turn away from that edge. There is still time left—though precious little, and less every day. Some of us are trying to do this by pledging to be this new generation of eco-warriors, fighting for something better.

It is a war for the last of the Amazon rainforest. It is a war to end our own grave digging in coal and oil mining. It is a war to defend the people caught in the cross fires of industrial pulverization. It is a war to defend the rights to life for nonhumans. And it is a war for the creation of a new world, one with renewable energy and a sustainable economy.

This war is being fought against the misinformers, denialists, and old guard of the fossil fuel regime that care only about profit, even at the expense of shortening our time here on Earth.

In short, it is a war for survival.

I believe it is appropriate to think of it as a war. Climate change alone is probably the greatest challenge humans have ever faced throughout our entire existence. The challenge is so great because the battle is not with external enemies but a war within ourselves. It is a war where we must stop ourselves in time to survive ourselves, with the planet as we know it hanging in the balance.

Our weapons for this battle are *not* daggers, firearms, or nukes but tools for social change, such as "mind bombs" of consciousness raising, energy alternatives, creativity to breed new solutions, and our fiery spirits for justice that brings humanity to new horizons. And the warriors themselves are not unwilling conscripts but willing participants who want to make a better world even in the face of great personal sacrifice, risks, and even at times personal endangerment.

This eco-war I speak of may seem of mythic proportions, yet it is the stark reality we must face, that we are in time of a war—a war for the planet and a war for ourselves. I think many of us know this ugly reality one way or another: we can feel the crumbling of the edge beneath our feet. We feel it with almost daily news of "weird" weather events like the flooding of Pakistan, the raging

PHOTO BY EMILY HUNTER

fires of Russia or the vanishing poles. It can make you feel as if the show is already over (for some of us, over before it even really began).

But it doesn't have to be this way. We can turn away from that edge. There is still time left—though precious little, and less every day. Some of us are trying to do this by pledging to be this new generation of eco-warriors, fighting for something better.

Therefore, in this book, I share with you the stories of men and women who have taken up this battle. This is by no means a *how-to guide* to save the planet: social change was never brought about through manuals or step-by-steps. Activism is a deeply personal journey and cannot be condensed into something so simplistic. Instead, many before me and many after me will note that the x factor for social change is storytelling. Stories are what have shaped our world and continue to shape it, whether through books, movies, or folktelling. And in continuing this effort of storytelling, this book provides just that: Stories from the next eco-warriors. Stories that attempt to reclaim hope in a world that seems to have very little.

These are the stories of the next eco-warriors. Read it, and know that this is your revolution too.

—*EMILY HUNTER*

THE NEXT
ECO
WARRIORS

EMILY HUNTER

▶ Twenty-six ▶ Canada ▶ Media Frontliner

PHOTO BY VANESSA LARKEY

Not the End, Just the Beginning!

Never believe that a few caring people can't change the world. For, indeed, that's all who ever have.

—*MARGARET MEAD*

THE CLOCK HAD JUST STRUCK MIDNIGHT. I stood in an empty warehouse. The lights were flickering, telling me to leave. A cleaning crew began sweeping up around me, from the mess of thousands of people before. Chairs and tables were being packed in. And a winter's breeze flew in, chilling my skin.

It was over.

I could hardly believe it. I couldn't accept the end. My body began trembling, and my heart ached. A friend tried showing me the exit door, but I didn't want to leave. I couldn't mentally grapple with it all. I kept looking up at a TV screen showcasing an empty room that held the negotiations. Hoping someone would come up to the podium and tell me the happy ending of this story.

But the happy ending wasn't coming.

It was a cold winter's night in 2009, the last day of the Copenhagen Climate Summit, an event that had been pitted as our "best and last chance" in the battle against climate change. Nearly two hundred heads of state had converged to finally tackle our impending *thermageddon*, with the United States leading the march.

There were forty-six thousand delegates from around the world participating in the summit to influence the leaders' decision, thousands more on the streets to protest if they made the wrong decision. Maybe even more important, the world was watching. All eyes were on Copenhagen and how it would unfold our climate's future. This was the *it* moment . . . and we lost it.

As I stood there in an activist convergence house on that final hour, I was grasping for hope. Hope that what became secret negotiations of a few individuals deciding the fate of the planet would spark something more than pure failure. But with silence in the room, I was beginning to know better. Hope was nothing more than a distant dream.

THINKING BACK TO MY FATHER, I felt as if I had failed him most of all. Five years earlier, I was in a hospital, staring death in the face—my dad's face. He was sweating bullets, just lying there, not moving an inch in the hospital bed. I couldn't seem to wet the cloth and wipe his forehead fast enough. These were the last moments I had with him. He was dying from a terminal cancer.

I had so much that I wanted to ask him before he left us. I wanted to carry on his eco-crusade into the next generation, but I needed to know how. Yet he couldn't say a word to me; he was unconscious and slipping by the second. I kept asking myself: Why him? Why now?

His name was Robert Hunter, and he was nothing short of a visionary and a leader. As a cofounder and the first president of Greenpeace, he was an unsung hero who was part of a band of individuals that began the modern-day environmental movement in the 1970s.

But to me, he was Dad. I used to skip school to hang around him in his cabin as he typed away, writing his books and articles outdoors. We would chat, with our heads lying on the grass, eyes wide open and staring at the sky, contemplating the cosmos, the meaning of life, and just how damn fucking lucky we were to be on this beautiful blue planet. He was my teacher, my guru, my best friend. And it seemed as if he was going away now when the Earth needed him most . . . when I needed him most.

Then there it was, his last breath. A last exhale, and it was all over. It was the end of him, the end of our relationship, and the end of an era.

AROUND THE TIME OF MY DAD'S ILLNESS, he had sent me on my first environmental campaign. I had traveled the world on my own and was sickened with what I had seen. It was the same old story anywhere I went: rapid development for the pursuit of jumping on an economic steam engine headed nowhere but to a mystical "progress" land, all at the cost of hacking the planet and killing people.

I had seen a man on a bicycle run over by a speeding truck in Guangzhou, China, because he literally couldn't keep up with development. I had seen one of the most beautiful places on Earth: heaven with waterfalls, crystal-clear water and life in all forms streaming from the island of Phi Phi, Thailand, and at the same time, its rape by mass-market tourism. I had seen a perpetual sunset in the sky in Irkutsk, Russia, from impenetrable smog. And I had seen enough; I knew I didn't want to just watch it any longer.

Knowing I was pulsing with a desire to fight, my father bought me a one-way ticket to the west end of Canada to jump on the ship belonging to his old pal Paul Watson. Paul's vessel was called the M/V *Farley Mowat,* and he ran his organization the Sea Shepherd out of the nuts-and-bolts boat. The *Farley,* as I came to call her, looked as if it was falling apart, but yet it was this ship that helped build the organization's reputation for being pirates for the oceans. Known for ramming other vessels and being taken hostages by their opposers, Sea Shepherd's members had saved countless marine lives, from whales and dolphins to tuna. But Sea Shepherd hadn't had much "action" in a couple of years, and I wasn't expecting much. I certainly wasn't expecting much as a member of the crew.

Growing up, I was surrounded by older hippie friends of my parents, recounting their "glory days" of the '70s environmental movement, as if it were some phenomenal event in history that was never to happen again. I was expecting nothing short of the same old hippies in these Sea Shepherd activists. Yet to my great surprise, I found exactly the opposite: young, courageous, spirited, risk takers that had so much passion and conviction it would make Gandhi weep.

One of the first people I met aboard the vessel was Peter Hammarstedt, a Swede who probably inspired me most of all. He was younger than me (and I was nineteen at the time), yet he had already fought on the frontlines to protect wild buffalo, would later come to be arrested (numerous times), was eventually exiled from Canada for his fight for seals, and worked his way to being the youngest first mate for Sea Shepherd in his efforts to save whales. Despite his tough-guy stance and militant veganism that might scare off some, he was more humane than anyone I had ever met in my generation. He was a warrior, but he had a deep core about him and a beautiful heart. He showed me the potential our generation really has within itself.

During that campaign, we sailed from Canada to the Galapagos Islands, and after several puke buckets later, I arrived on the majestic islands. The Galapagos Islands are one of the last places on Earth that are still mostly intact, with high numbers of endemic species found nowhere else in the world, both on land and in the ocean. It was Captain Watson's wish to try to keep the islands safe from humans' destructive nature.

I remember staring out at the volcanic island for the first time, lush with green vegetation and beaming with life in its waters. Yet, there I was, feeling unsure of myself and of what I was doing there. I had a burning urge inside me to do something, but I wasn't sure what I could do here in the Galapagos and what I could do with Sea Shepherd. I wasn't a sailor, as the puke buckets proved, and I had no seaman skills whatsoever. But I was soon put to work anyway.

We carried out precious cargo of spay and neuter medicine for veterinarians on the islands, as the foreign species like dogs were annihilating the Indigenous ones. We then patrolled the islands for weeks, arresting three illegal fishing vessels by spotting their location and calling in the navy. And, just when the campaign seemed to be winding down, that's when things got heated.

There had always been tensions between the fishermen and the conservationists on the islands, but the new demands by the fishermen were beyond obscene. There was a "gold rush" on the sea cucumbers in the Galapagos, as a pretty dollar was being earned from Asian markets for each one caught. While before there had been restrictions by the Galapagos National Park on allotted catch numbers, now the fishermen wanted full exploitation of the sea cucumbers. And who knows what would be next. It seemed few were fighting back, so we decided to intervene.

I jumped with five male crewmembers on a Zodiac, a type high-speed boat that activists often use, to the outer edge of the research station where the fishermen were holding their protest. They had barbed-wired the place and were surrounding every entrance but one, our landing strip. We jumped off the Zodiac and walked right into the midst of a battle between the navy with their guns and the fishermen with their Molotov cocktails and iron bats. No weapons had been used, but tension was mounting, and we certainly didn't make things any better.

We immediately stood our ground, holding a frontline just ahead of the navy and in front of the research station where scientists and park rangers were being held. I remember standing there as the only female activist; it was exhilarating but a bit scary. Men approached me within inches of my face and body, making sexually suggestive maneuvers and putting weapons in my face. Alex Cornelissen, the head of our pack, told me not to say a word and just hold my ground. Even with much desire to give a piece of my mind, I remembered the words my father used to say: "Always hold the moral high ground."

In that moment, a lot of what my father had told me over the years started to crystallize. Yet what heightened my heart rate, quickened my pulse, and made my head sweat wasn't just the adrenaline from the high of the action, but also the realization that what I was experiencing wasn't just those old stories anymore. This was a new narrative: my generation's story that we were writing. It was the sparks of a new movement. The idea alone made me want to squeal with delight right there and then, but I knew I needed to shut up, hold my ground, and look tough. Trying not to smile was the hardest thing I had to do in that moment.

Just then, Alex gave me the order to head inside the research station. I thought we were just regrouping. Instead I was told that the navy didn't want us in front anymore. They thought we were provoking the fishermen. We, who had no weapons and were standing peacefully, were provoking? Huh! Why is it that activists are always treated like criminals when the real criminals get the VIP treatment? Sure, I didn't think the fishermen themselves were the real criminals—more so were the multinational corporations for which they worked—but they were agents in this war, and they had picked a side nonetheless. A side I would fight against, whatever was to happen.

Within minutes, hanging low inside the research station turned into a hostage situation. The fishermen had the place surrounded, even with the navy around, and none of us could get out: the scientists, the park rangers, and us. I knew, sitting on the floor of the station and staring at the miserable people around me, that nobody in the world knew what was happening in our corner of the world. And I was of the belief that when a tree falls and nobody hears it, it hasn't really fallen. So with only being able to make one phone call, similar to being in jail, I made the one call that would get this story in the news: I called my dad. As he was the leading environmental journalist in Canada after his Greenpeace days and hosted his own hour talk show that night, I knew he would love the story. So I called him and said:

"Hey, Dad . . . I'm a hostage," starting off the conversation on a high note.

"What? What the fuck is going on?" he replied.

I explained the mess we were in. As a journalist and eco-media savant, he was jumping out of his seat for the story. But as my father, he was petrified for his "little girl."

"Now, but seriously, are you okay?" he said, with a slight panic in his throat.

I told him all was well, even though with the Molotov cocktails outside, I had no idea myself. We did the interview live on his show twenty minutes later. I got Paul on the show, Alex, and myself. The news began to spread, and after the interview we spoke again. He was bursting with pride, he told me, but the dad in him wanted me to call every chance I got.

"Your mother is going to be so pissed with me," he said, ending the conversation.

A couple of hours later, all of us were free and unharmed.

I remember looking at myself in the mirror the next morning, looking long and hard at my face. It looked a bit different. After nineteen years of not knowing what the hell I was doing with my life, I suddenly had a purpose and I could see it in my eyes. I knew I wanted to be an eco-shit-disturber till the day I die. We may not have won the battle for the sea cucumbers—victories in this eco-war are seldom, after all—but the beginning of a new movement was starting. It was right there with that young crew of Sea Shepherd activists.

———————

YEARS LATER, I COULD SEE THE GROWTH of the movement and the growth in myself as an activist. I joined Sea Shepherd in the Antarctic to help save whales. Over several years, I was a part of a mission with many young activists from around the world that saved more than a thousand whales. Later, I fought against the Canadian tar sands, a carbon-intensive oil project that is Canada's scar on the planet. I met many new activist contingents, including First Nations communities downstream of the project, who are confronting a slow industrial genocide and give a face to this fight. And as I traveled, meeting and greeting this movement's next generation, my own personal activism took on a new shape as an eco-media warrior of sorts.

Everywhere I went, I worked with mainstream media, shooting any and all environmental stories I could and exposing the movement's fight to the masses. There was a revolution in the camera. I had begun to understand that in the Galapagos but grew more passionate about it over the years. I believed that capturing environmental news from inside the battle exposed people to a world many didn't even know existed. To me, it was simply good journalism and effective activism—the two went hand in hand. So I was heading to Copenhagen, to cover the biggest story of them all, for it was sure to be this generation's biggest battle yet. But would it be enough?

Bouncing off the plane in Denmark, I was beaming. The airport was packed down the corridor with posters from Greenpeace and WWF alike, reminding us all what was at stake. A contrasting mosaic of individuals bustled out onto the subways, from habit-wearing nuns to Indigenous Peruvians in traditional wear, from cowboys to hippies, from corporate sellouts to top-tier negotiators. In the center of the city was a sixty-five-foot (19.8-meter) green globe you couldn't miss for miles, on which images of the Earth were projected, and a concert called "Hopenhagen Live," where companies like Coca-Cola sold "hope" in bottle form and the ignorant masses danced. It was a climate circus, and the feeling of being utterly alone began to sink in for the first time.

Everyone there had a purpose, everyone there had a mission, everyone there had a group of people they were with. Either you were affiliated with a nonprofit organization, a science body, or a governance of some sort, or you were in the way. Or at least that's the way it felt. Having lost a media gig and media partner just days before my flight, I was determined to still be in Copenhagen for this crucial moment in the *saga to save the planet*, and I was equally if not more determined to have an actual reason to be there, even if this all meant doing it by myself.

Desperate to find any job I could, I latched on to a volunteer correspondent opportunity for MTV News Canada. I would cover the Copenhagen summit, engaging youth back home in one of the most important issues of our time, maybe even inspiring others to get involved. This coverage would be a window into a world otherwise unrelatable to young people. I couldn't have asked for a better gig.

The only catch was I had to do it all alone: be my own camerawomen, reporter, editor, and techie, sending my clips through cyberspace and back in time for the six o'clock show in Toronto that day. Long days and little sleep were ahead, but I had done this before and I knew I could do it again. Yet what I was not ready for was what was about to happen inside the summit.

WITHIN THE FIRST FEW DAYS, a leaked document called the "Danish Text" exposed the inequalities of the summit before it had even really begun. The text was a draft climate proposal between the Group of Eight nations that virtually backroomed the negotiations, making a mockery of the multilateral United Nations process. It was also the quintessential blueprint for the negotiation procedures, dotting the lines for effectively excluding the most vulnerable countries, such as island states and developing nations. Those that will be most severely impacted, those that are the least responsible, and those pushing the most ambitious targets.

In response to the "Danish Text," the Group of Seventy-Seven leader, Lumumba Stanislaus Di-Aping, walked out of the conference in that first week in protest. Representing more than a hundred developing nations that felt sidelined, he temporarily shut down the negotiations. Despite this, the exclusivity continued into the second week. As security ramped up with heads of state beginning to arrive to the summit, thousands of members of accredited civil societies were closed off from the negotiations. By the end of the week, only three hundred of the twenty-four thousand civilians present were allowed to participate.

Being literally shut out of the gates myself, I knew it was more than just a security measure, but an attempt to stifle public involvement. As a friend of mine, Clive Tesar, who was working with WWF told me, "excluding civil society essentially strips the process of its passion and grounding."

Media too was being excluded. Orwellian "red zones" were established, restricting where, what, and who reporters could cover. The summit was essentially being censored, while the deal itself desperately needed questioning. In the final days, a leaked UN document showed that the climate deal on the table would mean a three-Celsius-degrees (5.4 Fahrenheit degrees) temperature rise—a far cry from the two Celsius degrees (3.6 Fahrenheit degrees) scientists say is safe and world leaders had agreed to. It was a deal that virtually guaranteed cooking the planet.

Then came the final day, the Obama day, the day the United States would pronounce its climate providence to the world. This was the sink-or-swim moment. It seemed as if all were holding their breaths. This could have been a defining time that changed the direction of the negotiations, if only politics back in the States weren't gridlocked by a few select senators. Instead, it was another well-written speech that fell empty.

For some, President Obama then attempted to salvage the pieces of a broken summit by holding a closed meeting with China, India, Brazil, and South Africa—which became known as the BASIC Group—to hash out an agreement among some of the world's biggest polluters in secret. For others, it was nothing more than that "Danish Text" realized, a well-orchestrated dress rehearsal that had finally come to its stage with its main actors: excluding most of the world leaders and the majority of people from having a say to instead allow the biggest polluters and their self-interests to decide the fate of our world. For me, the only thing worse would have been if a black hole had sucked up the universe in that instant.

I found myself at the activist convergence space, shaking, trembling, and defeated. I knew the summit was a wash at this point, but didn't want to say it out loud. Instead, just suicidal fantasies fogged my mind. I know that may sound overly dramatic, but I had made no difference whatsoever, none of us had. Despite all the best intentions, all the hard work, and years upon years of sacrificing for this moment—*poof*—it was all gone. Vanished with two words: Copenhagen Accord, the so-called climate deal that only added injury to an insulting failure of a conference.

After two years of intense negotiations to establish this treaty—some would say even twelve years' work with the Kyoto Protocol in 1997—it all ended in a few hours of a secret meeting with a few heads of state that created an alternative text. A noncommittal draft that circumnavigated the UN multilateral process and fell far below scientific demands. We didn't get any of our requests for a "binding, fair, and ambitious" deal. Civil society's message was so clear and yet we got none of it. If anything, this Accord had now created a path for climate tyranny, doing away with the shaping of a global treaty and putting most at the mercy of those few that predominantly created the problem.

Some might say that the only way to accomplish a climate deal is to negotiate strictly with the biggest polluters, and that the world is too divergent to unite on any single issue. Maybe there is some merit in that, but one thing I do know is that if I have ever seen one thing unite us, it is our very basic need to survive. In the last few years, people have crossed boundaries, divides, and oceans for the purposes of uniting on one issue. What many say is impossible may be impossible for the elites and politicians but is very probable for us, the masses. Despite all our differences, single issues, and criticism of one another, we are uniting, uniting in the face of climate change. It is the umbrella issue of our generation.

To testify to this, four thousand cities, in 128 countries, with nearly one billion people—that's nearly one-sixth the Earth's population—participated in Earth Hour in 2010, turning off their lights to support the fight against the climate crisis. In its first year, the *350.org* movement synchronized more than 5,200 events in more than 180 countries to perform climate rallies. CNN later called it "the most widespread day of political action in the planet's history."

In my home country of Canada, where I felt the environmental movement was in its grave, nearly five thousand individuals showed up in the nation's capital for Power Shift 2009, a youth-oriented demand for an energy shift. The reality is the movement was widespread and growing—from social justice spectrums to environmental justice spectrums to apathetic spectrums—all because climate change was uniting us, in a way that people like my father had only dreamed possible.

> *If I have ever seen one thing unite us, it is our very basic need to survive. In the last few years, people have crossed boundaries, divides, and oceans for the purposes of uniting in the face of climate change. It is the umbrella issue of our generation.*

So to say that the world cannot unite on one issue and that therefore only the elites should make the decisions for us is simply not true. The elite power structures have created the problem, not the solution. The only question is, can the masses defeat an elite tyranny in a time when the clock is ticking against our own self-made apocalypse? I guess only time will tell, and only the growth of this revolution—and I mean *revolution*—will save us.

———

JUST DAYS BEFORE THE MISERABLE END TO THE SUMMIT, I decided to do something. Instead of just watching complacently the slow death of the negotiations, I wanted to stand up against the climate tyranny. I took my camera to document the action I was about to be a part of and a chocolate bar to keep me happy. What can I say, I'm an emotional eater.

It was a usual rainy, bone-chilling morning in Copenhagen. But this morning, I was looking for trouble. In the wee hours, I searched for convergence spots in the city that had masses of activists and less cops, as I knew there were going to be takedowns. I met up with a guy named Dave Vasey, a Canadian anti–tar sands activist I had met in Copenhagen, and we decided to buddy up that day so at least one person would know if either one of us got caught and jailed.

Waiting outside at a subway station for a critical mass of activists, we could see that all of a sudden the police were getting ready to pounce. Letting other activists know as we skimmed our way past onlookers, we booked it for an empty highway. Just escaping arrest, we got completely lost on the stretch of cement that went as far as the eye could see, and we didn't know where else to go. Making the rounds of calls on his mobile, Dave soon found the location of a successful contingent of activists making their way to the summit grounds. We jumped a fence and ran for it.

Before I knew it, Dave and I arm-linked ourselves to strangers, connecting to more than four thousands activists in one block. The police had taken down the three other activist blocks already. But by noon, our block had made its way close to the summit grounds; we just had to get past a fortress of riot cops. We did. Pushing and squeezing, with some getting arrested, we broke past the police barricade and onto a bridge in front of the summit.

We were exactly where we wanted to be, the place some among us didn't believe we would reach. There we were, standing in front of the summit. To keep ourselves there, we had to hold our ground. We all became a wall holding the cops out to keep ourselves in. Dave and I were in the middle of it all. At first it was exhilarating. When push came to shove, we pushed back, and pushed back, and pushed back to keep our lines. Except soon the space between us activists became less and less and less. My body, my rib cage, my lungs felt as if they were being pressed, even flattened, until I almost couldn't inhale and couldn't see the top of anyone's head. I felt like a teenage girl in the mosh pit of a rock concert. Dave saw me and picked me out.

We moved, but we just happened to move to the frontlines. Standing there, catching my breath and bearings, I was arm-linked again to people from around the world, people who fought on diverse issues but were united in this one moment, people who were the faces of a new movement, and people I was proud to stand beside. But as I stood there on the frontlines, yet again staying quiet, holding my position, and trying to look tough in front of snarling guys (this time cops), I couldn't help but think about how in war, this is usually where the soldiers get killed.

I won't lie; I was petrified. I had already seen the police wrath firsthand in the push and shove, as they beat young and old with batons till they were bludgeoned, pepper-sprayed people directly in the eyes, and herded us like cattle. It was one of the scariest moments of my life when a cop riot van came up toward me looking as if it was going to run me over.

But I stood my ground; so did we all. In response to their attempt to silence our opposition on the streets and kill our future on the negotiating table, our generation finally stood up and said, "No more." We took a world stage in front of the conference center, with all the world's media paying attention to our fight. Creating a circle, activists held off the cops. Inside the circle, we began our own dialogue, a dialogue on the future we wanted, not that of a select few elites who would never come to see the consequences of their actions.

I knew right there and then this was the beginning of a new era. It wasn't just that the sparks were flying, as in my Sea Shepherd days, but that the fire was burning, and brightly.

There was a lot of things said—*an end to neoliberalism, down with capitalism, Copenhagen was an orchestrated failure, we need to make the movement accessible to all*—and then all of a sudden, I heard it:

"This is the dawning of a new movement," an anonymous activist yelled out on a megaphone.

After a week of being stepped on and beaten to the ground—at least that's what I felt had happened to my soul—I had the first genuine reason to have hope again. Why? Because I knew these words were true. As I stared at the brave faces of the women and men around me, who were fighting and constructing a new narrative, I knew right there and then this was the beginning of a new era. It wasn't just that the sparks were flying, as in my Sea Shepherd days, but that the fire was now burning, and brightly.

Possibly for the first time on a global scale, all movements, all issues, and all struggles were put in the same room together, or at least on the same street. Even outside of this one action on that rainy day, a dialogue had been stirring since the start of the Copenhagen summit that unified us in one movement. The young and old; the Indigenous, marginalized, elite, disempowered, and empowered; Africans, small Islanders, and Europeans; farmers, doctors, cyclists, white-collar and green-collar—we were all here, fighting for the most important thing of all: the battle for life itself.

On my travels back home, I came to realize that with the failure of Copenhagen came an opportunity. An opportunity to build a movement that was not just focused on events like this summit, but also on a generation's actions. An opportunity for a movement that is more global, inclusive, and stronger than ever before. An opportunity to be a movement whose fire burns within us all. Copenhagen was not the end, only the beginning.

PHOTO BY EMILY HUNTER

The movement is here. This is our moment.

––––––––––––

Emily Hunter continues to work as a freelance eco-journalist. She is the eco-correspondent for MTV News Canada, occasionally hosting a TV-documentary series called Impact, *covering such issues as the Canadian tar sands and the G20 Toronto protests. Currently, she is finding more ways to get herself in trouble and plans to eco-shit-disturb till the day she dies.*

JAMIE HENN

▶ Twenty-six ▶ United States ▶ Online Organizer

350: The Movement behind a Number

By defining our goal more clearly—by making it seem more manageable and less remote—we can help all people to see it, to draw hope from it, and to move irresistibly towards it.

—JOHN F. KENNEDY

I HEARD THE RALLY BEFORE I SAW IT. As I walked around the corner into Times Square with my colleague Jon, I instantly recognized the beat of Jay-Z's "Empire State of Mind," which we'd been listening to on repeat for the past week. Fists pumping in the air, our pace quickened, and our eyes yearned to see the results of more than a year of organizing. Until there they were: photo after photo of the day's thousands of climate rallies across the planet, streaming across the big screens of Times Square.

A photo of hundreds of schoolchildren in the Philippines preceded a picture of people forming a giant 350 in front of the Sydney Opera House. They were followed by another picture of a rally in Ghana, then Mexico, then the United States. For one day, those big screens that normally showed vodka and Hummer ads were displaying the vibrant, raucous, and powerful birth of the global climate movement.

The photos spinning across the screens at Times Square on that day, October 24, 2009, were part of the 350 International Day of Climate Action, which I helped lead and coordinate. The day synchronized more than 5,200 events in more than 180 countries. CNN later called it "the most widespread day of political action in the planet's history." At each event, whether in Beijing or Bujumbura, citizens made a strong call for climate action by displaying a simple but important number: 350. Currently, the levels of carbon dioxide in the atmosphere is 389 parts per million (ppm), while rising more than 2 ppm each year. But scientists now say the safe upper limit for our atmosphere should be 350 ppm. Essentially, this all means we are already in the danger zone.

The story of how a data point, as boring and unsexy as 350 ppm, somehow made it onto the screens of Times Square is intertwined with my own story of becoming a climate activist. As one of the founders of *350.org*, the campaign behind the October 24 day of action, I've fought over, despised, grappled with, and learned to love that 350 number. For me, it's become a symbol of what I love about this movement: the creativity and passion of its organizers, the radical ambition of its goals, the diversity of its global network, and the sense of caring and community that permeate throughout.

That number was little more than a factoid, however, when six college friends, environmental author Bill McKibben, and I launched the *350.org* campaign in early 2008. We'd been working together as climate activists since 2005, when a group of us got together over beers on Sunday nights at Middlebury College in Vermont and started to talk about how we could influence the national dialogue around climate change.

What started as a weekly meeting soon took over most of my time. I grew up in a progressive family in Cambridge, Massachusetts, and spent a lot of afternoons volunteering at soup kitchens and community groups in high school, but I'd never considered myself much of an activist. I'd always loved nature and the outdoors but had never been involved in efforts to protect them. Yet, there I was at college, scraping food scraps onto a giant scale to show students just how much we wasted in the dining halls, marching up to the state capitol in full hockey gear to demand that our governor protect winter pond hockey by slashing emissions, and taking an entire summer to help organize a national veggie oil bus tour called the "Road to Detroit" to push for cleaner cars. In 2006, our same group of friends helped organize a march across Vermont that turned out nearly five thousand people, practically a revolution for that small state.

The next year, my friends and I ran our first major campaign, Step It Up, which caught like wildfire across the United States and culminated on

April 4, 2007, with more than fourteen hundred events in all fifty states—the largest day of environmental demonstrations in a generation. I spent the final day of the campaign in a cramped office (more like a closet) that the League of Conservation Voters had lent us in their Washington, DC, office. I'd convinced all my professors to give me the week off from classes, and as I called event organizers to connect them with media outlets, I did my best to try to forget all the work that was piling up back at school. Watching the hundreds of photographs from around the country stream onto our website that afternoon was well worth the all-nighters I had to pull back at school to catch up.

I've fought over, despised, grappled with, and learned to love that 350 number. For me, it's become a symbol of what I love about this movement: the creativity and passion of its organizers, the radical ambition of its goals, the diversity of its global network, and the sense of caring and community that permeate throughout.

Step It Up was a big success, but I knew it wasn't enough. After all, they called it "global" warming for a reason. So, in late 2007, our team began exploring the idea of an international campaign. About the same time, Dr. James Hansen, one of the world's top climate scientists, published a paper that hit climate science like a "mind bomb." It showed that humanity needed to reduce the level of carbon dioxide in the atmosphere from its current 389 parts per million to no more than 350 ppm in order to "preserve a planet similar to that on which civilization developed and to which life on Earth is adapted." Those were strong words for a scientist. But Bill McKibben, who'd known Dr. Hansen since the late 1980s, seized on the 350 target as the symbol for our new campaign.

I was a bit more skeptical. Parts per million? Give me a break. Who's going to get that? Yet the more we discussed it, the more we all warmed up to our strange new symbol. After all, Arabic numerals are one of the few universally recognized symbols, making 350 mean the same thing in Cantonese as it did in English. It would become the ultimate global target: a clear benchmark that boiled what we needed to do to stop global warming down to three simple digits. It was a silver lining in a long and gloomy fight. And it was enough to start building a movement.

Over the following months, I settled into my new job as a full-time global climate activist with the beginning of *350.org*. Since there were seven of us on the team, we did the only logical thing we could think of: divide up the different continents and get to work. I picked East Asia and, in our usual organizing style, began to email everyone I could possibly think of who was connected to environmental issues in the region. Each day, I'd bike from my apartment in San Francisco to our windowless office in a rundown neighborhood of the city, sit down at the computer, and spend the next eight hours emailing, writing campaign plans, and trying to pull together the loose strands of activism I was seeing across East Asia. At certain points, I simply resorted to typing things like "Cambodia + environmental groups" into Google and seeing what showed up.

Little by little, a network began to emerge. One day in the spring of 2008, I received an email from a young Korean woman, Hyunjin Jeon, with a photo of her friend holding a big 350 sign in downtown Seoul. I was ecstatic and marched around our shared office space in San Francisco, making sure all the other tenants saw the photo. "Who's the Korean girl?" they asked. "I don't know!" I replied. "Isn't that amazing!"

Emails like Hyunjin's kept me going over the following months as I began to spend more and more time at the office. The day to day of building a campaign can feel like drudgery, and my eyes began to ache after hours of staring at the laptop. Yet, bit by bit, we began to receive more emails like Hyunjin's from places like Cameroon, China, Chile, and more. There was a buzz about 350; the wheels of the movement were beginning to turn. By December of 2008, after a year of building out our website and laying the groundwork with partner organizations, we announced plans for an International Day of Climate Action to take place October 24, 2009—just six weeks before the United Nations climate meetings in Copenhagen, when world leaders would meet to negotiate an international climate treaty.

Copenhagen helped focus public attention on climate as an international issue, and as the meetings approached, more and more people turned to

350.org as a way to do something about the issue. As usual, we welcomed everyone who wanted to chip in—other than corporations, which we couldn't ensure wouldn't just use our events for their own personal greenwash. But otherwise, we were confident that a diversity of partners would bring the type of creativity and energy we knew a successful campaign needed. Soon, artists and athletes were on board; churches, mosques, and temples were planning events; and students, always a strong base for us, were organizing alongside grandparents. We adopted the informal slogan "Just say yes!" and did our best to remain as transparent and responsive as possible, even as our email inbox began to reach the breaking point.

I was reminded every day in the office that our campaign wouldn't be possible without the new online tools that allowed us to communicate with people around the world. I often found myself in San Francisco G-Chatting with an organizer in Beijing while on a Skype call with a volunteer in Malaysia and editing a Google Doc with partners in Vietnam, while telling everyone about it on Twitter. One day, I tracked down a guy from Brunei on Facebook who seemed interested in climate change and told him about 350, and a few days later, he sent me back a link to a *350.org* Brunei Facebook group with more than three thousand members. I was thrilled but mostly stunned that no one had contacted him before. Despite the increasing prevalence of the Internet in our everyday lives, I think many organizations or campaigns still haven't grasped its full potential.

At the same time, I knew that online organizing wasn't enough. For one thing, even the Internet doesn't reach everywhere, and even when an email can get through, a face-to-face interaction is still preferable. So, tapping into some funding from a number of foundations that were willing to take a risk on our campaign, I took a few trips to Asia to try to track down potential partners in person. On my first trip to China, I met up with the Green Long March, a student conservation movement. We first met in Beijing, but the organizers invited me to join one of the ten marches across the country that they were holding that summer. I eagerly accepted and joined a group of students for a few days outside of Guangzhou. Watching student discuss climate change and other environmental challenges with local townspeople we met was a revelatory experience for me. I'd been talking for months about how people "all around the world" were taking action to fight climate change, but the phrase didn't really hit home until I was halfway across the planet.

On another trip, I spent three weeks traveling through Southeast Asia after attending a climate meeting in Bangkok. In Northern Thailand, I spoke with a monk I met outside a temple about Buddhism and protecting the environment. An hour later, he pledged to organize an event for October 24. In Laos, I tracked down the one environmental reporter in the country at the *Vientiane Times*, and we shared ideas about different storylines and articles he was working on. I squeezed in five meetings a day in Phnom Penh by hiring a motorcycle driver for ten dollars and zipping from meeting to meeting on the back of his bike, clutching my pamphlets. In Hanoi, I met up with ten Vietnamese journalists who thought that I was Dr. James Hansen—I guess *Jamie Henn* looks similar enough in Vietnamese—but who were still willing to talk with me when I admitted I wasn't a NASA scientist, rather an organizer fresh out of college.

Contact by contact, meeting by meeting, a network began to take shape. I remember being exhausted in the end, sitting in the youth hostel in downtown Bangkok, dripping in sweat but with a big smile on my face as I watched new friends make banners and signs to take back to their home countries for October 24.

Along with organizing East Asia, I took on the role of communications director. As October 24 approached, I began to try to map out how we could leverage the day to make a real impact on the public imagination. Soon, we'd assembled a global communications team with members ranging from individuals like Landry Ninteretse, who had to move from internet café to internet café as the power failed in his home city of Bujumbura to keep sending press releases, to a cheap public relations firm in India that committed to taking on the whole subcontinent. Linked together by Skype and Google Docs, our ragtag crew quickly prepared itself to try to channel the tidal wave of actions that we saw headed our way.

With a week left until October 24 and more than four thousand events registered across the planet, our core team of friends and some of our now thirty-five global staff convened on an office in downtown New York City for the final push. Those last few days felt like juggling a thousand balls at once, just trying to keep them moving through the air until the final moment when they were all supposed to fall into place. And as the pizza boxes began to stack higher and higher and our action counter skyrocketed up above five thousand rallies in more than 180 countries, we all began to get that tingling feeling that this whole crazy experiment might just work.

The day itself really proved to be the ultimate test for our open-source organizing. It was a nail-biting moment of waiting to see whether this would all end up as a failed dream or as a spectacular reality. Just forty-eight hours before October 24, I remember our South African media coordinator, Adam, was calling through to organizers on Skype to make sure they were actually doing their events. Two sisters of his were organizing an event. They'd come down to a workshop we'd run in South Africa before and gone back to Ethiopia fired up to organize, but we hadn't heard much from them since. Over a crackling Skype–to–cell phone connection, one of his sisters told Adam that not only were they having the event, but also that fifteen thousand schoolchildren would be in the streets the next day, marching for 350.

Adam and I nearly fell out of our chairs when we heard the news. Here was the event that could kick off the entire day! Ethiopia holding the first 350 event. Adam quickly asked them if they had a video camera and could send us footage of the rally. "Hmmm," said the sister, "we hadn't thought about that." Then Adam and I really fell on the ground. Here was our biggest event, and with just forty-eight hours to go, we had no way of getting the footage together to show the world. I think the technical public relations term for the situation was *we're screwed*.

Not ready to have our dreams shattered so quickly, Adam rushed to recharge his Skype account with more money and got busy tracking down someone to film the event. With only a few hours to go till the Ethiopian event would start, Adam ended up calling his father's friend's uncle's cousin's girlfriend—or something like that—and eventually tracked down a young woman. A woman who was not only near the 350 Ethiopian event, but also had a high-definition camera and would share the footage online. The next morning, the woman got on her bicycle, biked to the event, shot the footage, biked over to the one hotel in town that had high-speed Internet, bought an obligatory drink at the bar in order to use the connection, and uploaded the footage to our online video library. Sure enough, we got them out to the media a few hours later. Skype, plus cell phones, plus bicycles, plus cameras, plus Internet, plus laptops, (plus alcohol?) equals a new organizing frontier!

The images from Ethiopia were only some of the thousands of stunning photos that came across our laptops on October 24. I was captivated by images of thousands of people forming a giant sun in Mexico City, a human 350 with a peace symbol for the 0 in war-torn Serbia, and the video of climbers hanging with 350 banners off of Table Mountain in South Africa. I was driven to tears by the stories of the sweatshop workers in Bangladesh who held 350 signs at their sewing machines because they couldn't get off work to join an event and of the children in Indonesia who held banners that read NO ONE CARES ABOUT US, BUT WE CARE ABOUT THE PLANET outside of their orphanage. And I was inspired by the single young woman in Iraq who held a banner on her own because her friends were too afraid to join her; the citizens in El Salvador who marched through their tumultuous capital despite a ban on demonstrations of any kind; and the soldiers in Iraq who formed a 350 out of sandbags and told us they'd left their Hummers, walking on patrol to save gas.

In a single day, we'd put to rest the idea that the climate movement was just for rich, white people in Europe and North America. Instead, our photos were filled with young and old; poor and rich; black, brown, and white; faces and places that represented the entire planet.

Those were also the faces that made it onto front pages and newscasts around the world. Thanks to the efforts of thousands of organizers around the world, *350.org* hit the media jackpot on October 24, making it into nearly every major international news outlet and becoming the most popular story on Google News of the day—meaning it was the most covered event in the world.

———

OVER THE COURSE OF THE TWENTY-FIVE HOURS I was awake around October 24, I must have talked with one hundred reporters, doing my final interview with Radio Australia at two in the morning after the big day had finally come to a close in New York. After I hung up the phone, I sat for a while in the darkness of our rented Manhattan apartment where the rest of our team was asleep on their desks. I just stared into the blackness, exhausted and fulfilled, seeing image after image from the day in my mind. In that moment, I felt truly connected as a movement, as if every single person who took part in the day was reaching out from their photos, reminding me that we're all in this together.

In a single day, we'd put to rest the idea that the climate movement was just for rich, white people in Europe and North America.

Six weeks later, our team at *350.org* brought all those photographs and stories (and about fifty youth organizers from the global South) to the historic UN climate meetings in Copenhagen, Denmark. Our goal was to bring the full force of this growing movement to bear on our political leaders and push them to create a fair, ambitious, and legally binding climate treaty that could take the world back to 350 ppm carbon dioxide. From the outset, I knew this was near impossible: two weeks of meetings weren't going to suddenly convince the United States to take on ambitious policies or heal the divides between rich and poor countries. Nevertheless, I was hopeful. Copenhagen was a chance for the world, and our movement, to come together and chart a new course that at least pointed towards a sustainable and just future.

Sadly, Copenhagen proved to be a disappointment. I remember standing outside the AP Television room on the Saturday before the final weeks of negotiations and watching images of protestors being beaten by police outside the convention center. Stunning as the pictures were, I couldn't help but feel that the real crime was taking place inside, where negotiators from developed countries continued to block substantial progress on a strong treaty. Even though 117 countries adopted the 350 ppm target, they were, in a sense, the wrong 117—the poor and most vulnerable nations, not the rich and addicted ones.

Copenhagen didn't produce the treaty we desperately need, but it did strengthen our movement. Organizers and activists from around the world had the chance to work, celebrate, and protest together. As the meetings ended in failure, youth from around the world made a video repeating the phrase *You're not done yet. And neither are we*, in different languages. It was a message that I'd take home with me.

So, as I write this in the spring of 2010, I'm back to emailing everyone I know and helping get another campaign off the ground. On October 10, 2010, *350.org* hosted a Global Work Party, with actions in thousands of places around the world. Folks put up solar panels, dug community gardens, and laid out bike paths. Not because we think we'll solve climate change one bike path at a time—we won't. But because we want to send a strong message to our leaders: If we can get to work, so can you. If we can climb on the roof of the school and hammer in a solar panel, you can climb to the floor of the Senate or Parliament and pass a strong new climate policy.

> *We want to send a strong message to our leaders: If we can get to work, so can you. If we can climb on the roof of the school and hammer in a solar panel, you can climb to the floor of the Senate or Parliament and pass a strong new climate policy.*

Each new event for October 10 that I heard about was like a jolt of energy. Students in Malaysia installed homemade wind turbines. Across the United States, communities planned to retrofit schools and low-income homes. In Ghana, one town planted 350 trees. For me, it's proof that our movement is still strong and we're still growing. That even on the days when I'm feeling tired or hopeless about the state of the world, there's someone else out there who's also working hard to make a difference. Because now, we've got a movement.

Jamie Henn is the communications and East Asia director for 350.org. He contin-
ues to help lead 350.org's innovative efforts to use the web to connect a grassroots
climate movement around the world.

ENEI BEGAYE

▶ Thirty-two ▶ Diné ▶ Political Progressor

PHOTO BY CY WAGONER

The Lights over Black Mesa

It's crucial to understand that as a society, we can reorganize. We can reorganize socially, politically, and economically, and we can reorganize according to our values.

—REBECCA ADAMSON

ON THE NAVAJO RESERVATION IN THE 1980S, where I grew up, there were few lights in the dark night, other than the moon and the stars. Sitting outside and looking up upon the stars, my dad would tell me Diné winter stories of how First Woman and Coyote put the starlights in the sky. First Woman arranged with purpose and intention, while Coyote simply threw them randomly into the sky, the stars in the end creating their own pattern. The story reminds us of this world's many dualities and the struggle to balance them. Growing up, I would look out from the top of our small mountain and imagine the creation stories playing out across the dazzling points of starlight. On a moonless night, the sky became an endless dark canvas, and the brightly shining stars painted beautiful glittering images of men and women, animals and insects, and the worlds before this one. Where the dim shadow of the night sky touches the dark line of Black Mesa—the black mountain our home faces—that perfect set of intentional and random sparkling lights met a harsh glare of red and white illumination. These were the incandescent red and white bulbs flashing, unchanging atop the northern end of Black Mesa. The only artificial lights as far as I could see were these, the mine lights, Peabody Coal Company's mine lights to be exact. Still there today, they illuminate the coal mine's aircraft landing strip, then slide down Black Mesa's side, revealing the coal conveyor belt that strips our land of life and fuels madness elsewhere.

As a kid on our rural piece of "the rez" in northeastern Arizona, I used to think Peabody's lights were pretty amazing, glaring across a landscape of various shapes and shades of darkness. When you don't grow up surrounded by artificial lights and neon signs, these small flashy effects can really capture your attention. In my mind, it meant that one day we would have all the big-city luxuries. Only later did I understand the beauty and power our culture carries regardless of these electric lights. Only later did I realize the full cost we pay for these flashing lights.

Since 1970, Peabody Western Coal Company, a subsidiary of Peabody Energy, the largest coal company in the world, has operated two coal strip mines on Black Mesa. Together these mines made the Black Mesa operation one of the largest coal strip-mining operations in the United States. Coinciding with the mine opening, the United States Congress drew a line in the sand, deciding *for* the Navajo and Hopi people that our land would be put to use. To make way for mining, twelve thousand Navajos and sixty Hopis were forced to leave their homelands or forfeit rights. Navajo and Hopi communities who had long been good neighbors were pitted against one another for control of the "resources." My family was lucky to have just missed the line of forced relocation. But many families on and around Black Mesa were not as lucky.

Then, as if we owed the coal company more, for decades Peabody took our region's sole source of drinking water, mixed it with coal, and sent it hundreds of miles away, into what is known as coal slurry transport. It remains the only slurry transport existing in the United States, as it is such a shameful use of water. With bulldozers and chains, Peabody stripped the land of pine and juniper trees, sagebrush and wildflowers. For decades they have disturbed the red healing clay, *Chii*, and turned the earth gray. To power the Southwest, Peabody has dynamited hundreds of feet into Black Mesa for coal and water. Our land will never be the same again.

I grew up into a land that has been torn apart physically, culturally, spiritually, and socially by America's need for energy. Black Mesa is a female: Her head is Navajo Mountain, north of my home. Her body is the mesa stretching across the northeastern corner of Arizona. The coal is her liver—that organ that filters poisons from our bodies. And the water is her lifeblood;

this is what we are taught. Peabody has ripped her apart. As Diné people, we become a reflection of her, our mother—the Earth.

But in the 1960s, my people were promised riches in exchange for coal, jobs and electricity in exchange for our water. From an early age, I learned that coal meant jobs. Just about everyone I knew growing up had at least one relative that worked at the coal mine, yet I didn't see the promised riches. Like so many others, I grew up hauling water in fifty-five-gallon barrels over many miles to provide for my family's weekly water needs. With vehicles always breaking down from endless driving on dirt roads and bills that needed to be paid, the extreme lack of good-paying jobs is still a constant threat.

I'm thirty-two years old now, and most home sites still have no electricity or running water, no lights or refrigerators, just newer ice chests and fresh flashlight batteries. Navajo communities are disappearing as mothers and fathers are forced to leave their children with aging grandparents in order to find work in the cities off the reservation, while families living around the mine suffer from all sorts of respiratory illnesses.

So where are all the riches we were promised, the lights and income? The answer: Las Vegas, Phoenix, and Los Angeles—we have been sending it by train and slurry line for decades. Today's reality on the reservation is a stark reminder of the fairly recent colonization of our lands, always for mineral wealth. We were forced into concentration camps by U.S. Cavalry in the 1860s so the U.S. leader Kit Carson could search for gold freely. In the 1920s when coal, oil, and gas were found beneath our lands, the Diné were persuaded to set up a Navajo government system reflecting the United States' so that mineral leases could be signed "legally."

Today's reality on the reservation is a stark reminder of the fairly recent colonization of our lands, always for mineral wealth.

As I learned more about our history, connecting the dots with what I saw growing up, I knew it needed to be stopped and that I needed to act. There became no way to look at Black Mesa and be awed by Peabody's lights; seeing those flashing lights every night only made me angry and frustrated.

Going to college seemed the best way to learn how to fight these injustices and better understand them. But after several years and only one semester shy of graduating from Stanford University, I left it all behind to come home again and fight.

I REMEMBER SUMMER 2002 LIKE IT WAS yesterday. Driving to the public hearing took ages, as if we were actually driving through the ancient millennia that formed the red rocks and painted dunes surrounding us. The destination that day was Tuba City, Arizona—one of the "big cities" of the reservation. The little grocery store sign reads YA'AT'EEH (Navajo for *welcome*). There were two traffic lights, a strip of four-lane road lined by gas stations and fast-food joints, a trading post, a hotel for tourists, and federal institutions aplenty.

Some people might see a third world community, right at the intersection of poverty and the potential for modern prosperity. I see "home." I didn't grow up here, but it's fairly similar throughout the reservation—communities struggling, under the weight of McDonald's and Kentucky Fried Chicken, to find a balance between being Diné and being "American."

That day, my car, full of friends and organizers, was heading to the Tuba City Chapter House—the local government office, which is essentially a large meeting room with linoleum floors and florescent lights. The California Public Utilities Commission (CPUC), which regulates California utility companies, was holding a public hearing. The bigwigs had come out—commissioners and their staffers—and we rarely had visitors like that. This was a major meeting; they came to decide whether to give over a billion public dollars to keep one of Southern California's main power plants, the Mohave Generating Station, open. The plant provided power to the big cities of the Southwest. It is fed coal and water solely through a 275-mile (442.6-kilometer) long steel straw stretching all the way from my home, the Black Mesa region of the Navajo Nation.

Pulling up into the dirt parking lot of the Chapter House, we passed each other some of the stickers that read SHUT DOWN MOHAVE! in bold letters, slapping them on to our jackets and shirts. At first, nobody got out of the car; silently, we stared at the gate entrance. At the entrance stood a group of older Navajo men wearing Peabody Western Coal hats. *This is gonna be ugly,* I thought. I recognized a couple of the men as my friends' parents and clan relatives. We must have been pooling our strength silently in the car, because collectively we felt the push to keep going. Luckily, the worst we got as we squeezed through the gate's entrance were harsh stares and murmurs in Navajo. These were their jobs after all that we were threatening.

We arrived before the meeting began, but the list to speak had already filled three pages. I put my name down and my heart beat fast. When I looked at the list, it was filled with the names of Navajo employees of Peabody Coal Company. *Where were all the community people we had urged to come?* I wondered. We had spent days driving throughout the Black Mesa region, letting people know about this meeting, offering to pay peoples' gas expenses, telling them what's at stake. Many said they would come. My heart sank.

Inside the Chapter House, all the folding chairs were set out and filled; still more people stood against the walls. At the front of the room sat the commissioners, a professionally dressed group of older white men and women. The rest of the room was mostly Navajo with a few non-Navajo supporters mixed in. There were Navajo Peabody people, government people, grandmas and grandpas, and us—the only young people. We called ourselves the Black Mesa Water Coalition, a year-old group of which I was a leading member.

It turned out that more people opposed to the mine did show up, but in good Native time—late. We spent most of the morning listening to Peabody employees tell the CPUC commissioners why they had to keep the power plant open: jobs, college for their kids, a chance at the "American Dream." The same story you hear from many continuously oppressed communities. I grew more and more irritated hearing it.

But when I heard my name called as one of the next on the list to speak, my palms began sweating and I wondered if it was normal for my heart to beat this fast. I waited against the wall below the podium for the speaker before me to complete his three minutes. The mother of a good friend of mine from high school had just finished speaking. She worked for the mine, and she spoke about needing the coal income for her kids' education.

Walking down from the podium, she made a beeline for me. I braced myself; this was going to be painful. I hadn't seen her since my high school graduation, and now to see her here like this with my sticker blaring on my chest. I prepared for the worst. But she didn't attack me with mean words; instead she came over, leaned in close to me, and whispered, "Enei, think about what you are doing, think about what you are saying, think about my son, his college education—don't take that away from him," and then she left me.

Her words jabbed me harder than any insults could have. For a few seconds, I blinked back tears. Was I about to ruin people's lives? And then I got mad. Why did we have to be beholden to this exploiting corporation just to go to college? Peabody has already destroyed so much here. It was not me that was doing the harm.

When I found myself at the podium looking down at my notes, all I could see were indecipherable amounts of scribbles. I took a deep breath and just told the decision makers my truth from my heart:

I am "Red-Streak-Running-Through-The-Water" people, and I am born from "Bitter Water"; by these clans I am a Diné woman. I am from Shonto; I went to high school in Kayenta, both on Black Mesa's northern edge. And I went to college without Peabody's money. I am a member of the Black Mesa Water Coalition, and we represent young Navajo and Hopi people who say, "Shut down the Mohave Generating Station." I have seen the coal company give our people little things here and there to keep us "nice"—money for the school, machines to keep the dirt roads smooth— but I have also seen what the coal company has taken away from us: our water, our lands, our choices, our dignity. I grew up drinking the soft, sweet Navajo Aquifer water. And I have seen where the coal company pulls this sacred source of water from the female Black Mesa. Huge pipes pulse with a heartbeat as they take this life force from her and mix it with coal. Our communities have become economic hostages to the coal company. There has to be a way where we are not the exploited and disposable waste of the megacities' power and luxuries, of the overconsuming and all-consuming American Dream.

That CPUC hearing went on late into the night. This was just the beginning for us, young people picking up the reins of community organizing from so many older and exhausted community leaders. And it was this meeting that put many of us face-to-face with our first challengers—our own people, friends, family members, and relatives. If I had been alone at that meeting, I might not have had the courage to step forward and confront it all. But we were together, and so we kept right on going. For the next few years we organized just about anything we could think of—spiritual runs, protests, community meetings and trainings, nonviolent direct actions. With no money in our pockets but with passion in our hearts and bullhorns in our hands, we worked to elevate our community's voices.

On January 1, 2006, due to the work of many Native and non-Native individuals and organizations, the mine, the pipeline, and the power plant all closed. It was a bittersweet victory, however; jobs and tribal income would be lost. Like weeds in a freshly watered and tended garden, new coal proposals began popping up as solutions to this Navajo economic "crisis." It was no time to celebrate. I felt a crushing weight; we had helped do this, we had helped take away some of the few jobs on the rez and spur new desperate coal proposals. If we were ever going to be welcomed back to the community without side glares and distrust, we were going to have to do more. Our communities deserve a fair and just economic transition. Our work continued.

ALMOST FOUR YEARS AFTER THE BLACK MESA mine had been shut down and numerous restarts have failed, I found myself in the summer of 2009 sitting in the visitors' section of our tribal council chambers. It was the second day of the Navajo Nation Council summer legislative session, our government's Senate. I was in Window Rock, Arizona, for the Navajo Green Jobs vote.

As with my many other visits to our tribal nation's capitol, I tried to calm my urge to leave this place and head home, back to my children. I had spent the past four years of my daughter's life dragging her to public hearings, community meetings, and board meetings or leaving her at home with my sister. I longed to be home with my children, enjoying picking corn or feeding the chickens. I must remind myself that those wanted simplicities are the reason I am here today.

Black Mesa Water Coalition has grown up since the CPUC hearing. And as the codirector, I'd learned many lessons, most of them the hard way. Reprimanded or embarrassed by elders in the community over and over again, I learned there are times when you should not sit back and just watch the debate and other times when you have to shut up and listen, listen, listen, and you better know how to tell when is when. I had to partially unlearn my whole way of thinking that I received from college and relearn how to see myself as a part of everything around me. Every day is a constant melding of two worldviews: individualism versus communalism.

Our group itself had spent the past years in coalition with many other groups advocating for a just transition off coal dependence and on to green jobs. For us, green jobs mean good-paying jobs that don't pollute. They also mean more than cloaking a broken capitalist system in a sexy green dress. The green economy we propose would enable local Navajo communities to have jobs which are not only sustainable, but also utilize our traditional skills and knowledge.

That day, the Navajo Nation Council, with all its *Robert's Rules of Order* and formalities, was once again considering our proposal, the "Navajo Nation Green Economy Commission and Fund." This was more than bureaucratic political process; if the delegates supported this legislation, it would be the first step toward creating thousands of new, nonpolluting jobs on the reservation. The Commission and Fund would amass funding to provide communities with business and technical support. It would grant funds for job creation in everything from agriculture and green building initiatives to solar and wind community co-ops, as well as training programs for workforce development and management. It all boiled down to this.

We'd been to our capitol too many times to count, but that day was going to be different. We filled the visitors' section with green shirts and stickers. There were even some among the council delegates and staffers. Everything read NAVAJO GREEN JOBS Now! I tried to look calm and composed while sweating in the July heat. My fingers blazed along my phone's tiny computer screen as I sent out emails and texts to volunteers and staff here and at our office.

Finally the session started. The Speaker of the council entered the room. My dear friend and codirector, Wahleah Johns, and my clan brother, Tony Skrelunas, had been asked to join the Speaker to answer any delegate's questions. As they made their way to the front of the room, I could hardly contain my anticipation.

Before questions, the secretary read the legislation. As each line of the legislation was read, I thought about the almost two years we worked with just about everyone to build a policy that reflected the wide-ranging needs of a Navajo green economy. My mind flashed back to our first meeting with the Navajo legislative lawyer; on first sight, her only comment was, "You are going to need some older people with you." We were, for the most part, a group of people in our twenties and thirties, and that worried some. Legislative processes after all don't normally see many people under the age of fifty head-butting their way into policy shifts. But it's my future and my children's future that politicians are screwing with. Every day they are making decisions on things that will affect us far into the future. So there we were again, a group of young people, filling the Navajo Nation Council with green, letting our council know that we were watching their decision. And at that moment, across the country, Navajo college students and those working in cities were faxing, emailing, and calling their council delegate, letting them know that they were watching as well.

> *Green jobs mean good-paying jobs that don't pollute. They also mean more than cloaking a broken capitalist system in a sexy green dress. The green economy we propose would enable local Navajo communities to have jobs which are not only sustainable, but also utilize our traditional skills and knowledge.*

Then before I knew it, the motion was made in Navajo to close discussion and vote. My breath caught as I turned my eyes up to watch the large electronic scoreboard that hangs above the chambers and dangled our fate. Each delegate's name appeared with a red or green light next to it to indicate his or her vote. Green, green, green, green, red, green. . . . The seconds seemed like minutes, waiting for each to vote. But then there it was, the decision—62 to 1—it passed! For a second I looked around me, wondering to myself, *did it really just pass?* Anxious faces turned to huge smiles; we all jumped up and cheered. In this rural part of Arizona, the capitol of our Nation, where dirt roads are more abundant than paved ones and politics has often followed an unwavering commitment to coal and gas, this small victory felt like being at the center of a major seismic event.

<hr />

NOW, SITTING AT THE KITCHEN TABLE—LAPTOP OPEN; dishes piling up; in between juggling phone calls, emails, and kid's meals—I think about how far we have come. And yet, there is still so much work to be done: a need for multiangled and multistakeholder campaigns, a need to build equity on the same "green" side. Black Mesa is still being mined today for coal, with numerous proposals igniting to reopen the closed parts. I remind myself that change is happening step by step. I have proudly stood side by side with so many courageous people as we are called idealists, radicals, or inexperienced young people. I realize it is we—the young, idealistic radicals—who are not only demanding but also building some of the wisest solutions in our communities.

One of the biggest honors I have received in my life was being asked to present at my old high school's Career Day. This community, which for so long has been sustained by the coal mine, dealt with mine layoffs, and received mine payoffs, asked me to speak, and I went. I worried I might need a bulletproof vest, but instead I was greeted with open arms and smiles. Everyone seemed eager to talk about the positive changes the community is making now, and rather than being constantly challenged, I was treated with respect and appreciation. It was these subtle exchanges that were some of the highest acknowledgments and rewards for me. Looking back now, I know that some of the hardest and most heartwarming work to do is in our own communities. It is the tough and scary work of challenging our own family, friends, and people we've grown up with and daring them to dream bigger than we've ever been taught.

Some of the hardest and most heartwarming work to do is in our own communities. It is the tough and scary work of challenging our own family, friends, and people we've grown up with and daring them to dream bigger than we've ever been taught.

Peabody's lights still blink over Black Mesa, but one day soon they will be turned off, and, shining brightly, the moon and stars will remain. The stories, values, and teachings embedded within the night sky remain alive, and we must remember them as we reshape the world we want to see.

———————

Enei Begaye stepped down from directing the Black Mesa Water Coalition to make room for younger leadership, but she remains a senior advisor and active member. She is currently living in Alaska with her husband, Evon Peter, who is also a strong advocate within Alaska Native communities. Enei is enjoying time with their four children, strategizing on campaigns, and writing her reflections on the past ten years of community organizing on the reservation.

PHOTO BY AARON HUEY

WHITNEY BLACK

▶ Twenty-five ▶ United States ▶ Climate Comedian

PHOTO BY STEFFEN THALEMANN

The Yes Men: Surviving in a Time of Climate Chaos

First they ignore you, then they laugh at you, then they fight you, then you win.

—MAHATMA GANDHI

I WAS PERUSING THE SUSTAINABLY GROWN BLUEBERRIES at the downtown Manhattan Whole Foods store when the signal was given to suit up. With the precision of a well-trained ninja, I threw my large blue IKEA bag to the floor and laid out one cumbersome costume, the SurvivaBall. Within five minutes, I was inside the suit and maximum inflation had been attained. I shuffled up and down the aisles, following the sounds of my fellow protesters, yet I only managed to accomplish knocking over displays of sustainable fish and recycled paper products. The groceries weren't the real targets, just innocent bystanders, but I forged ahead despite the guilt. Amid the chaos of singing theater-goers, scrambling security guards, and highly confused store customers, my suit malfunctions. Frustrated and unable to see, I wonder to myself, *how the hell did I get here?*

The memories often pop in and out of my brain as if they were flashbacks from a war zone. But let me start at the beginning. I moved to New York to go to grad school and learn about how to help stop the impending doom of climate change. But I always felt a little different. I had grandiose ideas of using comedy and satire to help solve the world's problems. My prestigious and highly respected Columbia University climate science professors, although supportive, thought those ideas were just, well, "cute." Who knew vindication would come in the form of a SurvivaBall?

Before I started terrorizing the world with satirical activism, I was donning a shiny white lab coat and goggles while discoursing about oceanic biogeochemical compounds by day and sashaying in a kickline across the local community theater stage by night. I don't know what was weirder: having a *dream* that I could possibly combine creative theatrical style with my fervent ambition to humorously enlighten the world about climate change or that I actually *found* a way to combine the two.

The SurvivaBall is a six-foot- (1.8-meter-) diameter spherical beige suit tattooed with corporate logos that looks like a bloated tick with a human face. It was first birthed for the Catastrophic Loss Conference, where two men posing as Halliburton representatives demonstrated the functionality of the large inflatable suits. Dubbed a "gated community for one," the suit would protect the corporate elite from any number of future climate-induced calamities including drought, flood, extreme temperatures, sea-level rise, famine, hurricanes, and even impending ice age. Since such a technical phenomenon inevitably comes at an astronomical price, it would also conveniently protect one from the hundreds of thousands of future climate refugees who couldn't afford it.

The first time I came across a SurvivaBall, an email popped up in my inbox. "Worried about climate change? Don't be!" said the subject line. An absurd picture of a smiling beige blob popped up proclaiming to be a self-contained, completely sustainable climate-catastrophe-protection apparatus. The website read:

> We are America's largest companies, and we have a plan to save you from the wide range of catastrophes that are likely to come from our increasingly unstable climate.

> While others look to Senate bills or UN accords for a climate solution, we look to our best engineers. And our expert team has come up with a solution in perfect accord with our values. The SurvivaBall.

I covered myself in a layer of snot and tears after laughing so hard. The fact that there were others trying to work toward solving climate change and actually had a sense of humor about it was artificially comforting to me. Not that my sigh of relief was because there was a suit out there claiming to be the be-all, end-all solution for catastrophic weather, it was just nice to know that there were others that had the same thought processes that I do.

Most of the campaigns and messaging in environmentalism encompassed the "doom and gloom" approach, that if you don't help us save the world *right now*, we're *all* going to die, and it will be *all your fault*. While this message accurately conveys urgency and severity, having studied people's perceptions and reactions to climate change during my graduate studies, I knew that it was also ineffective and overused. If the environmental movement wanted to educate the mainstream public in order to inspire, mobilize, and take action, it would have to step out of its comfort zone. Let's face it, people like to be entertained, and besides, who said saving the world couldn't be fun?

If the environmental movement wants to educate the mainstream public, it has to step out of its comfort zone. Let's face it, people like to be entertained, and besides, who said saving the world couldn't be fun?

The SurvivaBall was the brainchild of a group called The Yes Men. In the activist world, they are well known for impersonating large corporations in order to publicly embarrass them and expose the truly disgusting world of corporate greed. One time they posed as Exxon executives and introduced a new fuel called Vivoleum made entirely out of climate change victims. Another time they posed as Dow Chemical on the BBC to announce complete remediation to the victims of the Bhopal tragedy. Naturally, these stunts garner lots of media attention, which then creates a level platform to talk about the real issues these companies hide behind expensive PR campaigns. Then, to further rub sand in the wound, The Yes Men make documentaries about all their exploits. But I had never actually heard of them until I read that email.

After grad school, I started working on a climate change documentary. I became fully enthralled with the documentary-film industry and soon was looking for other possibilities when the project started coming to a close. My producer, a mutual friend of The Yes Men, suggested I go help with their documentary. Fast-forward a few emails, and I found myself entering a claustrophobic little office currently serving as Yes Men HQ. Taken aback by the mess before me, I pushed a pile of papers aside to place my laptop down as I noticed tapes and books lining the walls while reams of (fake) newspapers barricaded the corner. This was no well-oiled machine; instead, I found myself immersed in a ragtag team of activists. I was trying to figure out where they kept the pitchforks and torches hidden in the haphazardly cluttered office when I met Larken, the artist who had once provided gourmet service on a NYC subway car. There was Joseph, who would occasionally find himself flailing on the floor wondering why he didn't have a real career as a respectable journalist. Then there was Andy and Mike, the original Yes Men, who went together like peanut butter and jelly, except peanut butter was a bit high maintenance. It wasn't until I met Rocco, the undocumented nomadic homeless guy, that I started wondering what I had gotten myself into.

Somehow, one week later, I got promoted to SurvivaBall Commander, a title I'm sure my parents and Columbia University were proud of. But there I was, suddenly in control of an army of twenty-five to be unleashed upon the city and around the country. It became my duty to showcase the stupidest costume known to humankind. I wanted to announce my sudden rise to power, but in the absence of a podium and a cheering crowd, I opted to send out an email instead.

The great part about using SurvivaBalls is their amazing ability to disarm any situation. It's one of the best suits for actions, because security doesn't know how to handle them, and someone has yet to find a way to handcuff someone inside. That's how I found myself in Whole Foods—it was the first time I wore the suit. We had been taking audiences that had seen the documentary out on actions. That particular night, the target was Whole Foods, since the CEO, John Mackey, had just released a tirade against health care reform. The U.S. population was up in arms over health care, as many of us who needed it didn't have it or couldn't afford it, since we're all not CEOs of major corporations over here. If we couldn't get health care right, the climate bill would have no hope.

I felt a bit ridiculous walking into the store with a deflated SurvivaBall suit and pretending to decide what brand of crackers to buy. Part of what makes a flash mob work so well is the ability to be inconspicuous beforehand, and I was failing miserably. Luckily, it's New York, and considering I had just seen Elmo walking home from work the other day, I probably fit in better than I thought. After the signal, I scrambled to assemble myself, first finding the flip-flops glued into the bottom of the costume in order to put my feet in. Then I took the helmet, adjusted the straps, and flipped on the fans before clipping it onto my head. The dual fans fastened above the helmet suck in air from the outside, turning me into a bulbous ticklike creature, free to roam about the world. Forgoing peripheral vision, I soon found out the real trick is trying not to knock things (including people) over.

I heard the whole store break out in song. It was 10:30 at night, and the security guards had no idea how to handle a mob of one hundred with six inflatable blobs roaming about. This was definitely not in their training manual. I sang along, although I couldn't remember all the words, and it was too hard to hold the piece of paper with the lyrics in my hand nubs.

Then I started having other problems. Inflatable suits tend to hold in heat, which is great for cold nights, but otherwise meant I started to sweat after about five minutes. My neck started to tire from holding up the fans, and my shins began to ache from only being able to walk with a six-inch stride. With screaming muscles and soaked in sweat, I tried to shuffle my way out of the store with the rest of the crowd but could only move so fast with my legs being shorter than two feet. I caught a glimpse of one of the security guards trying to manhandle Rocco, who was also in a suit. I couldn't help but smile as the poor guard got bowled over in slow motion ten seconds later.

As I made my way outside, I couldn't wait to get out of my sweaty enclosure. If only I could find my damn helper. The biggest irony of the SurvivaBall is that you really can't "survive" alone since someone from the outside has to zip you up in order to complete the ensemble. That means even though I'm suffering from near heat exhaustion and lactic acid buildup, I am still at the mercy of whoever wants to lend a hand because the person who has zipped me into the costume also has to unzip me. Perhaps the zippers should have been sewn on the inside. But we're not all engineers, after all.

Mechanics aside, there were bigger and better targets to humiliate. I was feeling quite cozy with the team of misfits I was now a part of as we piled up in our tiny office hatching the next plan. New York City was hosting Climate Week in support of the international climate summit being held by the United Nations. All the world leaders would meet in one place to discuss climate change, and we were going to do our part to make sure those heads of state got down to business. We wanted to blockade the UN with SurvivaBalls until everyone came to a fair agreement, but with the massive amounts of security and whole streets being blocked off, we knew even the SurvivaBall couldn't break that stronghold.

So we would pretend to approach the UN building by water instead of land by "wading" up the East River shore in hopes to create some media buzz. Ironically, the SurvivaBall cannot actually float. In fact, the water seeps in quite quickly and fills up the ball, creating a potentially gruesome death trap either by drowning or electrocution from the fans' batteries. But I was sure the volunteers would still be lining up to participate anyway.

The morning of, I arrived at the bank of the East River slightly downwind of midtown, donning my corporate attire with a veil of anxiety as an accessory. After the last couple of actions, I found out that even though I love the theatrics, I don't seem to quite have the stomach yet to deal with whatever unknown consequences us Yes Men tend to find ourselves in.

The balled army of twenty-five was out in full force and ready to surge ahead. I was not in a suit but playing the part of corporate hack, ready to pass out informational brochures to any willing or unwilling passerby (and also to help volunteers into and out of the suits). But to first rally the troops, I played a rousing round of our anthem, Gloria Gaynor's "I Will Survive," on the boom box. I marveled at the awe-inspiring spectacle: twenty-five six-foot- (1.8-meter-) diameter beige globoids adorned with corporate logos bouncing up and down as they try to navigate the shallow water and rocks along the bank.

Then I saw the police boats show up. All of a sudden, the coast guard appeared, with their sirens, probably bemused by the bizarre pageantry displayed before them. Then more police boats showed up. Then a helicopter. Then a man from inside the helicopter descended out of the aircraft and hovered over the water as if ready to spring into action. Oh, crap. My stomach pit of nervous excitement just turned into an ulcer.

I knew the SurvivaBall had an innate ability to attract stupid amounts of attention, including the occasional police officer, but never before had boats and helicopters been called to the scene. I never would have guessed that dancing beach balls on coastal waters would be considered quite the security risk. As if the police actually believed we would take the water by storm. I was torn between laughing at the ludicrous overreaction and my instinct to save myself and run for the high hills.

As I watched the circus unfold before me, the next act entered the ring. If at first by air and sea, the last piece of the puzzle was put in place when the police finally showed up by car. So I tended to the balls while keeping an eye out as the Yes Men, Andy and Mike, coyly approached the policeman and asked the unsubtle question, "What seems to be the problem, officer?"

I am not an aficionado at dealing with the police at actions, as I get quite apprehensive. In school, I learned things like chemistry and math, how to calculate solar flux, and the difference between carbon taxing and cap and trade, not how to work your way out of getting arrested. I had this image in my head of trying to shove SurvivaBalls into the back of a cop car and sitting behind bars. I fought my nervousness with logic. I knew they couldn't arrest us all, and I didn't think there was a law against running amok with large inflatable costumes. In the end, I watched as Andy was lead off to the clink on the charge of a previously unpaid bicycle ticket. Good job, cops, keeping the streets of New York safe from those rogue bicyclists who don't pay their tickets for riding through Washington Square Park. Later we would learn that the officer also lied through his teeth when filing the report, in that he stated he saw people jump the fence and ignore signs forbidding entrance to the beach, all of which was completely untrue.

However, for the Yes Men, getting arrested is rarely a lemon but rather more like a sugar-coated lemon taken with a shot of vodka. When Andy got arrested, this prompted CNN to cover the whole shenanigan, causing our symbol of stupidity to be seen by tens of millions of people. Yes, America: this is what you will look like if we don't take action now on climate change.

When Andy got arrested, this prompted CNN to cover the whole she-
nanigan, causing our symbol of stupidity to be seen by tens of millions of
people. Yes, America: this is what you will look like if we don't take action
now on climate change.

Throughout the Balls Across America campaign, I marched with the Yes Men crew in countless parades, rallied at 350 International Day of Climate Action in Times Square, maneuvered through the New York City Halloween Parade, brought the SurvivaBalls to countless actions around the country, and even traveled all the way to Copenhagen for the climate treaty negotiations to adorn famous statues and foreigners with the costume of the potential impending future. They broke all the time, didn't fit right, got ripped, had parts missing, and had to be repaired constantly. They always elicited the same reaction of confusion and hilarity from onlookers. Newscasters never spelled or pronounced the name right.

After all is said and done, I really hate SurvivaBalls. And I really don't want to live in one. It's only fun for an hour, not a whole lifetime. So I make it a point to use CFLs, eat less meat, buy renewable energy, recycle, and—most importantly—be an activist. Because in fifty years, I really don't want to have to survive in the world's stupidest costume.

As the balls travel around the world, I'm sitting here in my New York apartment fighting my dog for the spot next to the window on my bed while trying to figure out my next strategic step. Scientists say there are only a few years left before a crucial point of no return is passed. I've pulled out countless hairs obsessing, scrutinizing, and searching the depths of my mind every day, thinking, "Should I write? Should I educate? Should I fight? Should I go work in government? Where can I make the most amount of impact in this pivotal point in history?"

So instead I impersonated the U.S. Chamber of Commerce. But I can't tell that story until after the trial is over . . .

Whitney Black is currently still causing mayhem with the Yes Men, while simultaneously fending off the Chamber of Commerce lawsuit with a stick. She may or may not also have a real job by now. The SurvivaBalls have been sent out to travel the world but may soon be recalled for mass production upon the pronouncement of the death of the U.S. climate bill.

BENJAMIN POTTS

▶ Twenty-nine ▶ Australia ▶ Eco-Pirate

Taking the Whale War Hostage

The time has come when speaking is not enough, applauding is not enough. We have to act. I urge you, every time you have an opportunity, make your opinions known by physical presence. Do it!

—JACQUES COUSTEAU

THE DELTA INFLATABLE BOAT SPED ACROSS the large blue swells as I concentrated on trying to slow my racing heart and focus my wired nerves. Taking slow deep breaths and mentally preparing myself for confrontation, I kept reinvisioning myself scaling the rail onto the deck of the 1,025-ton (929.9-metric-ton) harpoon ship. If we managed to successfully board the ship, we would at least survive the action, though that could involve spending the next months or years in Japanese incarceration. If we failed, we could be crushed between the vessels or fall into the freezing Antarctic waters and be blended into a human smoothie by the massive propeller. Neither was an inviting prospect to someone who had really only just begun their foray into direct action.

But this was definitely not the time for doubt. I had decided a long time ago to dedicate my life to the defense of the Earth, and now that Captain Paul Watson had given me the opportunity, I was not about to back down. I had come aboard the Sea Shepherd Conservation Society's flagship, the M/V *Robert Hunter*, in July 2007 in Melbourne, Australia. Later to be renamed the M/V *Steve Irwin*, the ship still bore a large rusting scar ripped into the plate steel after a collision with a Japanese spotting vessel during the 2006 campaign. I would often stand out on the dock at night while on security watch and imagine what it would be like to stand on that bow as two great hunks of speeding metal came together in the frigid waters of the Antarctic.

The great boxy outline of the ships superstructure in the inky night sky, like some medieval fortress, spoke silently of purpose and the battle to come. The "*Stevesy*" waited patiently, creaking against the dockside for the time when the lines would be slipped and the race to save one thousand great whales in the southern oceans begun. My only wish was that I would be standing on that deck as she sailed out through the heads of Port Phillip Bay and due south to meet the roaring seas, shimmering ice, and ruthless whalers. My wish had been granted, and now come hell or high water. I would board a kill ship and let these whalers know face to face that I would not let them continue to kill whales in the Southern Ocean Whale Sanctuary without a fight.

Thank you for your offer of traditional Japanese hospitality. So far, our experience of it has been to be assaulted, tied up, and almost thrown overboard. But at least we were not harpooned and electrocuted first like the whales that you murder.

—Ben Potts & Giles Lane

The Japanese fleet's harpoon ships, of which there are three, are like Grim Reapers to the whales, menacing-looking vessels that taper into long, streamlined hulls and have raised bows where platforms for the harpoons are located. After a whale is hit in the guts with a grenade-tipped harpoon, it is then dragged into the ship to be peppered with rifle fire or electrocuted, then tied by their tail. With the whale inverted and drowning in its own blood, it is dragged back to the factory ship for butchering. These are ships designed to kill, but the design of the kill ship was also its weakness. Its low-lying deck, almost level with the waterline, opened itself up to a boarding from an inflatable boat.

The plan was to board one of these vessels and order the captain to cease his whaling operations, as it was in violation of the 1986 global moratorium on commercial whaling, Southern Ocean Whale Sanctuary, and CITES (Convention on International Trade in Endangered Species) treaty, as well as numerous other laws. The idea was just radical enough to potentially halt whaling operations and bring the issue to the forefront of the world's attention. At the end of the day, that was what we were here to do. The diplomatic talks, banner waving, and petitions of the world's governments and mainstream environmental corporations had failed for twenty years to bring about an end to whaling by Japan, Norway, and Iceland. It was time for a change.

The great decimation of whale populations during much of the 19th and 20th centuries resulted in the formation of the International Whaling Commission (IWC) in 1946 to regulate commercial whaling. But for decades, it had been deadlocked between nations who wished to transform it from a body that oversaw the continued exploitation of whales to one that would conserve and try to return whale populations from the brink of extinction. Since the 1986 moratorium, only scientific and cultural hunts were allowed, and Japan therefore claimed their annual hunt of nearly one thousand whales—including endangered whales in the Antarctic—as a matter of "science." Japan was using the "science" loophole to continue its commercial exploitation despite the development of nonlethal research methods. This simple relabeling of the hunt as "research" and the power Japan wields in international trade relations has fundamentally crippled the IWC and the conservation of all whale species.

> *Since the 1986 moratorium, only scientific and cultural hunts were allowed, and Japan therefore claimed their annual hunt of nearly one thousand whales—including endangered whales in the Antarctic—as a matter of "science."*

But on the day we boarded, January 15, 2008, the Australian Federal Court ruled that the Japanese company carrying out the whaling operations in the whale sanctuary were acting illegally under Australian law.

———

AS WE APPROACHED, THE GRAY STERN OF the harpoon ship grew larger until one could make out the name *Yushin Maru No. 2* printed in English and Japanese. *Yushin* means "brave new" and was meant to herald the resumption of Japan's commercial whaling industry with the construction of several ultramodern harpoon vessels. Yet in our action, we might take the industry back years in economic losses. In a stroke of luck, there was not one whaler in sight. The stink bombs, which the Delta crew had hurled all over the decks, had done their job in driving the whalers inside to escape the overwhelmingly acrid smell of rotten butter.

Dave, the boat operator, brought us in on the port side, but as we approached the gunnels, the harpoon boat increased speed and started to bank sharply from side to side—sending the lower deck, where we needed to board from the waterline, high into the air several meters above our heads and presenting us with a solid wall of slippery plate steel. The ensuing bow wave formed from the displacement of water from underneath the ship almost flipped our small boat upside down. Dave struggled to regain control and extract us from the precarious position.

As the ship leveled out, I found myself yelling into Dave's ear, "*Go go go go go!!*" I could see our chances slipping away and wanted to get onboard before the whalers came swarming out and onto the decks to repel us. The Delta increased power and pushed its starboard quarter into the slick gray side of the harpoon ship. My fellow boarder Giles Lane leapt from the bow over an access gate, while I struggled to move from the rear of the boat to gain a hold on the thick diameter railing used to secure the whales. My hands could barely hold the wet metal as the ship once again banked hard to port and the weight of my backpack combined with the downward motion of the railing almost sent me into the freezing water rushing below at a speed of twenty knots. *Just get over the railing!* was the only thought running through my head, and I threw a leg over and propelled myself headfirst onto the deck as Giles grabbed my backpack and helped haul me over.

In the time it took me to pull out a video camera, the crew responded, and one of the whalers ran down and grabbed me, pushing me up against the bulkhead, followed by several more, until both of us were pinned to the ship wall. Our Delta boat veered off, and we were alone with what was like a mob against us.

"Take us to the captain!" I yelled.

"We have a message for the captain," Giles said.

I tried to quickly produce the letter I had inside my Mustang suit, but my hands were forced away by one of the crew and then zip-tied to the handrailing, so I was all but immobilized. Soon after he was tied up, Giles's circulation was being cut off by his wrenched-down plastic cuffs, and he screamed out for them to be loosened. The whalers suddenly disappeared and left us on the open deck as the ship turned hard to port, sending chilling sub-zero water flooding over the lower deck and immersing us up to our waists. A chill set in; I hadn't considered water boarding the deck.

Minutes later, the water cascaded below, and the whalers returned in helmets and life jackets and proceeded to cut me free. The captain of the vessel, in his dark sunglasses, was yelling furiously from the upper deck and motioning with his hands to get us off. Two of the bigger members of the crew grabbed me underneath the arms, and the harpooner, with GUNNER written on his helmet, proceeded to lift me off the ground and toward the railing. There was no way I was going into the water from a ship traveling at such high speeds and from a position so close to the massive blender of a prop circulating below. I struggled with all my might and managed to free my leg from the harpooner's grip and kick off the railing, sending all four of us sprawling on the deck.

After the failure of trying to throw us back to the sea, the whalers marched us up a stairway onto the upper deck behind the wheelhouse. Ropes were produced from everywhere, and as in some *Looney Tunes* cartoon where the victim is tied in masses of rope to the railway tracks, we were securely fastened to the satellite dish mast. Even with the captain screaming in Japanese in my face, I was able to produce the letter from my shirt front. *"You're under arrest!"* I yelled rather ironically. The captain refused to take the document, but a tall guy dressed in black came over and took the letter from my hands. Giles and I were left in this position while the crew went off to man the fire hoses, taking aim at the Delta boat and our helicopter flying overhead with cameras rolling.

After what seemed like an eternity since we boarded, we were hustled in to the bridge and below for interrogation. The man dressed in black turned out to be the second officer of the ship and could speak rudimentary English. I pulled out my "dirty" Japanese dictionary full of colorful insults and humorous slang words and tried to find something appropriate to say from the extremely small selection. "Excuse my shitty Japanese," I pronounced terribly in Japanese.

This broke the ice a little, and the whalers all laughed. Then the second officer said, "Excuse my shitty English." We then informed him that their whaling operations are illegal under Australian and international law, that they were targeting endangered species, and that they should cease and desist and leave these waters immediately. We stated that we were here to deliver this message , pointing to the letter, and return to our ship, pointing out the porthole toward the Delta boat, which was still under chase outside. They were not impressed.

As the harpoon ship sped out of Australian waters and into international waters, the helicopter and small boat were forced to return to the *Irwin* without us, as they were running low on fuel. Giles and I were escorted to a cabin where a guard was placed by the door. We demanded contact with our ship and respective governments but were denied both. The whalers invited us to dine with the captain, but we sensed a publicity-photo setup and, not wishing to eat with a criminal, we refused and ate a vegetarian meal in our cabins. Later, we found out that the head of the Institute of Cetacean Research (ICR), the hack science body in Japan, had said that we had eaten whale meat. It was becoming a media war, while we were out of site and unable to tell the world what was really going on.

Meanwhile, footage of the action was being transmitted around the world via the *Steve Irwin*, and in the ensuing media storm, we became the center of worldwide attention and political negotiations at the highest levels. The Japanese were offering only to release us on the condition that Sea Shepherd would refrain from harassing their whaling operations and, in doing so, had turned this into a hostage situation. Making demands in exchange for the release of captives is a tactic usually reserved for terrorist organizations.

All this was unbeknownst to us at the time as we attempted to find an escape from the cabin we were confined to. Our greatest fear was that the whalers would begin hunting again with us on board. Should this have happened, or if we were taken back to Japan, we did not plan to make it easy for our captors by causing as much trouble as possible. Each hour we would demand to speak to the second officer, requesting contact with our respective government via satellite phone. But the captain refused each time, as he was waiting to receive instructions from Tokyo.

The whalers requested a statement from us saying that we were okay and being treated well, so that they could quell the international public outrage that was developing. We knew this was our only leverage in the situation, so our reply was this:

Thank you for your offer of traditional Japanese hospitality. So far, our experience of it has been to be assaulted, tied up, and almost thrown overboard. But at least we were not harpooned and electrocuted first like the whales that you murder.

—Ben Potts & Giles Lane

The statement was taken and faxed to the factory ship for translation and then forwarded to Tokyo. Half an hour later, the second officer, who was obviously under a lot of pressure, returned sweating profusely. "You cannot say this; please, please make another statement," he pleaded with us. We refused to make another statement until we had made contact with our governments. We knew this was our ticket to be transferred off the ship.

More time passed, and we counted the twenty-four-hour mark on our watches. We were beginning to think that we may be headed back to Japan. Giles paced back and forth across the tiny cabin like a caged animal, trying to think of an escape from this predicament. I was only too happy to rest on the top bunk. I figured to myself, there is an upside to all this. I had finally gotten out of the daily chores of cleaning toilets, scrubbing decks, and washing up the *Steve Irwin*—this was a well-earned break as far as I could determine. But as the hours ticked by, the claustrophobia of confinement began to creep into my consciousness.

I scanned out the porthole at the sun, which never sets at this latitude and this season, sitting low on the horizon. Its pale light reflected off the unusually calm ocean, and I tried to squash down the thoughts of incarceration in a foreign land and the possibility of having to endure the rest of the whaling season on this cetacean Death Star harpoon ship. Suddenly, the dark outline of a huge endangered fin whale broke the golden surface off the starboard side, and a great mist of breath was exhaled. The great leviathan sprouted again and, with its enormous black tail fluke raised high, waved us farewell as it descended to safety. At least one whale had been spared on this day because of our actions.

A young whaler no more than twenty years old who knew a little English had been stationed to guard our cabin door and gave us the opportunity to have a less serious dialogue than the ones we were having with the second officer. We asked him if this was a good job and whether he was earning good money. "No good job, no good money," he replied, shaking his head. A little time later, he knocked on our cabin door and was holding a videocassette. "I recommend, I recommend!" he motioned, bowing his head, showing a sign of respect.

I took the cassette, and we watched it on the TV that we had found in a cupboard in our cabin. The video was a Japanese animation called *Princess Mononoke,* a story of civilization's encroachment on the spirits of the forest and man's war against the natural world. The fact that this young whaler understood why we were there and had communicated this knowledge through this videotape gave me great hope that our actions would break through to the youth of Japan, despite the establishment's propaganda. In fact, our one action had finally pushed the issue of whaling through to the Japanese media, crushing the silence that had been there for decades. While a debate began to simmer in Japanese politics, one Japanese minister questioned why an industry that makes Japan no money, but which so severely damages its reputation overseas, continues to exist.

After sixty hours of tense negotiations between the prime minister of Australia and foreign ministers of Japan, coupled with a marathon of media assault by Captain Paul Watson, I received a knock on our cabin door. I was taken to a communications room, a radio mic was shoved in my face, and on the receiving end of it was an Australian government official. "Are you and Giles Lane willing to cooperate with Australian Customs, in a transfer to the *Oceanic Viking,* and from there to the *Steve Irwin?*" I exclaimed,

"Bloody oath! Come and get us." *No prison,* I thought to myself. *We live to fight another day.* Several hours after the phone call, an enormous blue and yellow ship appeared outside of our porthole. With great relief, we were escorted out onto the deck, as a smaller fast boat approached with a mean-looking armed boarding party. Just as I was leaving the cabin, I handed the young whaler a small koala bear with a t-shirt saying I LOVE AUSTRALIA. He smiled from ear to ear.

After a happy return to our crewmates on the *Steve Irwin,* big hugs, and congratulations, we learned the full extent of the publicity surrounding the incident. I was immediately placed to work, speaking to journalists from around the world to the point of exhaustion. Working sixteen, sometimes twenty hours straight. The story was front-page news from New York to Tokyo and made the world know that a commercial whale hunt was still continuing in the Southern Ocean off Antarctica, despite the laws. Most important, we had finally managed to breach the silence over the whaling debate within Japan itself. The action had also prevented the whaling fleet from whaling for more than a week during the chase—our boarding and subsequent release preventing the whalers from killing up to 10 whales a day. We took solace in the fact that our Sea Shepherd campaign in total had saved the lives of more than 500 whales—half of the Japanese target of 935 minke and 50 endangered fin whales—with a cost in the millions to the Japanese government and whaling industry.

> *Our Sea Shepherd campaign in total had saved the lives of more than 500 whales—with a cost in the millions to the Japanese government and whaling industry.*

Today, I am still serving with Sea Shepherd on board the M/V *Bob Barker* after having completed my third campaign to the Antarctic. The stakes have been raised. In 2010, one of our ships, the *Ady Gill,* was deliberately rammed and sunk, and its skipper, Pete Bethune, arrested and put on trial in Japan when he boarded another harpoon ship. Despite the costs and the risks,

PHOTO BY JO-ANNE MCARTHUR

we have saved thousands of whales from a brutal death. It's a battle for the sanctity of life in our vulnerable oceans. It's a battle of which I am proud to be a part. And it's a battle that continues today.

Benjamin Potts is a co-star on the hit TV series Whale Wars *on Animal Planet, bringing the plight of whales into the homes of millions of Americans. He is currently working with the pirates of Sea Shepherd in preparation for the next Antarctic whale defense campaign. The battle for whales continues in the Southern Ocean and Sea Shepherd will not surrender until the Japanese whaling fleet ceases their illegal operations.*

SUBHASHNI RAJ

▶ Twenty-five   ▶ Fiji   ▶ Speaker

PHOTO BY SUBHASHNI RAJ

A Fijian Storm

Nothing could be worse than the fear that one had given up too soon, and left one unexpended effort that might have saved the world.

—JANE ADDAMS

SUNLIGHT REFLECTING OFF THE CRYSTAL-CLEAR BLUE WATER glistened in my eyes. I perched myself on an old fisherman's boat, dancing my feet across the sand. The palm trees above me swayed in a calming rhythm. Scanning across the horizon, I was in search of something. This place was new to me. This Fijian island was my homeland, but I had never been to this coastal community before. I was scouting the area of Sigatoka for my research and a community by the name of Vuni Niu welcomed me in, sending their community grandmother, a *bubu,* to show me around. We had just ended our trek and took a rest on the shoreline. Standing tall and proud above me, the old bubu had a warm smile but an air of authority that one could only respect. Up until now, I had been so preoccupied with my scientific work on the Fijian reef that I had yet to think more about the people that inhabited this beautiful place. Bubu and I had been chatting politely when I suddenly turned to her and asked: "Has life changed much for you over the years?" I did not know what I was expecting, really. The words had left my lips before I had a chance to reconsider them.

But I will never forget what Bubu said to me. She shook her head and her face darkened slightly. She breathed in deeply and waved her hand over the landscape as she described another world. She told me of a time not so long ago when the oceans were streaming with fish, the white sandy beach stretched out far and wide, and the ocean surrendered, fleeting away from humans from time to time. She then told me of the world she sees now, where the fish are seldom and the ocean is alone. The beach is narrow and small, collapsing land as it erodes away. And the ocean is attacking, suffocating the community as it comes closer and closer. I didn't know what to say to her; I had no words to express. It was as if she was telling me the island of Fiji was disappearing before her very eyes. But I just stayed quiet, politely listening to her narrative and immediately filed her words in my memory, not realizing how important her brief speech would be to me later.

On the four-hour ride back to Suva, the capital and largest city of Fiji, I followed the sea with my eyes wide open. When I was younger, the sea was my friend, my childhood muse, where I could ponder my very existence. But as I grew older, I could see that the rising tides were becoming an evil, unrelenting menace. I realized that I had been very successful in life and was beaming with potential to do something but somehow still struggled under the expectations of my parents. I became a biologist and never considered any sort of activism, because I had become distracted with making ends meet in my day-to-day life. Now I could see that nature was fighting back by eating the coastline and livelihood of millions of people around the world, and I still felt helpless to react and do something about it. As the car tousled us around, I bombarded myself with excuses as to why I could not act or make a difference. These were probably the same reasons that many people have to justify inaction. I asked myself: I'm only one person, what difference can I really make? What about the political implications? Can't I just pass the buck to someone more capable? I still didn't feel that I had it in me to do what I thought needed to be done. What I didn't realize at the time was that everyone has it in them to do *something,* and I was no exception. But at that time, I was only beginning to put the dots together and I would have to overcome my fear first before I would evolve into more than just a bystander and a dreamer.

Several months later, on September 29, 2009, an 8.1-magnitude underwater earthquake rumbled off the coast of American Samoa. It was the largest earthquake of 2009 and generated a tsunami wave that New Zealand scientists determined would measure as high as forty-five feet (13.7 meters) off the Samoan coast. The tsunami warning in Fiji was taken as a joke. Instead of running for shelter, people lined up at the beach to see the wave come in, never expecting it to be large enough to cause any damage by the time it hit our coast.

If you have not experienced the ferociousness that is at the heart of a tsunami, it is a bit hard to comprehend how large the face of the wave is until it consumes the ground beneath your feet. More than 189 people died off the Samoan coast, while down the street from where I was, people gathered just far enough away from the destruction, watching as if it were a mere fireworks display, not really aware of the devastation being wreaked as they looked on. Later, news came in of the deaths, and we watched for days the videos of the waves and the magnitude of the destruction over and over again. Reality began to sink its teeth into my consciousness as the islands around me were also slightly sinking into the depths of the ocean. We could watch in awe, grateful it was not happening in our backyard. *At least not yet,* I thought.

A week later, another earthquake with a magnitude of 7.6 struck near Fiji, off the coast of Vanuatu. I was at work when the earthquake hit, and I ran into a colleague in my office who urgently told me, "There is a tsunami coming!" He pleaded with me to make sure that my family was safe. I thought he was kidding or maybe just paranoid. Where I live, tsunamis seem to be a constant threat but never materialize and warnings are canceled. This was quite out of the blue; I was not sure how to react. Should I take him seriously or go about my day as normal? He told me that this was the real thing and it could hit in the next sixty minutes. After all those deaths I saw, I was suddenly petrified of the possibilities. Sometimes you never realize how capable you really are until you are forced to act. In that moment, I leapt into action.

I ran back to my desk and snatched my cell phone. I clumsily dialed my brother's number. As I waited, holding my breath, I could see that outside the window the area around me was turning into chaos, with people hearing the news and becoming frantic. My feelings went from anger with my brother for not picking up the phone to immediate guilt and just wanting him to be safe until I saw him again. Just then, he picked up and said had not left for the university yet and was safe at home. Thank God, I thought.

In my heightened state of anxiety, I hadn't realized that almost everyone in the room either had a phone to their ear or was in the process of picking one up. Everyone was either calling whomever they could or receiving calls from whoever could get through the line. The sound in the room escalated as cries of frustration also rang. Just then, the networks became jammed. It was probably the worst thing that could have happened at that point. My co-workers and I did not leave, because we were at a high perch and needed to stay where we were. We heard news come in of major evacuation happening all over Fiji. No one was willing to take a risk this time.

Minutes passed. This seemed to be the quiet before the storm. Not being able to do anything but wait, I sat on my desk and looked around me. The phones were still not working and we were not able to leave, so the only connection we had was with other people around us. I found it hard to concentrate on chatting, because the chatter in my own head was too loud. I was thinking about when I was in Sigatoka and what Bubu had said about the rising waters. I had not really taken the time to think about the consequences then, but now that was all I could do.

The entire infrastructure of most islands is on the coast. I could not conceive the costs that would be involved in moving whole cities away from the coast. In some cases, moving would not even be an option because there is no higher land to move to. Even if the option were presented, I was sure that many locals would refuse to leave their ways of life and would rather die on the land they know then move to territories that were unknown. I knew that there are places like Tuvalu that were already being hit hard by rising sea levels and face-high gushes of seawater flowing through the streets at king (high) tide. Or places like the Carteret Islands, Papua New Guinea, where nothing will grow because the water sources have been polluted by the ocean's salt.

So as the hour wore on, I began to pray. I put my palms together and prayed to God. I prayed that the tsunami would return to the depths from which it was summoned and keep my family and friends safe. Then, with only minutes remaining, I had a moment of clarity. All of a sudden, I knew that even if we survived this tsunami today, we had an even larger wave looming over us—the climate change wave. Rising sea levels from the melting polar ice caps will consume our island forevermore. The ocean will continue to hammer us till there is nothing left. I didn't believe these earthquakes and tsunamis were linked to climate change, but they did have something in common with it: they could bring the death of us on these islands. While the threat I faced today was of a natural origin, the one I faced tomorrow was a juggernaut of our own making, and one that we could stop if we so wanted.

The entire infrastructure of most islands is on the coast. I could not conceive the costs that would be involved in moving whole cities away from the coast. In some cases, moving would not be an option because there is no higher land to move to. Even if the option were presented, I was sure that many locals would refuse to leave their ways of life and would rather die on the land they know.

I felt fueled by my fear of the possibility of everyone I knew being consumed by water, and I turned to my laptop, grateful to find that the Internet was working. I fired off an email to my friend James. I told him what was happening and that if we survived this, I was going to speak to world leaders, stand up for what I believed in, and work with others to do the same. Despite my fears of stepping up, I needed to do this for my people. I turned away from my laptop and went to a window looking out to the ocean and shook my head as I saw people gathering below to wait for the wave to come in. With only a couple minutes left, we held our breaths, expecting the worst. We waited in anticipation, and just as the final moments drew upon us, we were given a red light, the tsunami warning was yet again canceled. People tried to get back to whatever they were doing in a fog and frenzied state. But for me, I now had a vision, and I was not even close to letting it go. Adrenaline can force you to make crazy decisions, and just as it was wearing off, in my head I yelled out, *"Copenhagen, here I come!"*

My focus kept fighting off the anxiety of the new horizons that were becoming apparent. I knew I needed to find a way to the Copenhagen

Climate Conference, and I started to look around for inspiration. I learned from my friend David about the *350.org* campaign that he was working on, and he invited me to join. An international campaign, *350.org* works to unite the world around one solution, lowering our carbon in the atmosphere to 350 parts per million, what many say is the sustainable number for our future. Across geopolitical borders, we would be working to raise awareness and be a much larger voice than just one person—there was something very powerful in that. I realized that this was exactly what I wanted to be doing with my life. I was where I belonged. I had purpose. And it was a beautiful feeling.

I didn't believe earthquakes and tsunamis were linked to climate change, but they did have something in common with it: they could bring the death of us on these islands. While the threat I faced today was of a natural origin, the one I faced tomorrow was a juggernaut of our own making, and one that we could stop if we so wanted.

I spent close to three weeks missing sleep and food. I was balancing the pressure of helping organize the Fiji 350 campaign, securing sponsorship, and my already heavy workload at my office. I did it with much joy nonetheless, because finally I was trying to be part of the solution. As I changed all the house bulbs, explained to my mother and brother over and over again the need to switch off lights, I saw their behavior slowly change. I felt what I was trying to do was not in vain and that people could make changes with the hope that the effects would multiply.

And then before I knew it, it was the big day, October 24, 2009. That day, the Suva waters were calm while several hundred young voices carried the 350 chant. I walked with the sea never leaving my side, and the blue-sky breezy day reminded me there was a reason I worked so hard for this campaign. I needed to give back instead of continuing to take away from an already overtaxed planet. That was the first time in the city where I was born that I cried out for change, and man, did it ever feel good.

I tried to capture it all in photographs so that the world could see the Islands were also demanding 350 ppm in time for the Copenhagen Climate Summit. Media took notice of our rally; we got spots in the *Fiji Times* newspaper and on Fiji TV. Weeks later, I got word that *350.org* would like me to go with them to Copenhagen as their Pacific representative. I thought it was a joke at first. I refused to believe it and many emails later, I was jumping, yelling, and clapping all at once. It was very distracting for my mother, who could not understand how anything short of winning the lottery could justify such emotions.

Bags packed and five flights and three continents later, I landed in cold, chilly Copenhagen of Denmark. I came to share the Pacific's story with the hope that the leaders would listen. But the first day was jarring, because there wasn't a single person that I could call my friend. I was lonely and scared, and it took time to find my bearings. Anyone could see I was brand new. I was not a seasoned campaigner or activist, but I had a story that needed to be heard. This was reinforced when I found that many of the islands were missing representatives inside the conference center.

Soon, I would get the opportunity to share my story, many times over, but the one that would stick in everyone's minds was my real moment in the spotlight. It was called the *Rainstorm Action,* an art performance inside the conference center that mimicked the flooding of island states due to climate change and gave a speaking opportunity with all the world's media paying attention. I was blown away at being given the opportunity. This was huge. This was my opportunity on the world stage. There were nerves. There was fear. Not of public speaking—I had many awards for that. But I was afraid that I might not be able to speak honestly, that I would not be able to deliver on the reality of the situation, that in that moment I would not be able to make it connect for the audience—but I needed to. Many people back home had faith that I would, and the *350.org* team was relying on me. This was the most important piece of public speaking that I had ever done, and I could not fail.

As a *350.org* member called out my name and I stepped up to hold the microphone, I thought back to my conversation with Bubu, and saw the journey I had made since then. I was making a difference, in my own way. I knew what I did at the grassroots level was just as important as efforts on the top level, because I was helping to make a movement, which is the central force for all other change. Today, I was going to take what Bubu told me and retell it in my own way to the world.

I took a deep breath and tried. I felt as if I was getting nowhere by citing journal article facts, so I paused and asked for patience. I explained that this was a significant event and that I was overwhelmed. I was met with kind eyes from the crowd, as everyone could relate. I took another deep breath and began again. I stumbled through the most important speech of my life, concluding with:

> If climate change was something we could deal with on our own, we would do so, but unfortunately we cannot. For us to save our homes from the devastation that climate change is sure to bring, we need your help. If this was war, and you asked the Islands to fight for you, you know we would, and we have. This time we need you to step up for us.

I returned to Fiji soon after, disappointed by the failures of the Copenhagen Climate Summit. Yet as I reflect, I have come to see that the only person whose actions I can control is me. If I can make a difference, then I must. I am tired of the broken political promises, circular rhetoric, and public lip service by our world "leaders" that consistently fail to deliver any substantial change. Instead, I know now the value of grassroots activism to build a movement and revolutionize communities. This is the change one person can make; that is what I can do.

So don't give up, because I am just getting started.

Subhashni Raj is currently working with 350.org to help build a climate movement in the Pacific Island countries. She's helping the sparks fly with securing funding for climate workshops, leadership training sessions, and youth-led environmental initiatives.

PHOTO BY SUBHASHNI RAJ

ALLANA BELTRAN

▶ Twenty-five ▶ Australia ▶ Performance Artist

PHOTO BY MATTHEW NEWTON

Tasmania: We Will Always Be Together in the Forest

The difference between a soldier and a warrior is that the warrior is a lover...

—MATTHEW FOX

ARRIVING ON TASMANIAN SHORES BY BOAT, I felt magic in the air. Fresh, icy wind blowing on my face from the land's ancient forested mountains. I know I need to be here, but I do not yet know I will help create a powerful and internationally recognized symbol for saving the last of Tasmania's ancient forests. Nor do I know that I will fall in love and that my life will never really be the same again.

As I stand there, embracing the moment, a tall, beautiful, and mysterious man named Ben Morrow approaches. He takes me on a tour of the forests, and it's like standing inside a cathedral of creation's most delicate sculptural masterpieces. This is enlightenment in the form of bright greens, yellows, deep umbers, and sparkling fragments of gold hovering effortlessly around me. Light refracting like crystals through dew-filled spider webs. Tiny, tweeting blue fairy wrens flutter and sweep through the ornate myrtle branches and giant flowering man ferns. The floor and walls are carpeted in soft breathing moss and lichen. And a loud echo reverberates through the forest, a sound I had never heard before: *koo koo koo koo ... koooo koo.* "That's the cry of the currawong," Ben tells me.

He leads me down a winding stone path. Something catches my eye in the distance. I look up and witness the tallest, most majestic tree I have ever seen. Its massive, ancient body reminds me of depictions of mammoths in museums, yet it is alive. These trees are relics of Gondwanaland, a southern supercontinent that existed over five hundred million years ago and whose land masses still exist here in parts. I had never before seen a tree of this size in my life; it must have been about three hundred feet high (91.4 meters) and possibly sixty-five feet (19.8 meters) in diameter. As I am an artist who has been passionately drawing trees since I can first remember, I wanted to capture this vision right there and then, to paint and draw the subtle white and burnt umber shades and intricate swirling patterns.

"It's a *Eucalyptus regnans*," Ben tells me. "They are the tallest hardwood trees on Earth, and they are endemic to the southeast forests of Australia. The Weld Valley is one of the last surviving strands of this carbon-dense forest." The compassionate tone of his voice shows me the heart-filled integrity of caring he feels for this place. Ben's eyes shine brightly, mimicking the forest's green. We look deeply into each other's eyes, as if we were long lost friends, he smiles at me, and I look away shyly with butterflies in my stomach.

I sit down to question. Where does this tree end and the ground that supports it start? Like the water that falls from the skies and flows through the streams, it is one and the same. I can start to see how each organism is a part of an interconnected and interdependent whole. I can feel it is the same relationship that we share with nature.

I follow the stony path along, greeting the ferns, flowers, and fungi with a gentle touch from my fingertips to show my appreciation. I am walking along with a spring in my step, humming a little song to myself, lost in the beauty, breathing in the pure, clean air and smelling the flowers.

Then, suddenly, to my pure shock, I find myself standing on the crumbling crust of a new logging road in Tasmania's Weld Valley, a literal hell on Earth. The air is filled with smoky smells of the burning flesh of rare animal species and ancient trees that had once been teeming with pure, unadulterated life. Before me was a whole mountainside of bare, blackened land, the equivalent of forty football fields littered with the carcasses of chain-sawed forest giants.

The air is filled with smoky smells of the burning flesh of rare animal species and ancient trees that had once been teeming with pure, unadulterated life. Before me was a whole mountainside of bare, blackened land, the equivalent of forty football fields littered with the carcasses of chainsawed forest giants.

My heart has just been ripped from my chest and stomped on. Ben watches my utter distress as my eyes start to flood, my throat chokes up, and tingles of desperation start to resonate up my spine. "Are you okay?" he asks. I shrug my shoulders, looking at the devastation around me, trying to hold back the tears. "What can I do to stop this?" I ask, feeling low and powerless against this shattering destruction. He comes over to me and gives me a big hug and whispers in my ear a comforting comment: "A lot of people really care about the Weld Valley, and we're doing all we can to stop this madness."

Set against this sea of forest is a curious sight: a life-sized pirate ship blocking the new logging road. The *Weld Ark*, as the ship is named, is a protest site. *What a spectacular and startling sight,* I think. This brightly painted, hand-built, life-sized pirate ship is blocking a logging road in the middle of nowhere.

To me it is like one big, living art installation resembling Peter Pan's Neverland home. Dozens of people buzz happily around the site, climbing on the ship, swinging from and living in the trees. They are stopping this road from going ahead, from cutting into a sensitive tract of wild old-growth forest in the north Weld Valley. An imposing wooden fortress barricades the area, like a medieval village. It is surreal but welcoming, and I instantly feel at home in this ancient land occupied by busy, passionate forest pirates.

I CAME TO TASMANIA, TO THIS ISLAND, to make art, collect images, and research for my first solo exhibition at a large gallery in Sydney. I had an artistic and personal goal to convey the magic of the forest and the determination of those who were trying to save it. I wanted to capture this wilderness, but it ended up capturing me.

Ben told me stories about the forest and the fight to save it. He talked to me about the plans of companies like Gunns Limited to cut roads into the heart of this wilderness and clear-fell the forests. About the hellish fires that were lit on the remains of the forest to burn away their legacy and leave the charred soil free for a virtual monoculture of regrowth, destined to be cut and burned again in another human lifetime. But out of all this madness, he also taught me hope.

Working harmoniously together, a core crew of about fifteen grassroots activists kept track of the logging operations across the various forests in our area. Night after night, I ventured out with my crew to secure logging equipment. Using lock-ons—made by welding together metal poles to lock our arms—tree-sits, and tripods, we constantly put our lives on the line as our last option to halt the destruction. Into the dawn, we would be met with an entourage of heavy-handed and easily angered loggers. I would often stand in the way of their chain saws and bulldozers as they either threatened the trees or myself with their deadly weapons. We hoped the publicity of our multiple arrests would help the world hear the forest's silent screams.

In the blissful summer days, Ben taught me to climb the ancient trees, to tie knots and so halt the destruction. I felt strong like a true Earth warrior living this way. I watched Ben come alive in the forest, swinging over branches, building this astounding monument of peaceful resistance. I admired his gentle strength and heard his slow, thoughtful words. I developed a profound respect for Ben, stronger than I had ever felt for another human being before. I fell deeply and madly in love with the forest and with this man who seemed such a part of it.

Ben and I had the same strong, driven conviction to save these forests. Our love grew and solidified with the forest's changing seasons. We had found true soul mates in each other and a home together in the forest. It was beautiful!

And life took on a new form. I spent six months living in a tree-sit. This involves living on a 3-by-6-foot (0.9-by-1.8-meter) platform 150 feet (45.7 meters) above the ground. Each night at about 4 AM, I would crawl out of Ben's warm arms in our comfortable bed on the pirate ship and climb my ancient tree, entering into the icy cold air, standing on a branch.

As I climbed around my tree swaying in the breeze, it felt as if I were climbing into a sea of stars and planets, the sky a brightly lit backdrop for tall, dancing silhouettes of forest giants. I felt more at home here than I ever had before. It is something difficult to put into words, but put simply, I was becoming one with this land. It vitalized and rejuvenated me, and in return, I vowed to protect it.

Other activists also lived in trees. Together, we formed a human spider web through the forest. If any logging machinery tried to enter the valley, it would become entangled, unable to cut without the risk of harming human life, something we all seem to respect more than anything else, including the very air we breathe.

Soon, art became more than just my voice; it was also my tool to protect the forest that had become my love and home. I prolifically drew and painted, filmed and made animations. I felt inspiration and an awakening passion to create. But I knew that this passion was bigger, deeper than any single project or piece. I decided to forsake my solo exhibition in Sydney. My art would work to a higher purpose. I began to donate my works to highlight the destruction. I started to make a film that would document the life of the camp and the passionate struggle to keep this valley wild.

One night, Ben and I, putted out from the forest in our old battered Subaru with a carload of other activists to a fundraising function in Hobart. We left a skeleton crew to guard the pirate ship. I felt nervous. Next morning, Ben and I awoke to sounds of crying. Then the door burst open and our friend Laura was in the room, a shattered look written on her face.

"Camp's been busted," she said, wiping tears from her cheeks.

It was the moment we had dreaded and prepared for. I felt the blood drain from my body and wanted to vomit. We jumped out of bed, our instincts sharp. Without hesitation or words, we went straight into action mode, clambered into the car, and headed back for the forest.

It was raining, a freezing thirty-five degrees Fahrenheit (1.7 degrees Celsius), and our packs were painfully heavy. We walked six miles (9.7 kilometers) through thick scrub and tall cutting grass that sliced up our arms, hands, and faces, while making our way though almost impenetrable horizontal forest. As we approached the now demolished pirate ship, we could see dozens of police trucks, bulldozers, and other logging machinery invading the forest where our home had been. Already, they were felling the ancient trees that were behind the camp. The sadness that ran though me like scorching tea was for more than for myself or the trees, but for the human race.

Scores of people—activists, media, forestry workers, police—were converging on our quiet corner of the world. A desperate battle had begun. Daily, for the next three weeks, I would sneak six miles (9.7 kilometers) into the forest with my video camera to create a film on their killing and our actions to stop it. I was living with constant high adrenaline—every time I heard a car I would thrust my weary body into the bushes to escape arrest. I don't really know how I kept going; it was possibly the thought of new generations of children being born into this world without the importance and beauty of old-growth forests that pushed me on.

One afternoon, running through the undergrowth, desperate to meet a media deadline, I felt so exhausted that I collapsed in the forest and cried. What was this madness? My mind was flooded with thoughts like millions of pouring raindrops. I thought, if we can see and feel that as we destroy the Earth we also destroy ourselves, only then will we actually have the conviction to really do something about it, and only then will we have a chance to turn around the effects of this impending doom of catastrophic climate change. But how do I present this idea? As the saying goes, a picture paints a thousand words!

It was in this moment that I imagined what would become known as the Weld Angel. She would be a cry for the beauty and innocence of the forest. A painted white messenger atop a huge tripod, who would block the entrance to the threatened ancient forest. She would wear the wings that I had made for more than two years, carefully hand-sewing the discarded feathers I had scavenged from the earth's floor into a wire and canvas frame. They would have to arrest this angel and drag her from her tripod in handcuffs in order to evict her from the forest.

What a contradiction . . . what a powerful image, I thought. This performance art action would be my plea for a purer world.

Within days I found myself volunteering to be an "arrestable" for the stop-work actions our crew was planning. And at 5 AM on April 29, 2007, I got my chance. With my heart racing, I climbed my thirty-three-foot (10.1-meter) tripod, a three-poled platform, and I sat on its top in the freezing night air. In that moment, I felt incredible strength; I was united with all people who have ever gone against the given paradigm and stood up for justice and peace, like Joan of Arc, Mother Teresa, and Gandhi. I knew what it was like to risk oneself for a bigger cause.

But within hours, I was surrounded by dozens of police, professional negotiators, media, loggers, and Forestry Tasmania employees. They yelled and gestured at me. Finally, they produced a megaphone and began to threaten me. "*When we get you down, you are going to jail,*" they shouted. "*You are looking at a minimum sentence of two years.*"

If we can see and feel that as we destroy the Earth we also destroy ourselves, only then will we actually have the conviction to really do something about it, and only then will we have a chance to turn around the effects of this impending doom of catastrophic climate change.

As I sat there, legs dangling between the hard poles of the tripod, my wings swaying in the breeze, I looked out to the forest that surrounded me and called for its support. I felt at one with the swaying branches and the glistening leaves. I was part of the Earth defending itself. I looked down at the frustrated men milling below my feet. *Bring it on,* I thought. *Just you try to put an Angel in jail.*

I knew in my whole heart that what I was doing was pure, true, and right. The laws that safeguard corporate profits while abandoning the Earth's life-support system are wrong. I had the moral high ground.

Once they had given up on any negotiations, they brought in a crane to get me down. They did. But the Angel's story, and my personal journey with her, had only just begun.

ONE MORNING, SOME MONTHS AFTER THE ANGEL'S first adventure, my partner, Ben, answered a knock at the door. "Hey, babe," he said, "the cops are here." And I already knew why they had come. "Allana Beltran, you are being sued for ten thousand dollars," a police officer said with a smirk, handing me the compensation claim.

The day after I was served, the Weld Angel made front-page news, with a breathtaking full-color photo. My case was featured in countless newspaper articles across the country, TV news stories, radio interviews, and debates with forestry spin doctors. There were even international magazine articles, including an eight-page spread in Italy's *Vanity Fair*. The Weld Angel was being publicly described as Tasmania's heroine.

As I nerve-wrackingly faced the multitudes of cameras and microphones, an incredible calm would instantly come over me when I spoke. I felt as if it were not me speaking, as if I were simply a vessel in which the grace of the forest's plight could flow.

I felt a turning point for the campaign when I had a farmer call me and pour his heart out to me over the phone. "I have always supported the logging practices of this state, but what you are saying makes sense. I just want you to know that I will pay your charges if you lose the case."

I smiled . . . the blood, sweat, and tears were actually paying off.

IT WAS AT THIS TIME THAT MY life went in a different direction.

Ben had been feeling unwell for some time. Soon after I had managed to convince him to see a doctor, we received the chilling news. Ben had been diagnosed with aggressive terminal bowel cancer. He needed emergency major operations and chemotherapy. I was shocked, and my heart ached, but I quickly assured him we would find a way through this. Ben was so young, only thirty-two. And I was just twenty-two. I felt confused, empty. But my love for Ben was boundless.

For two months, I lived by Ben's bedside in the hospital. I watched this vibrant, energetic man debilitated by a barrage of traumatic treatments. Ben still loved the forest, and all through his treatment, he continued to inspire me with ideas and wisdom as I continued with the Angel's case. We were both still fighting to save the Weld and the wild landscape where our love was forged. Through the campaign to win back the forests, we felt we could somehow win Ben's life back too.

The court case lasted for just over six months. There was an incredible growing public outcry to save the forests and to save the Angel. In the end of the long and tedious legal endeavors, we won the case. And Ben was growing stronger. At times, he seemed to be winning the fight with his health. He even started to surf again, a popular Australian pastime.

Fighting as hard we could, we did everything we could to diminish the cancer. But it was too strong for the both of us. One day, a year and a half after diagnosis, as a frail Ben sat in the sunny backyard of our urban beachside home, a beautiful white-masked barn owl landed in a tree and sat looking at him.

"Allana, come check out this owl," he called out. Little did he know, I had been told about the importance of this significant event before. An Australian aboriginal elder had taught me that white owls came to his people as spirit messengers to help them cross to the other side before they die. This was my proof that Ben really lived at one with the Earth, and that he was leaving soon.

I will never forget his last words to me, just as I will never forget those first dazzling but unsettling glimpses of the valley where we met. He turned to me on his bed and whispered, "we will always be together in the forest."

It's been a very trying and painful year since his passing. I still visit the Weld Valley when I am able. The landscape there is haunted by my great sadness and a mourning for the loss of Ben, as well as for the wounds imposed on its wilderness. The trees where we held court under that ocean of stars are gone. Clear-fells, more horrendous than those I witnessed on my first visit, scar the hills. But there is magical core of old-growth forests, unprotected and still beyond reach. I know Ben's spirit is there.

Since Ben's death, I have watched the forest industry falling on its head. No one wants to buy old-growth woodchips anymore. It looks as if the forests we have been campaigning for will soon be protected. I can rest assured that Ben lived a full, happy, and meaningful life, and although short it was never in vain.

My experience with the Angel, Ben, and the forests has taught me so much about the power of creativity, art, love, and compassion to overcome the injustices and obstacles that exist on our Earth. The Angel is a caring archetype, a symbol of love within us all. When I stood firm as the Angel, trying in my way to protect the life of the forests, plants and trees, rivers and animals, I was acting on the same impulse that compels a lover, daughter, parent to protect the life of a loved one. There is no difference.

This story is dedicated to Ben Morrow.

PHOTO BY MATTHEW NEWTON

Allana Beltran continues to campaign and use her artistic talent as a tool to protect Tasmania's old-growth forests, creatively bridging the gaps between the human world and the natural world. Tasmania's forests are still wild and still threatened, however, due to the growing strength of the international campaign, the demand for Tasmanian old-growth woodchips has dramatically declined. Change does look close for these forests.

ROB STEWART

▶ Thirty ▶ Canada . ▶ Filmmaker

PHOTO BY VERUSCHKA MATCHETT

Sharkwater: The Rising Tide to Save an Ocean Predator

Whatever you can do or dream you can, begin it. Boldness has genius, power, and magic in it. Begin it now.

—JOHANN GOETHE

I TAKE A LAST DEEP BREATH BEFORE diving underwater. As I kick deeper, bands of sunlight dance across the reef on Grand Cayman Island. I'm trying to stay calm and move gracefully so I can stay down longer and not frighten the teeming life around me.

The yellowtail jacks grow accustomed to my presence and swim closer. I try to reach out and touch them. The school—an undulating wall of fish— parts perfectly around my arm. I'm only eight years old; it is another five years until I'm old enough to start scuba diving lessons. For now though, the way I've learned to explore the ocean is through free diving and holding my breath for as long as I can.

The longer I stay underwater, the less the fish are afraid of me. They're very sensitive, moving every time my heart beats. Underwater, for a couple minutes at a time, I get to fly in this magical and colorful world, meeting and interacting with creatures beyond my wildest imagination. As much as I love the colorful fish and coral formations, I'm really in search of one animal in particular—a shark.

Peering out from behind a rock, I finally see the telltale shape of a Caribbean reef shark just slightly bigger than me. I watch as it moves closer, swimming gracefully and without effort.

I try to stay calm but am overwhelmed with excitement. The animal I wanted to meet most was finally in front of me, the closest thing to a dragon or dinosaur possible, but even cooler because it was real and existed.

After just a few seconds, I make a break for the surface for air. The shark notices me, and instead of moving in for the attack, it flees. How impossible, I thought, the shark is scared of *me*.

Watching one of the oldest and most feared predators in the world retreat in fear changed something in me forever. I realized that if the shark, this fearsome beast, was afraid of me, a little boy, then I knew that despite all the fear-mongering stories in the world, I had nothing to be afraid of. From that point on, I spent as much time underwater as possible, not only to take advantage of my newfound freedom, but also to try to hang out with these fascinating predators.

In revolutions of the past—from the end of slavery to movements for cultural or gender equality, from ending whaling to slowing the depletion of the ozone layer—there are some commonalities: they were always preceded by a growing awareness of an injustice. Things weren't right, and the public, when educated, forced change upon the world.

Twelve years later, I had a biology degree and was chief photographer for *Canadian Wildlife* magazine. I soon found myself on an eighteen-hour boat ride to Darwin and Wolf Islands, one of the most important gathering places for sharks, some 160 miles (257.5 kilometers) north of the Galapagos Archipelago, 900 miles (1,448.4 kilometers) from Ecuador. I was on assignment to photograph hammerhead sharks, my favorite sharks, for the first time in my life. Here, hammerhead sharks congregate in greater concentrations than anywhere else in the world, to socialize and find mates.

I woke up at four in the morning to see if we were any closer to these mystical islands. As I looked out over the waves, I started to see little black flags sticking out of the water. Not knowing what they were, I imagined they were secret dive sites or flags to mark particularly shark-rich areas. But I would soon find out that these little, tattered flags were actually attached to longlines, which were catching and killing the very animals I had come to film.

Longlining is a brutal and indiscriminate fishing method explicitly banned in the Galapagos. A single longline can have up to sixteen thousand hooks on a sixty-two-mile (99.8-kilometer) line, almost long enough to stretch from Earth to outer space. Despite targeting specific species, they kill indiscriminately, taking seals, dolphins, sea turtles, and sea birds, contributing to humans wasting fifty-four billion pounds (24.5 billion kilograms) of fish each year as bycatch—animals that are killed and thrown back because they aren't the target species.

We spent the entire day pulling in thirty-seven miles (59.5 kilometers) of longlines, releasing the couple dozen sharks that were still alive, and throwing hundreds of dead sharks back into the sea. We were in a UNESCO World Heritage Site protected by the Ecuadorian military, supposedly one of the most protected marine reserves on the planet. If sharks are being fished here so blatantly, I feared they must be in even worse trouble in the rest of the ocean, which is mostly unprotected.

I soon found out that more than one hundred million sharks were being killed each year, and that shark populations were plummeting worldwide. What's worse, to my horror, no one cared—largely, I believed, because everyone was afraid of them.

As a photographer, I turned my efforts toward educating the public about the plight of sharks through magazine and newspaper articles. I also set up a fund so readers could donate money toward putting a patrol boat at Darwin and Wolf Islands in the Galapagos.

This became my mission not just because I loved sharks but also because I loved the ocean. Sharks have been here for more than 450 million years—150 million years before the dinosaurs. They're the world's ultimate survivors. Having lived through five mass extinctions, they evolved into one of the most highly adapted and successful animals on Earth. They're the world's foremost predator, responsible for shaping today's oceans and much of the life in it.

Sharks sit on top of oceanic ecosystems, the very ecosystems that consume carbon dioxide and provide the oxygen in the air we breathe. If we look to basic biology, we know that if sharks are eliminated, the species below them in the food chain will dramatically increase in population, setting off a chain reaction that would reshape the marine ecosystem. At the bottom of this chain, we find tiny plants that convert carbon dioxide into oxygen, producing more than half the oxygen in our atmosphere. Removing the top predator from the most important ecosystem on this planet could have huge consequences for our own survival.

But why were people killing them?

The simple answer is money. There is an enormous and growing demand for shark fin soup. Through much of Asia, but most popularly China, shark fin soup is a status symbol and is served as a sign of respect. Now a ubiquitous dish at banquets and weddings, a single pound (.5 kilogram) of shark fin sells for more than three hundred dollars. Once reserved for emperors, the booming middle class in China has created such a massive demand that a single whale shark fin can fetch more than fifty thousand dollars. Shark bodies are less valuable and spoil quickly, so fishermen started finning to increase profits. They cut the fins off and throw the rest, 95 percent of it, overboard. By drying the fins, fishermen can avoid expensive refrigeration systems, and even the most decrepit boats can fin sharks and turn a huge profit. Though this practice has been outlawed in many countries, it continues unmonitored and unabated in international waters, spurred on by what is estimated to be a multibillion-dollar market worldwide.

I soon found out that more than one hundred million sharks were being killed each year, and that shark populations were plummeting worldwide. What's worse, to my horror, no one cared. . . .

The huge demand for fins and poor fishing regulations have decimated shark populations in every ocean on Earth. Studies from Dalhousie University show that shark and large predator populations in the oceans have dropped an estimated 90 percent in the last fifty years. The U.S. National Marine Fisheries Service says some species of shark, such as tiger, bull, mako, and great white, have dropped by more than 95 percent and are on the verge of extinction.

Realizing the gravity of the situation and my lack of success using print media, I knew I needed a more powerful weapon. I needed to not just educate the public about the plight of sharks but also reverse the media's portrayal of sharks as menacing predators to people—something Hollywood had perfected. As long as people believed all sharks were like the ones portrayed in *Jaws*, nobody would want to protect them.

Once I was back in my home city of Toronto, my dad told me about a new kind of video camera that George Lucas was using to shoot *Star Wars*. High-definition cameras were brand new and were high-enough resolution for their images to be printed in magazines. With this new technology, I started plotting out a film that would visually capture the public's attention while changing its views of sharks.

I immediately started looking around for equipment and financing and, most important, people who were willing to undertake this journey with me. There were, however, few organizations working to protect sharks. I heard about the Sea Shepherd Conservation Society and the work they were doing with whale conservation. I got in contact with their leader, Captain Paul Watson, to look into a campaign to save sharks. Watson has been battling illegal whaling for years. He's been shot at and rammed and sunk a whole Norwegian whaling fleet in the process. Watson invited me to join a campaign on their 165-foot (50.3-meter) ship, the *Ocean Warrior*, to confront shark poaching in the oceans of South and Central America.

Getting into gear as fast as I could, I assembled a makeshift crew out of a couple of longtime friends and borrowed enough money to rent HD cameras. We quickly jumped on a plane and met Watson and the crew of the *Ocean Warrior* in Los Angeles.

Boarding one of the most radical marine conservation ships in the world, we started a two-week trip south to Costa Rica. Costa Rica's Cocos Island is home to some of the greatest concentrations of sharks in the world. Without the ability to effectively protect their waters from foreign poaching, Costa Rica's president had asked for Sea Shepherd's help. Twelve days into our journey, in Guatemalan waters, we came across our first illegal shark-fishing boat.

It was called the *Varadero*, a Costa Rican longliner, pulling in sharks and cutting off their fins, which is illegal in Guatemala. Sea Shepherd contacted the Guatemalan authorities, who then asked Sea Shepherd to bring the boat into port for arrest. As much as Sea Shepherd was known for being radicals, in this moment we were working within the law.

Captain Watson hailed the pirate boat on our radio and ordered them to stop. He informed them that they were illegally fishing and ordered them to release the sharks on their lines. I ran out on deck and began filming as the fishermen ignored Watson's demands and continued killing sharks.

Racing the *Ocean Warrior* ahead, Sea Shepherd tried to intercept the lines and free the sharks. The *Ocean Warrior* was a much bigger and faster ship, but the *Varadero* darted ahead and seemed always to have another longline to pull in. Disabling them was the next tactic. Using a high-pressure water cannon, Sea Shepherd attempted to spray their boat to try to flood their engines.

Doggedly pursuing them with the water cannon on full blast, Sea Shepherd's translator kept repeating over the radio in Spanish, "You are illegally fishing in these waters. Guatemalan authorities have ordered you to stop." This had no effect, and the chase went on for hours. But just then, almost in a flash, I heard lots of commotion and screaming, and then: "We're going to hit!"

I grabbed a railing with one hand and filmed with the other as we collided with the pirate fishing boat. Then it was a shudder to the side of the ship and a loud thud as the boats crashed into one another. Finally, the *Varadero* agreed to follow us into port to meet the Guatemalan authorities.

Halfway to Guatemala, Watson heard from the authorities that they were on the way to arrest both the *Varadero* and the *Ocean Warrior*. They asked us to stay put until they arrived, at which point we would be escorted back to shore to meet with the authorities.

I couldn't believe it. We were in trouble for enforcing their laws. Figuring some strings had been pulled, and not wanting to risk time in prison, Watson made the only decision he could in order to not compromise the entire mission. We ditched the *Varadero* and hightailed it to international waters, onward to Costa Rica.

Arriving in Costa Rica, the situation was not any better. We were charged with seven counts of attempted murder. The Costa Rican Coast Guard boarded the ship to search for evidence and told us we were going to be thrown in jail for trying to kill the fishermen aboard the *Varadero*. It was crazy. We were confined to port under house arrest and couldn't move, despite the forty-three testimonials and footage from three video cameras. The trials lasted weeks, with each case being thrown out with our overwhelming evidence and immediately reinstated with a new judge and prosecutor. Almost daily, the court sent prosecutors and judges to our boat to interview us, search the boat, and see the footage of the incident. Realizing the tapes might be confiscated and that we might need foreign pressure to get out of this, I shipped the tapes to Canada just in time, as they scoured the ship looking for them.

I couldn't believe that Costa Rica was putting us through all this when they were the ones who invited us to help them fight shark poaching. When we met William, an ex–shark fisherman, it became very clear that this was a much bigger issue than we had thought.

We sneaked ashore in Puntarenas, and William took us to where he believed the shark-finning mafia had illegal operations. Combing the high seas for a particular fishing vessel is like trying to find a needle in a haystack, but all fins have to be brought back to land to be dried and packed before being sold to the dealers. This was our chance to find out what was really going on with shark fishing in Costa Rica.

In a secluded area of town were warehouses on the water surrounded by high cement walls, barbed wire, and security cameras. We parked a few blocks away and headed back on foot, camera in hand. Unable to see anything at first, I climbed onto a transport truck so I could see over the huge walls and into the operation.

As far as the eye could see, there were tens of thousands of shark fins drying on the roofs of these warehouses. I started filming immediately, zooming in on the field of fins laid out to dry in the hot sun. Only visible from above, this whole area was a secret port where fins could be landed unchecked by authorities and dried out of sight.

I hadn't been up there for more than thirty seconds before I was spotted. Immediately, a few men climbed onto the roofs of the closest building, shoving the fins off the roof and out of sight. They had seen the camera and were clearly panicking, kicking and pushing the fins off the roof. There were far too many to cover up, and they must have realized that I was filming the cover-up as well.

Then a group of men with guns ran out of the warehouse, screaming and pointing at me. There were millions of dollars worth of shark fins on those roofs, and I was bad for business. I hurriedly scampered off the roof and sprinted to the waiting car, yelling at the driver to "Go! Go! Go!" I quickly jumped in, and so did our group, and within minutes we sped away. We headed for the center of town, where there would be the most people and the most cars—basically the most witnesses to anything that might go down. As we arrived, the mafia were nowhere to be seen. We'd lost them. I knew we had just made it and were lucky to be alive.

PHOTO BY SHARKWATER PRODUCTIONS

Back onboard the *Ocean Warrior*, we got a call from our lawyer asking us what we had done. Apparently we had aggravated the situation, and instead of keeping us under house arrest, they were going to imprison Captain Watson indefinitely. There was only one way out of this, to make a break for it. Watson made the order to quickly pull anchor, leaving a couple volunteers on shore, and we headed for international waters.

Only minutes from port, with the Sea Shepherd's engines on full throttle, the coast guard's ship caught up with us and ordered us back to port. They were waving machine guns, telling us they were going to shoot unless we stopped. We wrapped the ship in barbed wire so they couldn't jump onboard and raced on.

Manning the battle stations to face any boarding attempt, the activists' faces were tense as I continued to film. This was it. If we were stopped here, we could spend months, if not years in Costa Rican prison. As we crossed the line into international waters, the coast guard gave up pursuit, and the activists aboard the *Ocean Warrior* exploded in cheers. I breathed a big sigh of relief. We had escaped, but just barely (again and in the same day). Sailing out into the open ocean, I looked back, knowing it would be a while before I went back to Costa Rica.

This adventure, along with many more from a dozen other countries eventually became the film *Sharkwater*, which took me five years to complete. When I started, I was twenty-two years old, had never shot a video camera, and had no film experience or professional help. I jumped in way over my head, and in the process, I was hospitalized, lost at sea, and indebted to many. I had flesh-eating disease, West Nile virus, tuberculosis, and dengue fever. I had to beg, plead, borrow, learn, mature, grow, and become a filmmaker to get this film done. What started as a film became a mission and a way of life. Giving up was never an option, because people need this information for positive change to be effected in the world.

In revolutions of the past—from the end of slavery to movements for cultural or gender equality, from ending whaling to slowing the depletion of the ozone layer—there are some commonalities: they were always preceded by a growing awareness of an injustice. Things weren't right, and the public, when educated, forced change upon the world. My form

PHOTO BY VERUSCHKA MATCHETT

of activism is making films, because they can educate, inspire, and create change.

Sharkwater went on to become the second-highest-grossing Canadian theatrical documentary of all time and had successful theatrical releases around the world. It's been cited as the inspiration for changing government policy in at least four countries and has helped spawn shark conservation groups. We amassed a massive shark conservation army, and recently, Hawaii became the first place in the world to ban shark fin soup and the possession, sale, and distribution of shark fins. When I started filming *Sharkwater*, there were only four countries that had banned finning. Now there are more than eighty. Change is happening, but we're finding out that the problem is much bigger than we thought. It's not just about saving sharks anymore; it's also about saving humanity.

By midcentury, scientists predict the end of fisheries, rainforests, and coral reefs; huge food and water shortages; and a population of nine billion people on a planet that can sustain far less. We'll have mass displacement due to rising sea levels, flooding, and desertification. This isn't just an issue, this is *the* biggest issue humanity has ever faced, and it's our own survival that's in jeopardy now.

Now, more than ever, the world needs heroes, and lots of them. And that is where you come in.

Rob Stewart's film Sharkwater *exposed the shark-finning industry to audiences and spawned conservation movements worldwide.* Sharkwater *has won thirty-five international awards and had its Asian premier in Hong Kong last summer, the epicenter for shark fin consumption. He continues to promote ocean conservation and is currently working on his next film: a how-to guide to start the revolution necessary to save the planet and, ultimately, humanity.*

BEN POWLESS

▶ Twenty-five ▶ Mohawk ▶ Communicator

PHOTO BY BEN POWLESS

A Peruvian Massacre

You can imprison a man, but not an idea. You can exile a man, but not an idea. You can kill a man, but not an idea.

—BENAZIR BHUTTO

MY FLIGHT WAS MEANT TO LEAVE THAT NIGHT, June 5, 2009. I was in Lima-Callao International Airport, checking my emails when I first got word. A massacre was taking place in the Amazon of northern Peru. I was stunned—the killing was only a few hours' travel away, and I had just made friends with some people who were probably being slain. Life carried on normally at the airport, with a surreal edge as scenes of the violence played out on the waiting-lounge TVs. I scrambled to write a quick article in English about what was going on, as the only news at the time was in Spanish.

The guilt was overwhelming. I had to leave Peru right at this moment of crisis. But money was tight, and I didn't have the capacity to buy another ticket. Yet an hour before I was about to board, my flight to Canada was canceled, and I knew then that I had to stay.

Behind the scenes, there had been an organization representing Peru's four hundred thousand Amazonian Indigenous Peoples, AIDESEP (Asociación Interétnica de Desarrollo de la Selva Peruana; translated in English, it means the National Organization of the Amazon Indigenous People of Peru). This group and its leader, Alberto Pizango, whom I had met the week before, were the prime targets of the government now because AIDESEP had led a two-month-long protest against the government. The night my flight was canceled, I got their address from their website, and the next morning, a cool and overcast Saturday, I showed up at the AIDESEP office. The office turned out to be a humble home behind huge gates—not what I had expected. When I entered, I waited in the reception area as people came in and out, talking of the violence in the Amazon their family members had witnessed. After explaining myself, they made me a place in the communications office and set me up to translate a few things into English and communicate with the English media.

Being at the office felt like being in the center of a storm. The day before, Alberto Pizango held a press conference, where he blamed that day's deaths of thirty-three people on the government. Shortly after, the government charged him with sedition, accusing him of being behind the deaths, and he disappeared. We learned a few days later he had been granted asylum in the Nicaraguan Embassy, but at that moment, we feared the worst. People in the office were worried the police might kick the door down at any moment, or that the jungle might erupt again into bloodshed.

It was important for me to try to figure out what had really happened. There were many contradictory accounts in the media—who had shot first, who in the government had ordered the military to stop a peaceful protest, even how many people were killed. The next day, though, I managed to get a phone number for a young Belgian lady who had witnessed the incident herself. She filled in many parts of the story that the news and government were withholding. There had been very few reporters in the area, and the media was only reporting the government version because most reporters wouldn't go into the jungle themselves.

We watched what the government was saying on television in the communications office, and it had us all scared. The president, Alan García, went on the air and accused the Amazonian peoples of being "savages, barbarians, and second-class citizens"—obviously racist remarks. He called them terrorists, saying they were stopping "our progress and our democracy," as if they were not Peruvian, and said they were even controlled by "international communism" and foreign governments. I couldn't believe what was being said but felt as if the government might be trying to justify the use of more violence.

Meanwhile, we were getting more and more firsthand testimony in the office from people who had been there. We were all intent on making sure that the international media knew what was going on, so that the government of Peru couldn't resort to more violence. We also wanted to make sure international human rights and environmental groups knew about the situation and could respond and assist. I struggled to make a list of all the different organizations and media sources that I could and concentrated on sending out information.

After three days in the office, I was told that AIDESEP had prepared a delegation to go into the Amazon, and they wanted me to go along with them. They asked me to document my trip, write about it, and take pictures, while trying to figure out what exactly had occurred and what was still happening. The delegation included another Indigenous leader and members of the media.

The whole trip was a tense one, where we didn't talk openly about what we were doing. We flew from Lima to Chiclayo and drove overnight in a beat-up jeep to Jaén. Bagua, our real destination, was still under military curfew. It wasn't until the next morning that we proceeded directly to the Devil's Curve (*La Curva del Diablo*), just outside Bagua. This was where the violence had occurred, just a few days before. The district attorney had just completed his first investigation of the area, turning up little evidence.

For our quest, we were mainly looking for any evidence of missing persons. We had heard reports of fires on the mountain and that the police had taken a number of bodies into their helicopters and had been seen throwing them into the water. Five days had passed since the violence, however, and the military hadn't let anyone in the area until now, so there was much speculation that they simply sanitized the area. That day, we found nothing.

Attempting again to put the pieces of this puzzle together, we headed back into town the next day to talk to others who had been at the battle. Most people had already headed back to their communities long before, except for those unlucky enough to be stuck in the hospital. There, we found a number of vanloads of wounded, off to trek back into the jungle. All were young men, in such a rush that we could only get one person's story.

Inside the hospital, there were another five men who had been shot, a few of them multiple times. Four of them had been on the Devil's Curve, too close to the soldiers to escape their bullets. One older gentleman, accompanied by his wife, had been walking through town when the police there opened fire. They all wondered how the government could do this to them, for which we didn't have an answer.

We were forced to skip town to avoid the curfew, and headed back to Jaén for the night. The whole time, I was reminded to stay inconspicuous, as military patrols were out on every corner. That night I spent writing about what we had seen, responding to emails, and uploading photos.

A large part of my work was comprised of informing and updating various human rights, Indigenous, and environmental groups around the world, as well as international media. I felt this was crucial to help communicate what we were seeing and being told and to generate support for the Amazonian peoples.

The rainforest was their grocery store, pharmacy, school, life. They didn't see why the government or any company should be allowed to take away their land and pollute it—especially since they had never given up their rights to the land.

The next morning, I was back at the Devil's Curve. Here, another search was already under way by local Indigenous leaders who wanted to see for themselves if there was any more evidence.

We chanced upon a family who happened to live on the side of the road. There was an older woman and her granddaughter Marilu, ten years old, who had witnessed the violence in their backyard. They recounted that after the initial violence subsided, police were going door to door, looking for any Natives who were hiding.

Forcing their way into the house, the police put a gun to the little girl's chest and demanded that her family reveal the whereabouts of anyone hiding. The family told them to leave them alone, that they weren't hiding anyone. This warranted the policeman to ask his commander if he should just shoot them. A simple response saved their lives: "No, let's go." Marilu showed us the tear gas canister and spear she had discovered in her backyard—the first pieces of evidence we found.

We spent some more time scouring the mountains. Much of it was burned now, but we called out anyway, just in case there had been any survivors overlooked. After hours in the hot sun, we had to give up, partially happy not to make any gruesome discoveries but dismayed that we were no closer to having any more information. That's when we knew we weren't going to learn any more from the mountain. We needed to go into the jungle.

We started off at the crack of dawn in a packed station wagon. At one point, we got stuck in thick mud, but we got out and pushed our way free with the brute force of our bodies against the vehicle. We winded our way on the sides of mountains covered with tropical forests, following alongside one of the Amazon River's tributaries.

Hours later, I arrived at the community of Wawas, which we had to take a boat to enter. I got out of the boat and hiked through dense jungle to meet the family of Felipe Sabio César, who had been killed in the violence. His mother brought us to see his wife and five children, one of whom was born the day before he died. Family members told of how he had become a respected leader of the community through radio broadcasting and by serving as a translator, volunteering on the protest lines. I felt alone sitting there with the widow, Violeta, who wore her pain on her face. I hadn't expected this moment and wasn't sure now what to say, except offer condolences and make sure his story was shared with the world.

I went down to meet with a few others who had been shot in the violence. I wanted to hear why they had been protesting in the first place and what happened to them.

The Peruvian government had signed free trade agreements with the United States and Canada and changed its laws to let mining, oil, and forestry companies come in. Immediately, Indigenous groups recognized it was their land the companies and the government were after. When their demands to have some of the laws changed fell on deaf ears, they decided to protest. For two months, they had shut down the highway near the Devil's Curve and blocked access to some oil facilities in the jungle.

About fifty people from that community had participated in the protests from the beginning, concerned about what the laws would do to their forests and water. They knew that climate change was a big problem and claimed they were acting to protect the environment for the rest of the world. As much as it was a matter of protecting their rainforest, it was also about protecting their culture.

Many people told us that the rainforest was their grocery store, pharmacy, school, life. They didn't see why the government or any company should be allowed to take away their land and pollute it—especially since they had never given up their rights to the land. But all I could do was agree and take notes.

In the end, more than thirty thousand people participated in the protests. They told us that the morning of the violence, the police hadn't come to talk but to shoot and kill. Many had to flee higher into the mountains to escape; others headed into Bagua, where there was more shooting. They had decided to stand up to protect the forests that cannot speak for themselves, and were shot for it.

Down the road a few hours, we next arrived in the community of La Curva. There we met with the family of David Jausito Mashigkash, who was only nineteen when he was shot and killed in the mountains. David had recently returned to his region to study nursing, after having been gone eleven years to attend school. His cousins and a few others from the community had gone to the protest, and David joined them soon after graduating.

The morning of June 5, he had gone with a few others to find out who was coming down the mountains to see the protestors. Some people had thought that they might be another group of Indigenous supporters. Instead, it was the police. That was the last time his cousins saw him alive.

The family was still visibly mourning, and I felt somewhat intrusive to be there, as a dozen family members were gathered in remembrance at the bamboo house in which he had lived. At the same time, they were also glad to have David's story told. When we talked to others in the community, they felt betrayed that the government hurt its own citizens—especially when they had made an agreement to peacefully remove the blockades. A number of them were even military veterans who had fought for Peru against Ecuador before, and were even more hurt. They were not angry at the government officers that had been sent and were only doing their job, but rather with the government itself, which could have avoided all bloodshed if they just decided to talk first.

Before sundown, we made our last trip to a community called Nazareth, to meet with Solomón Aguanash, president of the Regional Strike Committee. He was in charge of negotiating with the government during the protest and gave us the most authoritative version of events.

He told us of an agreement between armed forces and Indigenous groups to take down the barricades on June 5. This agreement was negotiated the night before, where Solomón had met with the top military commander in the region.

Instead of sticking to the agreement, police, helicopters, and armored carriers began an eviction of sorts, ignoring pleas against violence. In the confusion of people fleeing or even trying to defend themselves with spears, many were shot and lay wounded on the battlefield. While eighty-five people were still missing after the incident, some returned to their communities after the battle; some were gone forever.

When questioned about the reasons for the protest, Solomón replied:

We do not accept the kind of "development" that the president offers us, because it is not sustainable, and it threatens the Amazon rainforest. If the government insists on sidelining us, we will no longer block roads but will instead draw our own limits.

Our territory is our market, our mother. Everything we need for our survival is in the rainforest. That's why we are defending it with our lives. The struggle will continue until the laws are gone. What happens next is up to the government.

He was referring to the many laws passed by the government to open up the Amazon to foreign oil and mining operations.

That night, we were lucky to find a hotel room in a small Amazon town that even had Internet. The next morning, we took off for Station 6, the oil facility in the heart of the rainforest that was another site of violence. We somehow got very lucky, as we passed through a number of military checkpoints and they never asked for ID. However, we were disappointed, arriving at Station 6 hours later.

We got there, finally, but the military troops who now ran the station refused to talk to us. Even worse, they got angry when I tried to take pictures, saying it wasn't allowed. We drove off, frustrated that we had come all that way for nothing.

When we were on our way back out of the jungle, our driver noticed an oil spill on the side of the road. We got out of the car and quickly found some people from the neighboring community who were also wondering what was going on. Gobs of oil, like a river of black, pooled in puddles on the side of the road. We managed to follow the oil stream up a hillside, which had been recently cut down. Scrambling to the top, the other photographer and I discovered all the trees had been cut down, and the ground was covered in sheen.

> The issue of oil companies going into the Amazon didn't seem so theoretical anymore. Community members had been sharing their fears of oil companies coming in, taking away their land, and poisoning them. And now, here it was, happening before our very eyes. . . .

We had found ourselves in the middle of an old-fashioned oil spill. Not far away, a crew worked on an exposed oil pipeline, as lots of young men picked up contaminated vegetation and tossed it into garbage bags. They stopped for a bit when they saw us but went back to work. A security guard by the pipeline spotted us. I worked quickly to get some photos and document the spill.

The security guard came by, telling us not to take photos. The other photographer began negotiating with him, distracting him. I got some more photos, but he had called in the military. Soon, a few soldiers arrived to tell us it was illegal to take photos, waving machine guns around. Intimidated, I slowly came down the hill, where there was now a group of about thirty local villagers who had come by to see what was happening.

The villagers were very concerned about the oil pipeline leaking into the river and contaminating their source of food and water. Like us, the company and military wouldn't tell them what happened, or even what company they were from. The soldiers seemed to be working for the company, even doing their media relations for them, telling us we would have to direct any questions to their headquarters, a headquarters they wouldn't name. The villagers were distraught, and our chance visit would be their only way to let the world know.

The issue of oil companies going into the Amazon didn't seem so theoretical anymore. The whole time, community members had been sharing their fears of oil companies coming in, taking away their land, and poisoning them. And now, here it was, happening before our very eyes, almost unbelievable that it was so real, plainly in front of us.

This is why the people had started their fifty-five-day protest. It seemed they had very good reasons to want to protect their homes, families, ways of life. In total, more than thirty thousand people in the Amazon had participated in the protests, including communities like Bagua. With the news of what really took place, people around the world rallied to the cause, and in Peru, thousands of people marched in the streets against the government. In the end, the protest was successful, and the government backed down on many of the laws in question after huge domestic and international pressure was placed on Peru.

For me, after helping spread the word of what happened, I soon had to return to Canada. Being back at home, I sometimes felt a lot less useful, but I kept in contact with Peru and did many speaking events and media interviews about the massacre, continuing to tell the world what happened. It was important to share this story in Canada, as many of the mining companies in the Amazon are Canadian. And with Canada recently signing a free trade agreement with Peru to secure access to formerly remote areas, communities like the ones I was in have become expendable.

The case of Peru really challenges me to consider how the things we value and the way we live have an impact around the world. That will be the defining challenge of our generation, and this is the message that many Indigenous Peoples in the Amazon and beyond are bringing to the world. Whether we as people are able to come together and deal with our crises—of racial violence, environmental justice, and climate change—will depend on our relationships with each other and our only home, planet Earth.

We are in a time where profound transformations of relationships are needed. What we need to do is consider how all our actions, every day, can contribute to the world we live in. We are all connected, and it's time we started living like it.

Considering this myself, I went back to Peru almost a year later. Many of the Indigenous communities were still suffering from the wounds inflicted, people were still in jail, Pizango was still in exile. Today, their biggest threat isn't from oil, however. It is from a Canadian gold-mining company trying to invade their territories. In the future, their real threat will continue to be from a world indifferent to their survival and the survival of our planet.

PHOTO BY SHADIA FAYNE WOOD

Ben Powless continues to support Indigenous Peoples across the world through his work with the Indigenous Environmental Network and freelance reporting.

DAVID NICKARZ

▶ Thirty-eight ▶ Canada ▶ Survivor

PHOTO BY BARBARA VEIGA

Toxic City: A Cancer Survivor's Struggle

The Earth is not dying—it is being killed. And the people who are killing it have names and addresses.

—U. UTAH PHILLIPS

WE WERE SITTING CROSS-LEGGED, staring up at one of those huge Mac trucks, one that was revving its engine just inches from our faces. It was one of those moments when all reason would have you get up and leave. This ten-ton truck could have crushed us like flies before it even reached second gear. But force wasn't going to win this battle; it was a classic case of peaceful civil disobedience in the tradition of Thoreau, Gandhi and Martin Luther King. We had strength in our weakness.

There were, after all, two other exits to the municipal yard that weren't being blocked. But the head of the Winnipeg Insect Control Department was determined to break through the blockade we had set up. It was a symbolic moment for both of us, and it had turned into a standoff.

The cops were playing nice, milling around and asking us politely to leave, knowing full well that we weren't going to do so unless it was in handcuffs or with a promise that the pesticide trucks would not leave the yard today.

The "fogging" trucks have been around as long as I can remember, driving through my neighborhood and leaving giant clouds of pesticides in their wake. It's just like a scene from one of those 1950s films of DDT trucks spraying clean-cut American kids and sunglass-wearing mothers just after World War II. But DDT was banned for its toxicity, most notably for its links to cancer in humans and softening the shells of bird eggs. It's hard to believe that with this clear association in the public mind, the city of Winnipeg still dares run these same spray trucks in the 21st century, poisoning the citizens of our city with a different toxic chemical, ostensibly to save us from the evil disease-carrying mosquitoes that arrive every summer.

The truck drivers were clearly agitated. They were gunning their engines, releasing big clouds of black smoke. Then a friendly face arrived. He was a suit-wearing bureaucrat from the city and he invited us into his office to negotiate an end to the blockade.

Four of us agreed to follow him, while the rest stayed at the yard exit to maintain the blockade. He sat us down, offered us a cup of coffee and smiled, saying he understood why we were angry and that we had every right to make our opinion heard, but this wasn't the best way.

I had seen this good cop, bad cop act before and I wasn't going to have any of it. As he was midway through his pitch on why we should be lobbying our municipal councilors instead of sitting in front of the pesticide trucks, I just cut him off. Lobbying could come later, but today one thing was for sure: there would be no spraying, period.

We walked back out to the blockade and into the melee. The press had shown up and there were TV cameras and photographers galore. The bright lights were on us as we took up our positions on the blockade once more. But just as we were settling in for the long haul, the tie-wearing city worker marched out of his office and announced to the cameras that all spraying was suspended till further notice.

Victory! We stood up and gave each other high-fives. We hugged each other and then turned to the media to explain why this was an important victory for public health. "Winnipegers, young and old, would be better off without clouds of chemicals floating across their lawns and their gardens, into their houses and their lungs," I said to the cameras.

But force wasn't going to win this battle; it was a classic case of peaceful civil disobedience in the tradition of Thoreau, Gandhi and Martin Luther King. We had strength in our weakness.

I was jubilant. I thought that we had shown that the voices of citizens can be heard, that popular sentiment can overcome business interests and, in short, that the system works. But three days later, our victory would fall short. I would get a call saying that the trucks were getting ready to head out of the yard again, and I knew that it wasn't going to be as easy as I'd thought.

IN AN EFFORT TO KILL MOSQUITOES, THE City of Winnipeg employs the pesticide Malathion, sprayed in a fine mist in the middle of the night. Their hope is that the droplets of poison will kill a significant number of mosquitoes that hit the city, and thereby reduce the nuisance of getting bitten, as well as reduce the exaggerated risk of West Nile disease that had everyone in crisis mode in the early 2000's.

Besides the fact that the risk mosquitoes pose is negligible, this 1950s-style solution doesn't work, and the authorities know it. Fogging with Malathion does nothing to kill mosquitoes, but it does poison everything in the local environment that has a brain, human and animal alike.

In fact, to say that Malathion harms human health is an understatement. There is no debate as to the toxicity of Malathion. There are numerous studies showing the health effects of Malathion and it would take this whole chapter just to cite them. Malathion has shown to cause intestinal disorders in children, leukemia, birth defects, brain damage, chromosome defects, gene loss, lung damage, weakening of the immune system and many other deleterious effects on wildlife. It's also been shown to do damage at very low doses.

Yet the majority of our citizens are convinced that fogging is a good idea. As soon as the mosquitoes start biting, it is as if everyone is trained to start looking around for the fogging trucks to come to the rescue. Only slowly are residents becoming concerned about the health effects of pesticides, but the loud voices of support for the fogging program always seem to be winning.

Yet there was a small hardcore group of local activists who decided to take action despite the popularity of the fogging. Back in 2002, several groups of activists on bikes blocked the fogging trucks. I wasn't active on the issue at this point, but I remember the bikers wearing bandanas for some protection from the poison fog. It made them look like villains from the old west.

I decided to explore and took my camera with me. I don't really know when I crossed the line from observer to participant, but I soon found myself acting as a self-appointed media liaison. There were journalists and photographers milling around, but they weren't seeing the bigger picture. I knew that this was an important issue and I could tell that these activists felt strongly that the fogging should be stopped. We never heard their side of the story and I just thought that their protest should be covered so that as many people as possible could see it. I started directing journalists towards the blockades and offering up my photos for their articles.

There was one wild-west biker in particular who caught my eye. She was sitting in the middle of the street, right in front of one of those massive trucks, and the cops were trying to convince her to move. She was adamant and wouldn't budge. Apparently, the truck driver had had enough, so he revved his engine and inched his truck forward. The truck actually bumped the masked woman and then she lost it.

She jumped up screaming and climbed onto the hood of the truck telling the driver just what she thought of his intimidation tactics. It was an image that I'll never forget, this small woman standing up against the big truck and its tattooed driver. Maybe it was then that I decided whose side I was on.

My first act was to help organize the buffer zone requests. We had found a loophole in the municipal bylaws that allowed people to exclude their houses from the fogging. Once a request has been filed with the city, the trucks have to stay 100 meters away from your property. The impact of each exception is pretty minimal, but if you can get three or four people on your block to sign up, the trucks will have to skip your whole street. If you can convince 30 or 40 neighbors, you can get the whole neighborhood exempted.

We went door to door speaking to people, explaining the issue and the science behind Malathion and urged people to sign up for the fogging exclusion. The whole time the newspaper continued to publish unquestioning articles reiterating the politicians' platitudes about how safe the fogging was, and how those against it were just simply "crazy."

We weren't gaining popular support, but one house at a time we were fighting the spraying. Street by street, block by block, we were reclaiming territory from the pesticides.

THE SUMMER OF 2004 WAS A PARTICULARLY bad one for mosquitoes. The spring had been really rainy and reports that the West Nile virus was arriving in Manitoba were widely repeated in the media. The city declared a health emergency, which automatically nullified any exclusions. All our work was lost overnight, and the city was now fogging people against their will. In July, the city fogged people without the usual announcements in the local media. People were outraged that they didn't have the chance to at least close their windows to prevent the nerve toxin fog from drifting into their lungs while they slept.

Then we had a win. A big story appeared in the *Winnipeg Free Press* that for the first time didn't blindly accept the city's claims that Malathion was safe. Finally, we had broken through the media blockade. For years we had been telling the media about the toxic effects of pesticides like Malathion, as well as the poor effect it has on the mosquito population. The newspaper went with the story after finally getting the statistics on the fogging program. The official numbers proved our argument. The fogging program had no effect on the mosquito population whatsoever.

This was our chance. Our issue was on the tip of everyone's tongue and we knew now was the time to act big. We headed down to the depot where the fogging trucks parked for the night and sat down, beginning a two day blockade at the municipal yard. We blocked the fogging trucks, even at the odds of their intimidation tactics, with revved engines just inches from our faces. Keeping our ground, we frustrated the city into canceling all spraying until further notice. It was a high point for me personally and collectively for our group.

But we didn't have much time to celebrate. Three days later, the city announced they would be fogging again. So we did what we had to. The lines in the sand had been drawn; we would now have to put our bodies on the frontline for what we believed in.

We knew we were going to be arrested. We prepared by writing lawyers' numbers on our arms and arranging for bail ahead of time. Eight of us went back down to the depot to blockade the trucks. Three of us were promptly arrested in front of the national media. The issue had now grown beyond the bounds of our city and province. Now the whole country was exposed to what was going on in our little toxic city. The debate was in the public spotlight. We hadn't won yet, but we were winning. Or so we thought.

AS SPRING 2005 ARRIVED, WE GEARED UP for another season of blockades and activism. It was another heavy year for mosquitoes and people had already started to complain to politicians. The fogging trucks were quickly dispatched onto our streets and the clouds of pesticides hung over our city once more. We foolishly thought that using the same tactics as the previous year was a good idea. But blockading the fogging trucks did not have the same effect this time around. The media turned on us and the public was uncomfortable.

After celebrating the media breakthrough of the year before, we were shocked to see journalists act as if they had forgotten everything they had printed. In the year before they were printing stories about the toxicity of pesticides and the fact that fogging wasn't effective at reducing mosquito populations. Yet this year they were asking us what evidence we had for our claims. I was exasperated. I couldn't believe the gall of these journalists. I did the only thing I could think of. I referred them to their own newspapers.

Years earlier, a forest activist colleague of mine had developed cancer. Alice would eventually die of the disease, but she stayed active on forest defense until the end. I had worked with her for years, taking trips into the Boreal Forest investigating clear cuts and logging roads. When she was sick, she offered me some advice.

"This is a terrible disease, Dave. Don't get cancer, just don't," she told me. I did my best to follow her advice, but just like her I had no choice in the matter. Only a month after our blockades began in 2005, I found out I had testicular cancer.

I can't say with certainty that Malathion caused my cancer. We are exposed to so many different chemicals that it's impossible to know which one got through my defenses. But whether it was due to the fogging or not, the links between indiscriminate use of under-tested and misunderstood chemicals and our increasingly sophisticated illnesses are clear.

At that point, survival was my only focus. I needed to stay alive to finish our battle. So I did the only thing I could: I turned off my emotions and did what I needed to do to live. I walked briskly and purposefully into the surgery that removed the offending organ, which had grown to the size of my fist.

A few days after the surgery, a CT scan showed that the cancer had already spread to the lymph nodes in my abdomen and there were already new tumors. I didn't know whether it was the worst, most aggressive form of cancer, which would mean I had only a short time to live. The doctors performed a biopsy and determined that I had a very aggressive form of cancer—but not the worst. If left untreated, it would spread to my lungs and brain and end my life in a few short months.

So I had to undergo months of chemotherapy. The irony wasn't lost on me. I was an activist that protested against toxins and now I would be knowingly poisoning myself, hoping the cancer inside me would die. I spent three long months hooked up to chemicals that dripped into my blood for hours every day, while the tumors in my abdomen were pressing painfully on my back. This was the worst time for me. It was like my own personal hell. After two weeks, I lost my long hair. Eventually I would lose my facial hair and eyebrows as well. Our bodies have natural defenses against this kind of poison. We get nauseous and throw up the offending substance. But when you submit to voluntary chemical treatment like I did, you need to take more drugs to kill the nausea. I can still taste that chemical tinge on my tongue and I sometimes think I can smell it on my body.

I'm usually a very social person, but the chemotherapy kept me shut indoors. I had to stay away from people for fear of developing a fever from a cold or flu. I was weak and delicate with sickness. Just walking up a flight of stairs would leave me out of breath and my head pounding.

After three months on chemotherapy, I was declared cancer free and began my recovery. I was young, so I recovered fast. I started work again fixing things in peoples' homes. At first, I would work only half days before becoming too tired to go on. But after a month or so I was able to work full time again. I had come through a deadly illness alive and wanted to get back to the battle.

I hate to say it, but this time it was personal. Not in the action-hero sense you see in the movies, but my battle was no longer abstract for me. I had been sick with a deadly disease, caused by human pollution and I didn't go back to being the same person, doing the same activism.

I could no longer sit in front of fogging trucks and breathe in that poison anymore. I did not want to chat with the poisoners cheerfully and try to engage them in a non-violent and respectful conversation about their jobs. They were giving cancer to people for the illusion of insect control. They think that fooling people into believing they are being taken care of is more important than not poisoning them in the first place.

Instead, I lobbied the city government to enact a pesticide ban, like so many places around Canada were doing. The entire province of Quebec had banned the use of Malathion outright. Ontario was going to enact a pesticide ban. Millions of Canadians were living with much less pesticide exposure. I joined with a couple of cancer survivors to lend more credibility to our cause. Forming this survivor group got us some attention from the mainstream media, but not enough to make the policy change I so desperately wanted.

That was because I was up against something everyone knew all too well: annoying mosquitoes. And my only weapon was something abstract: a cancer that most people can't even imagine getting.

Years later now, the city still hasn't banned pesticides. They now require you to put a sign on your lawn indicating that people should stay off. That's all we got—a sign. It was frustrating to watch places like Quebec, Ontario and the Maritime Provinces enact municipal bans on pesticides and then see Winnipeg just ignore the issue all together.

The good news is that more and more places in Canada and around the world are going pesticide free. People with chemical sensitivities are reporting being able to breathe easier in those places. I hope it's only a matter of time before it comes to my city.

The change of policy has been achingly slow. I am deeply frustrated and angry about the slow pace of change. Winnipeg is a very conservative city. Even after all we've been through, people still seem to want their chemicals. But there are a group of us who continue to fight and as long as we are alive, there is always a fighting chance for that thing called change.

———————

David Nickarz continues to oppose pesticide use in his home city of Winnipeg. When not working against toxins, he's campaigning against logging and animal rights or teaches direct action to new activists. His health has returned to normal after his bout with cancer and he has recently celebrated five years cancer free.

ELIZABETH REDMOND

▶ Twenty-six   ▶ United States   ▶ Energy Innovator

PHOTO BY MATT TYSON

A POWERleap

We cannot solve our problems with the same thinking we used when we created them.

—ALBERT EINSTEIN

I SCOURED THE AISLES OF A SECONDHAND STORE on a mission for any pair of sneakers I could find from the late '90s. The smell of disinfectant flooded my nostrils, and I was overcome with a feeling of panic. *I mean, how hard could it be to find a pair of shoes that lit up when someone walked in them?* I asked myself ironically. While I poured over bins of discarded clothes and household items, I reflected on the academic project I had taken on during my final year at the University of Michigan.

On the first day of school, I had gone to my mentors and informed them that I wanted to create the next form of alternative energy. I tingled with excitement as I told them my idea—I was going to design systems that generated electricity from human kinetic energy. But I was only met with dumbfounded looks on my professors' faces. My heart sank as they gently reminded me, "This is fantastic, but you are a designer and artist—not an engineer."

Just then a dirty white and red sneaker caught my eye. At last! I picked it up and whacked it against my hand, sending the light at the bottom rocketing into bright, perfectly timed flashes. Relief washed over me. This was exactly the type of energy I wanted to harness, only on a much larger scale.

I had been working my way through a physics class and meetings with brilliant minds in university when I stumbled upon the idea of piezoelectricity, a type of kinetic energy that sparks an electric charge through applied physical strain. It's a naturally occurring phenomenon present in materials like sand, ceramics, and quartz. If you ever dragged your feet on the beach on a hot, dry day and heard a squeaking noise, that was the piezoelectric effect. I knew how to generate electricity with big clunky motors that need to rotate and move back and forth, but I was searching for a way to generate electricity on an entirely new scale: a nano- or at least microscale. I needed to harvest vibrations, rather than movement.

Once I felt brave enough to open my eyes to the joyous wonder of the group's reaction, I noticed the very evident truth that people were sharing my vision. They were dancing, jumping, walking, running, and even doing handstands on my mock-up.

That is much easier said than done. But I am not a woman that shies away from hard work, the value of which was made clear to me at the tender age of three when I learned how to ride a two-wheeled bike. My family lived out in the country on a dirt road, and anyone who has ever tried to ride with training wheels on gravel would understand why I wanted them taken off—the gravel makes it nearly impossible to balance. One day, my dad brought home a beautiful brass bicycle horn and told me it would be mine when I learned how to ride on a two-wheel bike. The horn was the first thing I remember receiving that I didn't really *need* and that wasn't a hand-me-down. I was honored and determined.

Every night when my dad got home from work, we went outside and practiced long after it got dark. At the end of our lessons, I got to honk my horn just once to remind me what I was working toward. I was intoxicated with motivation and a desire for graduation. After a few tirelessly long weeks, I finally rode all the way across the twenty-foot (6.1-meter) concrete landing to the other side, up and down ten times on my two wheels. I was a cyclist! I don't remember honking the horn much after we actually installed it on my bike, but it did continue to play an iconic role in my life as I grew up. I transplanted the horn from bike to bike as I outgrew old ones. It has become a symbolic part of my life. It proved that with a little determination, I could accomplish what I set out to do.

But despite my I-can-do-anything-I-put-my-mind-to ambition, I was beginning to think that I was in over my head with this project. You see, I had set out to accomplish something that had never been proven by anyone in the world while only taking junior-level physics. My task at hand included finding piezoelectric components, identifying the correct wattage output, the certain impedance match to the electronics, and so on. I was beginning to let my doubt lead me into pits of discouragement. It was then that my mentor came to me and said, "Remember those light-up sneakers kids wore some years back?" He told me there were piezoelectric generators in them that were used to activate the circuit of lights. With those words, I felt the hairs on the back of my neck raise with excitement. *How do I find out?* I asked myself. *Go find yourself a pair and take them apart!* I left my studio desk and drove straight to the Salvation Army resale.

I left the store with three pairs of light-up shoes. Once back at the studio, what I discovered was a little piezoceramic sheet that, when stimulated, created a charge. The charge was great enough to send a signal to the circuit board, which told the lights to dance in the shoes. Ah, ha! It worked! Inspired, I rigged the shoe circuits up in a set of small glass and concrete tiles that I had cast in a ceramic studio. When one stepped on the tile, the glass moved down to stimulate the circuit and send the lights into action. Four tiles lined up in a strip; a walk across it would create energy with endless uses. I knew that the mock-up I was constructing may seem unimpressive. It was only, after all, six pairs of L.A. Gear light-up shoes from the Salvation Army, cast concrete from Home Depot, and cuts of glass from an artist friend. The mock-up to most probably looked whipped together like any old art school project, but to me, it held the key to a world of possibility.

That next week, I organized a little installation at a gallery opening in town to test the mock-up against a little foot traffic. My excitement regarding the technological progress I had made was quickly replaced by anxiety. Would people understand it? Would they share my vision? My goal was to see if my newfound gadget could handle the heavy traffic and how people would react to the idea of generating their own electricity. The morning of the event, I braced myself for the feedback I would receive, skipping breakfast while coping with waves of anxiety. There was no turning back now . . . all I could do was step aside and watch as the technology was utilized by my unknowing test subjects.

I watched as people took tentative steps across the tiles, creating tiny flashes of lights as they shuffled. One by one, each person registered a look of shock and awe as they realized that they had harnessed their own energy, marveling at the possibilities.

We began to party.

The exhibition was a huge success. At first, I could barely stand to look at the people in the art gallery, in fear that they couldn't "get it" or would think the whole idea was stupid. Once I felt brave enough to open my eyes to the joyous wonder of the group's reaction, I noticed the very evident truth that people were sharing my vision. They were dancing, jumping, walking, running, and even doing handstands on my mock-up.

That day was only the beginning. The nagging fear and doubt was cast aside, and intuitively, I knew I was about to create something that could change the world. The success of my innovation had resulted in a prestigious undergraduate award, which I quickly put to use to pay for the incredibly expensive materials for my final thesis prototype.

But I was hooked. The high from my exhibition fueled my passion for the project. I knew I needed to go forward; burning out was not an option, but burned out I was. The last year had been a whirlwind of activity, and I was emotionally and financially exhausted. Sick and tired of being broke, I took a job working for my sister, Sara Snow, as an assistant on her TV show *Get Fresh with Sara Snow*. My days were filled with research, content consulting, and contacting guests for the show. My sister and I referred to this time as "the apprenticeship program." While I wasn't sure what my next step was in life, I knew that I was anxious to discover it.

It was a day off, and I was taking the afternoon to get caught up on some magazine reading. When I was a student, I enjoyed perusing design magazines, but working full time had left little time for leisure reading. I lay across my bed with a hot cup of tea and leafed through *Metropolis Magazine* until I came across a page with these words in big, bold letters: NEXT GENERATION DESIGN COMPETITION. I nearly choked on my tea as I read the theme for the 2007 competition: Energy. The call for entries was practically begging for my thesis work. My break was over. It was time to get back to my own work and inspire the next wave of energy innovation.

I went to work putting together my submission. The process went smooth, and I had a strong feeling that I was meant to do this. I labeled the application "Project Power Struggle" and mailed it to the magazine. I occupied myself in my work for my sister, anxiously waiting to hear back. While it was exciting to think about what it might be like to win, and I had high hopes, I knew I might not. This was an international competition, and while my work had been well received by the experts at the art exhibit, I had no idea how it would fare after being judged by leading experts in the field. They would love it or hate it, I suppose. Either way, it was worth trying.

We are a global network. All our individual choices create a ripple effect and will eventually impact millions. Once we realize that, we can each find our own place and let the ripples move further and further out.

I didn't have to wait long. I was on a long weekend from work and went to Ohio to visit my good friend from college Mavilya (Mia) Chubarova. Mia was my partner in crime at university. Our art studios were next to each other, and we were the only ones who stayed into the wee hours of the night plugging away at our projects. We had passion, and we were like sisters. As you can imagine, the magazine submission was far from my mind the moment I arrived in Columbus and saw Mia. As we sat giggling over a shared joke, my cell phone rang. I answered it for some reason, which is rare because I am a notorious screener.

It was the editor from *Metropolis Magazine*. My heart skipped a beat as she informed me that I had been selected as a runner-up in the competition. Her voice was warm and friendly, and her support for the project became clear: "Now I only request one thing—that you come up with a better name than Project Power Struggle. What is that? This is a fantastic and exciting product that can change people's behavior and the world! Show it!"

As I hung up the phone, I had goose bumps from her words. It took a moment to truly realize the potential of this opportunity. I looked at Mia; she knew exactly what had just ensued. We cried with excitement, opened a bottle of champagne, and immediately took out a piece of paper to start brainstorming names as we used to do in school. Our favorites: the Electric Stride and POWERleap.

After the weekend, I immediately went back to work on the project, as I had to prepare for a reception ceremony in San Francisco. It would be the first time I would present my innovation under its new name, POWERleap. After the excitement of the editor's phone call, doubt and anxiety crept back into my life. I realized that although my idea was fresh, I didn't have a proto-type that I felt was appropriate to show off at the reception. Suddenly, I felt too young and foolish to be taken seriously. After all, I would be competing against seasoned engineers and professional designers. Who was I? I was a recent graduate working for my sister.

The night before the reception, I couldn't sleep. I kept thinking about my pitch and how I would talk about POWERleap. I was overwhelmed by con-fusion—so much to say and only one shot! I was scared of being made out a fool, to say the least. That morning I had breakfast with my brother Joe in San Francisco. Joe is four years older than me, and he was always one of my biggest fans. Sitting across from my eggs over easy and toast, he could tell my head was hanging low. He reminded me of the day I learned how to ride a bike. "Remember how determined you were? You were taken over by this goal. Just remember what it is you want to accomplish today, and you are going to touch the masses." That conversation stuck with me all day, and when I walked into the showroom, all of my fears had melted away. I didn't have an idle moment.

The week after the reception ceremony, I was contacted by Mohawk Group—a global commercial carpet manufacturer. They were cosponsors of the competition that year and, to my great pleasure, they took quite a liking to POWERleap. They followed up after the reception with some phone and email correspondence to learn more about my project and its direction. Before I knew it, I was being flown into Atlanta for a meeting. As a result of the meeting, they agreed to give me a ten-thousand-dollar grant to build my Next Generation prototype to be showcased on a segment for the Sundance Channel. Working day and night, I frantically studied and tried putting everything together before the television shoot. Everything started

PHOTO BY POWERLEAP

to come together quickly—I incorporated my business, collected two business partners, launched a website, spoke with fifty-plus potential commercial customers, and filed a provisional patent. I started getting emails and calls from media outlets like National Public Radio, the *New York Times*, and *TreeHugger.com* all remarking on the possibilities of the project and wanting to report it to the world.

At the time of this writing, we are finalizing a business agreement and planning our first set of commercial pilot installations. We have a number of customers lined up to be our initial testers, and finally I can tell them approximately when our doors will open. POWERleap today is not just a new source of alternative energy, it also represents an alternative pathway of how we can think about and take responsibility for the energy we use.

I consider myself an entrepreneur working for the planet. I realize that working within corporate models for change isn't seen as the traditional form of activism, but I feel as though I have defined my own form of activism. I never imagined myself owning an American business and sustaining myself through a capitalist market system. Yet when the opportunity presented itself, I didn't turn it away. I don't operate my business in a way that lets life go by, selfishly taking without giving back. Instead, I found a way to harness my passion and commitment to environmental activism into full-time work that is rewarding personally, financially, and environmentally. I strongly feel that we are a global network. All our individual choices create a ripple effect and will eventually impact millions. Once we realize that, we can each find our own place and let the ripples move further and further out. For this reason, I remain dedicated to developing technology that goes beyond harnessing the energy of the wind and sun. To truly make the switch from dirty fossil fuels, we need to exhaust every possibility of energy production, which calls for continual research, innovation, and guts. And I'm happy to drive that train in any way I can.

When I was a three-year-old learning to ride a bike, I refused to let go of a dream. Today, that dream is not a brass horn, but a new kind of energy future. And for me to achieve that dream, it means running a company that will hopefully one day change the way we use energy in a more sustainable and productive way. With the state of our planet right now, that day can't come soon enough.

Elizabeth Redmond is the president and director of POWERleap Inc., a cleantech company that generates electricity from pedestrian and vehicular traffic. Since its inception in 2006, POWERleap has now grown to become a global corporation showcased on the Discovery Channel, Sundance Channel, The New York Times, and Forbes. Elizabeth plans to continue to use design to fuel the engines of change and innovate alternatives for our future.

PETER HAMMARSTEDT

▶ Twenty-five   ▶ Sweden   ▶ Animal Defender

In Defense of Seals

Bring on your tear gas, bring on your grenades, your new supplies of mace, your state troopers, and even your national guards. But let the record show, we ain't going to be turned around.

—RALPH DAVID ABERNATHY

IT WAS APRIL, 12, 2008, when a heavily armed tactical response unit of the Royal Canadian Mounted Police (RCMP) boarded my vessel by force in international waters. They stormed the wheelhouse and pushed me and the captain down to the deck at gunpoint. I was told to put my hands on my head and not to move. Throughout the ship, the heavy thud of combat boots echoed down narrow wooden companionways, drowning out the screams of the rest of the crew as they too were forced to the deck. Five minutes after boarding, the storm troopers had secured the ship.

In groups of four, we were moved onto a Canadian Coast Guard icebreaker. We were handcuffed to a railing that ran along the vessel's starboard side. From there, I could see the RCMP comb through the ship, referred to affectionately by the crew as "the old *Farley*," that had been my home for almost five years. We were taken to Sydney, Nova Scotia, past the heavy ice floes that we'd negotiated several days earlier when first entering the Gulf of St. Lawrence. The M/V *Farley Mowat* was put under tow, and the single-largest mass slaughter of marine mammals in the world, the Canadian seal hunt, would continue virtually unopposed dozens of miles in our wake.

The captain of my vessel, Alex Cornelissen, and I were subsequently moved to an RCMP detention center on a First Nations reservation, twenty-five minutes out of Sydney. I was brought in front of Canadian Customs as if

I had flown into the country rather than having been forced in at gunpoint. As I stood in front of them, all my possessions having been confiscated, all of my clothes beyond a t-shirt and pants taken away from me, they asked me if I had "anything to declare." I didn't answer. They proceeded to ask me the usual Canadian Customs questions: if I was bringing any plants or animals into the country, if I was bringing ten thousand dollars or more into the country. I chose to remain silent.

As I pulled up my first hook and saw it gleam under the moonlight, I knew that that specific hook wasn't going to kill another seal, sea turtle, or tuna ever again. And to think that it didn't make a difference was completely wrong—it made all the difference in the world to that one animal.

Every year, 275,000 baby harp seals, most between four and six weeks old, are clubbed to death on the ice floes of the Gulf of St. Lawrence and along the lonely coast of Labrador. The pups that find care by their mother's side—expecting to lose their molting hairs before taking to the water for the first time—only fall prey to barbarians with spiked clubs. Individuals paid to convert living, feeling beings into leather jackets and omega-3 supplement capsules. The Canadian government legitimizes this hunt by blaming the seals for the disappearance of the codfish—the cod comprising only a miniscule part of the seal's diet—rather than scrutinizing their own mismanagement of the fishing sector.

Every year, the organization I work with, the Sea Shepherd Conservation Society, heads to Canada, sometimes by helicopter, often by ship, to bring back video evidence to the world that the slaughter of harp seals in Canada is unsustainable and incredibly cruel. The Canadian Veterinary Medical Association paints an accurate picture of the seal hunt, I think, when it draws the parallel between men running around on a field filled with puppies, smashing their heads in with baseball bats. But it doesn't just end with spiking these seals; 60 percent of the seals are skinned alive. In 2008, the Sea Shepherd crew was once again able to bring back footage of seals being skinned alive, showing the lie of the so-called sustainable hunt. I've seen it firsthand take five or six blows with a spiked club to render a seal pup unconscious. I've seen seals kicked and stomped to death. I've seen the carcass that remains after being skinned alive. After seeing all of this, it's a hunt I'm committed to stopping.

Upon arriving in Sydney, Nova Scotia, Alex and I were put in separate vehicles and driven to our respective interrogations. For the task, the Canadian Department of Fisheries and Oceans had enlisted the help of the RCMP Serious Crimes Unit. But as the moment the RCMP had pushed me to the deck at gunpoint after illegally boarding the *Farley Mowat* in the Cabot Strait, my lips were sealed, and that silence continued until I was released on bail.

Maybe we couldn't save the world, but we could save the whole world for this one animal. And nothing that the government thugs from Ottawa dished out was comparable to what this innocent creature would experience if there were nobody on the ice to protect her.

I was put in a small concrete room, furnished with a table, three chairs, and a plain bookshelf. An hour and a half into the "interview," the interrogating officer trudged into the room, removed my hat from my head, and yelled in my face, "When I look at you, I see a twelve-year old Palestinian boy with a backpack full of nails walking into a shopping center in Israel. Are you that boy? Are you?" It was enough for me to almost forget for an instant that the only thing that I was being charged with was allegedly being within a half nautical mile (3,038 feet or 926 meters) of a fisherman butchering a defenseless seal pup. I was then told that the only reason I could have to keep quiet was if I was "planning something like the next 9/11," which was then compared to photographing a seal being skinned alive, the "crime" that Alex and myself stood accused of.

When all else fails, the police draw out the interrogation for as long as they can and believe that if they yell enough terrible things at you, you'll eventually crack. Typically, if you don't know your rights, it's very effective. You're made to feel that the only way out of the situation is to "cooperate." The distempered interrogation officer suddenly spit out, "You're like a prisoner of war. You just say your name and your rank. But even prisoners of war say what they're fighting for. They say, 'I'm fighting for freedom, I'm fighting for America.' Well, what the hell are you fighting for?"

What the hell was I fighting for? As the door to my jail cell slammed shut behind me at the end of a four-hour long interrogation, I began to reflect on the long road that got me there. Unbeknownst to me, at the same time a court clerk at the Sydney Court House was counting 2,500 two-dollar coins delivered by Sea Shepherd president, Captain Paul Watson, paid for by Farley Mowat. A sure slap in the face to Canadian national pride, two of Canada's most famous conservationists getting the so-called eco-pirates, Alex and myself, out on bail. But for me, there was nothing left to do but think. It wasn't the first time that I'd been to jail in Canada. Almost exactly three years earlier, I'd been arrested for the same thing—allegedly being within half a nautical mile of a barbarian butchering a seal.

IT HAD BEEN THREE YEARS SINCE I was grabbed by the nape of my neck, kicked behind the knee, and thrown to the ice by a Department of Fisheries and Oceans officer desperate to keep footage of the seal hunt from reaching the mass media. With my face firmly pressed against the cold, hard ice, the government thug had twisted one arm behind my back, bent my wrist at ninety degrees, and thrust his knee into my back. I yelled out in pain. Between bursts of crude vulgarity, he whispered into my ear, "I hope that this is hurting you enough, you bastard," and answered my cries with another twist of my wrist.

Far beyond my line of sight, a crew of six seal butchers walked back to their ship accompanied by officers of the RCMP. Between bashing in the soft skulls of four- to six-week-old seal pups, they had assaulted five of our crew, broken the nose of another and deliberately targeted our property and person. They were free to go. We were not.

As I tuned out the raging officer sitting on top of me, I tried to make sense of it all. Witnessing a seal being killed equaled interrogation, fines, and jail time. While mercilessly slaughtering defenseless seals and assaulting members of the international media community equaled pats on the back and seventy dollars per pelt. Out of the corner of my eye, I saw one friend and shipmate hauled away in handcuffs. Just past him, another friend was dragged by her feet into an awaiting coast guard helicopter. With the purest of intentions, we had come to the ice floes of Canada to defend life and were being treated as criminals. Two of the most compassionate people that I knew were about to be put behind bars. Overnight, my world had gone twisted from the inside out.

It was then that I saw her, somewhere between my two arrested friends: a gray and black spotted seal stared at me with her big black eyes. She was thirty-three feet (10.1 meters) away and seemingly oblivious to all of the chaos around her. I thought to myself, because of our intervention, at least she was safe. At least the sealers were being escorted back to their ship, their day of sealing prematurely over. Maybe we couldn't save the world, but we could save the whole world for this one animal. And nothing that the government thugs from Ottawa dished out was comparable to what this innocent creature would experience if there were nobody on the ice to protect her. She was my anchor in reality. At least something still made sense. Defending her was right. No fine, jail term, or physical violence would convince me otherwise.

That was 2005. It was because of the nightmares that followed me after this, of seeing so many defenseless seal pups bludgeoned to death repeat in my mind, that I'd once again made the trip to the ice floes. I had seen a white expanse of ice stained blood red overnight, and you can never really turn away from that. Now being in jail gave me the opportunity to reflect on the twists and turns in my life that brought me to this stage, where I could safely say that I would risk my life to save that of a seal or any animal for that matter. But again, my expedition to the Gulf of St. Lawrence essentially began a decade earlier.

When I was fourteen, I met a dog named Marlboro through the chain-link fencing of an animal shelter housing pen. I had been volunteering at the shelter for two months, and when his deep brown eyes met mine, there was instantly nothing more important to me than finding this dog a loving home. Marlboro never said a word; neither a bark nor a whimper escaped his lips for the duration of his two-month stay. But he spoke volumes about the way our society views animals—not as feeling, thinking, unique individuals, but as disposable things. For me, I would come to call him my best friend.

For an entire summer, we tried to make the best of the cards that Marlboro had been dealt. Every morning for two months, the concrete floor turned to mud and grass and steel fencing crumbled to a sun that kept us playing around the large oak tree that marked the end of the property for the better part of each day. From that oak tree, the kennel seemed far away.

But one Saturday morning, I came in to find Marlboro's cage empty. He'd been moved. But not to the wide expanse of a country home that I'd dreamed up for him, but to a set of cages down the road referred to as death row. Marlboro had inadvertently bit a volunteer. And because of that, he was condemned to die. The day before he was put down was the first time that Marlboro ever spoke to me. As I said my last goodbyes and turned to walk away, my quiet friend let out a howl and threw the entire weight of his body against the cage door. I ran home crying, feeling helpless. The next day, a Rottweiler named Holly stood in Marlboro's old cell. She found a home one month later.

Marlboro taught me more than has any other individual I've ever come across. He would help set the course of the rest of my life, and because of that, I am forever in his debt. Marlboro taught me that every single animal—human and nonhuman alike—is a completely unique individual. Until the end of time, there will never be anyone else exactly like you or exactly like me or exactly like Marlboro. A rookery of seals is a collection of distinct personalities. For me, that has always been one of the most powerful arguments for animal rights. That we have more in common than not. That's what my best four-legged friend taught me many years ago—that animals are worth fighting for.

The day I ran from the caged rows that separated Marlboro from the rest of the canine population, I made a promise: never again, when put in the position to save an animal's life here and now, would I turn my back. Now I found myself in a Canadian jail cell for the second time, hoping that our intervention had brought us one step closer to ending the seal slaughter. Not just because of the hakapiks that were scheduled to fall over the heads of 275,000 baby harp seals, but also so that Marlboro would understand that not for a single day had he been forgotten.

Not more than a year after meeting Marlboro, I stumbled upon a photograph of a whale being harpooned in Antarctica. I knew right away that there was nowhere in the world that I'd rather be than between that whale and that harpoon, to use my body to directly stop bloodthirsty pirates of profit from mercilessly pursuing marine mammals. There was nothing left for me to do but to sign up to be a part of the Sea Shepherd Conservation Society. As soon as I turned eighteen, I submitted a crew application. I responded to the question, "Would you be willing to risk personal injury to save the life of a whale?" with a resounding yes. I was by no means suicidal, but I recognized that power cedes nothing without demand. Within a few months, I was off to the Galapagos to help Sea Shepherd patrol for illegal fishing, allowing me the opportunity to keep the promise that I had made years earlier.

It took seventeen days to get from Seattle to Galapagos, but it only took an hour or two to find an illegal longline in the Galapagos Marine Reserve. Longlines are essentially the nuclear warhead of the ocean, as they are incapable of discriminating between species, killing hundreds of diverse creatures in their wake. Our first night on patrol had us pulling up dozens of miles of line and releasing any animals caught. I remember feeling distraught, knowing that very same night that there was enough line set in the oceans to wrap around the world eighty times. But as I pulled up my first hook and saw it gleam under the moonlight, I knew that that specific hook wasn't going to kill another seal, sea turtle, or tuna ever again. And to think that it didn't make a difference was completely wrong—it made all the difference in the world to that one animal. Since that day, I've worked to save as many lives as I can, lives of individuals as capable of suffering as you and me, but incapable of defending or speaking for themselves.

> *Every single animal—human and nonhuman alike—is a completely unique individual; and a rookery of seals is a collection of distinct personalities. For me, that has always been one of the most powerful arguments for animal rights.*

On April, 13, 2008, the day after I was put at gunpoint, I sat in my jail cell and remembered that nothing that could ever happen to me could compare to what billions of animals are put through every year. I thought about the seal whose eyes I met on the ice three years earlier; I remembered Marlboro's howl, which was as clear as it was a decade ago; and it was as if I could feel the hook that I pulled out of the water in the Galapagos in my hand once more. I remembered that a promise is forever. And then I fell asleep on my concrete bunk.

———

Peter Hammarstedt was later convicted for his role as first mate on the Sea Shepherd Seal Defense Campaign 2008. The Provincial Court of Nova Scotia fined him $22,400 for two counts of being within a half nautical mile of the Canadian seal hunt. Peter was unable to attend his own trial due to an outstanding deportation order.

Today, he works as crew coordinator for the Sea Shepherd Conservation Society, when not out at sea. As of spring 2010, he was preparing for Sea Shepherd's sixth expedition to the Antarctic to shut down the illegal Japanese whaling fleet and prevent the killing of more than one thousand whales.

PHOTO BY JO-ANNE MCARTHUR

WEN BO

▶ Thirty-eight ▶ China ▶ Awareness Raiser

The Lone Warrior of China

You are not Atlas carrying the world on your shoulder. It is good to remember that the planet is carrying you.

—VANDANA SHIVA

I FIRST TRAVELED TO YUNNAN PROVINCE in the southwest of China in 1992, when I was backpacking there as a student. At the time, I loved the wild quality of the land, how pristine and undisturbed it all seemed. The Yunnan countryside is enchanting and beautiful, with steep gorges dropping into rivers that feed the Yangtze, snowy mountain ranges with perilous roads cut between them and climbing up their slopes, towering old-growth forest stretching to the horizon, and in the south there are rainforests harboring rich wild fauna and flora. Yunnan is known within China for being the "land of elephants and peacocks," just two of the colorful inhabitants that make it easy to fall in love with the place.

Yunnan is just as diverse culturally and ethnically as it is geographically. The province borders on Tibet to the northwest and Burma to the south, so there are Tibetan people, Dai, and many other minorities living along the border and in the southern parts of the province. It's an unforgettable land—remote to get to, but hard to leave once you're there. When I was a child, the pictures of the rainforests in southern Yunnan caught my imagination. I had always wanted to be a rainforest researcher, studying its ecology and wildlife. The colorful wildlife and scenery seemed to have been dreamed up in a fairy tale.

But now, as I walked along a narrow road dug into the side of a cliff with thirty other students, our local tour guides, and the horses carrying our luggage, I knew better. This land was far from untouched: uncontrolled clear-cut logging of the old-growth forest had devastated many parts of the province, and wildlife habitats were being destroyed at an alarming rate. As I looked out to the horizon, jagged scars abruptly gouged the landscape every so often, a brutal reminder of the industrial machines that were chewing up the ground and the ancient forests that stood there. That's why I and my small group of students, activists, and journalists had come here—to see this destruction firsthand and try to alert the rest of the country to the destruction ravaging the landscape and its wildlife.

I was lost in thought as I walked, following behind one of the packhorses plodding slowly up the narrow path on the cliff. Wanting to get ahead, I tried to quickly pass the horse, but as I came into its view from behind, it startled, and, bucking and snorting, blundered into me. Hardly realizing the danger, I turned and saw I was staring one thousand feet (304.8 meters) straight down into the gorge and the rushing water below.

It took what seemed like a lifetime to regain my balance and scramble back from the edge—though of course, in reality, it was only a fraction of a second. But that brief moment I spent staring into the gorge, I felt a terrifying rush, the feeling that whatever the price of this endeavor, I was totally committed, even if it put my life at risk. There was something about that realization that scared me—but it also confirmed that I was doing exactly what I was meant to do.

We had come from Beijing to meet the local people, the provincial and local officials, the Tibetan lamas, and representatives of the logging companies that were working there. Ironically, though, it was not the fate of millions of acres of forest that had set this journey in motion; it was the fate of a few small monkeys.

One of the many rare species of primates in the province is the Yunnan snub-nosed monkey. These black-and-white monkeys, notable for the small black noses they're named for and distinctive red lips, live in the mountainous alpine forests found at high altitudes. By the time of our trip, in 1998, the logging in Yunnan had severely depleted much of their habitat, and they were in danger of vanishing forever.

I had first heard about the danger to the Yunnan snub-nosed monkeys from a retired editor of the Chinese-language *Great Nature* magazine, Tang Xiyang, while I was a student at the China School of Journalism. We had invited him to speak to our student group in Beijing, the China Green Student Forum, about conservation issues in China. He stalked the room as he talked, giving us a fiery speech about the thousands of years of natural history being wiped out by industrial logging. The scale of the loss was nearly too much to bear. It was an electric performance, and Tang's passion was infectious. Previously, we were nothing more than a small group of students who met every once in a while to talk about our interest in environmentalism and swap stories. But by the time Tang finished his presentation, we were much more—seized with a desire to not just talk about the environment any more, but also to take action.

We determined that it was time to act on what we knew and try to make a real difference on the ground. The situation in Yunnan presented an irresistible opportunity: we would travel to the area, meet with representatives from the many different constituencies there, and generate as much publicity as possible, hopefully pressuring the Chinese central government into acting, and finally stopping the logging scheme.

Starting from just a few individuals planning to go and do some volunteer work in Yunnan, it quickly grew to become a grand tour, with more than thirty students and conservationists traveling to northwest Yunnan for three weeks. With so many people involved, word got around quickly. Media interest grew, and soon we were bringing much-needed media attention to report on what we were observing. The *China Green Times* was the primary newspaper to cover the trip and sent timely reports back to Beijing on our little band of travelers and our adventures in Yunnan.

———

THOUGH I LIVED IN AN APARTMENT, nature was abundant around me growing up: Trees, frogs, and butterflies were part of my childhood memories, and the starry night sky beckoned me to explore the unknown world outside. However, as the urbanization process picked up its pace, and China's economic boom required wider roads and more building, the natural environment around me gradually disappeared. The natural places that haunted my childhood memories were forever lost. That was the dawning of my environmental consciousness. I'd always enjoyed nature and the outdoors, but it wasn't until the day that a news report came on television about whaling and the dumping of toxic chemicals into the ocean that I began to seriously consider the natural world as something that needed consideration and protection.

The news report I saw was of Greenpeace activists harassing and blocking the activities of a whaling boat in the Pacific Ocean. The Chinese government was fond of these kinds of Greenpeace stories because it was an opportunity to highlight some distinctly Western problems, such as whaling and environmental degradation—this, of course, being around the time that China's own environmentally destructive industrialization was accelerating as never before. There was little to watch then on Chinese television, and the daily newscasts often featured such stories, translated from Western TV feeds. The slaughter of whales, and the actions of the activists to stop it, wrenched at my conscience. I decided that environmental action—the kind that Greenpeace took on a regular basis—was what I wanted to do. Starting Greenpeace in China was my new life goal.

Greenpeace was the first instance I had ever heard of in which citizens had organized to promote their cause independently. Each time I watched these news accounts of Greenpeace's bold action in the Pacific Ocean, individuals putting themselves in front of boats and in harm's way, my excitement grew. Every day around China Television news time, I would have been expecting a piece of news on Greenpeace. I must have been Greenpeace's number one fan in China by the middle of the 1980s. In 1986, when I was fourteen years old, I started my own unofficial Greenpeace group and started lecturing my friends and classmates about environmental issues.

But meeting that goal of starting an actual Greenpeace movement in China proved to be more difficult. For one thing, there was no Internet then and no practical way to get connected with the real Greenpeace. And given the lack of communication with the outside world, being a fan of Greenpeace was, at the time, a lonely thing to be in China.

When I graduated from my first university degree in Changsha, there was still no Greenpeace in China—or *any* environmental group, for that matter, that I could consider working for. So I decided to continue my studies at the China School of Journalism for my second degree. Having moved to Beijing for graduate school, I had more time and started to connect with other people interested in issues of ecology and conservation and introduced them to each other. Eventually, these other student leaders and I started the China Green Student Forum, a network for college students interested in environmental issues. We met to exchange ideas, tactics, and contacts.

That kind of student gathering could be dangerous in the years after the Tiananmen Square protest of 1989. In 1991, when I put up posters around university campuses in Changsha to tell people about Earth Day, I was taken in for questioning by Hunan Medical University police.

I remember the day clearly: just as I was putting up a poster promoting things students could do to celebrate Earth Day, a man in plainclothes watched me intently. Moments later, he asked me what I was doing, and I explained about Earth Day and why I wanted to tell people about it. I was about to leave, but he asked me to go with him, which is when it became clear that he was an undercover police officer. He questioned me, asking me who paid me to do this. I told him no one did—it was something I was doing on my own initiative.

He called my own university, and a group of people, including police officers from my university and faculty members from my department, soon arrived. They huddled over my poster in a separate room, looking for unacceptable political messages—and, naturally, couldn't find any. After being transferred to my university, I was taken to the police office at my campus, unable to leave. The officers continued to question me on my motivation and whether or not someone else was funding my activities. I gave them a lengthy talk about my past involvement in environmental efforts, from middle school to college. I enjoyed presenting my confession—I turned it into another energetic lecture on the need for urgent conservation efforts in China—and the police dutifully took notes.

Finally I was allowed to go back to sleep at my dorm the next morning, but I had to write a "self-criticism report." Instead of criticizing myself for these actions, I wrote a report about the crucial need for environmental action by the government. They didn't like that very much, and so I gained a reputation for being a problematic student, one potentially having "dangerous links with the international community."

These police investigations—there were others—never led anywhere, but I always treated it as an opportunity to talk with the government officials about the importance of conservation. And I knew from watching Greenpeace on TV that being arrested was an important part of the process. I wore those arrests like a badge of honor. I felt like I was already a part of Greenpeace, whether officially or not.

IN YUNNAN, OUR ACTIVISM WASN'T DRAWING the attention of police, but of the national media. For several weeks, we rode in buses around the province meeting people. But northwest Yunnan, being rugged terrain, wasn't always the most hospitable place for a bus full of people. So from time to time, we would hike to remote villages to talk with the locals, or to Tibetan temples perched on mountaintops to meet with the lamas who lived there. Everywhere we went, the people were kind and warmhearted. We visited several villagers and were welcomed to dine and dance with them upon first meet.

In Deqin, a small town in the farthest northwest corner of Yunnan, right on the Tibetan border, we conducted social research on such issues as household income, child schooling, family structure, and so on. The encounters were eye-opening. Many villagers relied on collecting and selling pine mushrooms, which were being exported to Japan to earn extra income. It was a vivid example of how locals needed a healthy environment to sustain their own livelihood.

The local people lived largely in small villages, surrounded on every side by forest, and many had a deep knowledge of the land formed by decades of living there. They loved their forest and valued having it intact. But many people were also quite poor. Therefore, when local government advertised their logging schemes as a way to generate extra revenue for the local economy, it could be misleading. And for the government-owned logging companies, it was always an easy argument to turn publicly owned forests into resources that would feed their profits.

Political action is crucial to saving vibrant ecologies, because government is the one institution that can mediate the many different concerns of industry, citizens, and the land, the sea, and those that cannot speak for themselves—at least, not in our language. Activism, on the other hand, is knowing when to challenge governments. But the key is to know when to work hand in hand with both.

We saw clear-cut sites where logging companies had stripped everything from the ground, leaving acres of scarred land in their wake. Local officials explained their decisions to allow logging on these lands, and they consistently told us the same things the villagers had: there was every economic incentive to treat the forest as a resource to be exploited, and little economic incentive to treat it as either a source of sustainable livelihood or an environmental heritage to be preserved. Local governments needed money to provide services, and logging was one of the few activities that brought in the money.

We met Long Yongcheng, a researcher of the Yunnan snub-nosed monkeys who had lived and studied the animals in their natural habitat for eight years. As a group of mostly city-dwellers, we felt it was important to not just look at the logging and complain about it, but also to learn as much as possible about the whole situation from people who knew much more about it. Long, having studied the monkeys for years, was a wealth of information to our group. He knew the wildlife and the habitat extremely well, but he was also someone who actually lived in the area, who had friends and connections in the community. A group of outsiders who were leaving after their three-week trip can still have a role to play, as we learned, but it is citizens with deep links in the community and the environment that can achieve the most impressive and lasting results.

After nearly three weeks of riding down roads in our bus, hiking over newly deforested alpine slopes, and stumbling up and down mountainsides, we headed back to Beijing, armed with knowledge of the issues particular to Yunnan, and ready to propose real solutions that would protect the environment and the people as well. The question at that point was, would anyone care or listen?

That was the dawning of my environmental consciousness. I'd always enjoyed nature and the outdoors, but it wasn't until the day that a news report came on television about whaling and the dumping of toxic chemicals into the ocean that I began to seriously consider the natural world as something that needed consideration and protection.

As it turns out, our journey had been a sensation in Beijing, and the central government had taken note of our time on the road. Media reports of our exploration in Yunnan were widespread, provoking a long-overdue national conversation about balancing China's need for economic development with the need to protect natural environments.

Shortly after our trip, the central government offered ten million dollars to the local prefecture to invest in their efforts to reduce poverty and announced that they would halt logging of old-growth forests in Yunnan. The following year, in 1997, after severe flooding in the Yangtze River region, the late Prime Minister Zhu Rongji ordered the immediate ban on logging of all natural forests across China. The Yunnan snub-nosed monkeys—and thousands more species—would be protected from the logging that was devastating them, and local people would benefit economically and environmentally.

For me, the whole experience reshaped much of my thinking about environmentalism and ecological activism. Environmental problems are complex, and so are their solutions. Protecting a single species of wildlife is easy for people to understand, but ultimately, I decided the goal must be more than simply securing a piece of forest for a few endangered monkeys—it must be a comprehensive effort to protect whole ecosystems, ensure the human and social development of local communities, and integrate those two worlds in a way that improves both. Such solutions are never easy to find, but when they work, they are world changing.

Environmental activism, I concluded, *is* political activism. The two are inseparable. Political action is crucial to saving vibrant ecologies, because government is the one institution that can mediate the many different concerns of industry, citizens, and the land, the sea, and those that cannot speak for themselves—at least, not in our language. Activism, on the other hand, is knowing when to challenge governments. But the key is to know when to work hand in hand with both. Both techniques are necessary to successfully preserve fragile environments.

Today, as with the original Yunnan trip, my dream from the time I was a teenager still propels me. That unofficial Greenpeace office I started at fourteen years old finally, over a decade of work, became real when I helped establish the first Greenpeace office in Beijing and became the first Greenpeace staff person working in mainland China. The daring actions of those original Greenpeace activists all those years ago, which dazzled me as a child, still inspire me today. It shows how activism—committed, long-term, and fearless—can effect not just immediate change, but also transform the world for decades to come. I'm proud to be part of that change today, and hope that I can similarly inspire the next generation of Chinese environmental activists.

Wen Bo is currently the China coordinator for Global Greengrants Fund. Time Magazine *says his work to fuel an environmental movement in China has "lit sparks amid the darkness of public indifference." He received a Pew Fellowship in Marine Conservation and is now investigating marine endangered species trade in East Asia, trying to save sea turtles, sharks, and coral species.*

ANDY RIDLEY

▶ Thirty-eight ▶ Britain ▶ Movement Builder

PHOTO BY ANDY RIDLEY

Earth Hour: The Hour Is upon Us

A pessimist sees the difficulty in every opportunity; an optimist sees the opportunity in every difficulty.

—WINSTON CHURCHILL

I WAS DESPERATE FOR A CIGARETTE. Booked for a hip replacement in two weeks time, I'd given up smoking under advice from my surgeon. I hadn't smoked for five months. But none of this seemed to matter now. Standing there looking at the skyline of Sydney, shock took over. The amazing project that had become Earth Hour had succeeded on its first attempt. The beautiful skyline was lit up, not by glittering office lights but instead by a full moon glistening off the harbor. A city not asleep but fully awakened to an issue that the government had claimed did not concern people or was only the domain of "greenies."

I felt a friendly hand on my shoulder. It was my good friend Phil McLean. "Don't forget to breathe it in," he said. "Just take a couple of minutes." We were standing down by Fleet Steps in the Botanic Gardens, looking across a dark city, far away from the Earth Hour event in order to see it all. For months, my world had been a buzz of hectic preparations, and it wasn't until now that I'd had a chance to appreciate exactly what we were doing.

It was hard to believe that such a simple idea had taken off in such a big way in Sydney, when earlier there were walls of resistance to our fight. That same year, 2007, the Australian government would not even refer to the issue as climate change. Officially to them it was "climate variability," not necessarily human-made. This government was not only skeptical about climate change, but was also doing its best to stifle the science and the debate. This wasn't the only roadblock. Around this time, it was dawning on some of us at the World Wildlife Fund that we were unable to connect to the public beyond a small percentage of people that we already knew. Our climate campaigns were failing. Yet the evidence grew stronger day by day. I knew then that we had to get out of our comfort zone and think again about how we approached not just the subject of climate change, but also, in its very essence, the subject of the planet.

To be honest, back then I could relate to those who were questioning what climate change was all about. I was pretty much your average guy, and issues like this had only recently come to the forefront of my concerns since I had joined WWF Australia in 2002. My journey in conservation to date had been amazing and inspiring but was often also fueled by frustration. I'd met some heroic characters who had shown what could be done, but I'd also struggled against a bureaucratic element within the conservation movement that, at least in my view, saw conservation as endless policy discussions and committee meetings. I had come very close on a number of occasions to finding myself being "managed out" of the organization.

Yet for me, conservation was more than committee meetings—it had been my life. One of my dreams growing up as a kid in rural England was to dive on the Great Barrier Reef. Within a week of first arriving in Australia when I was thirty-two, I got the opportunity to do just that. I quickly found myself on the back of a dive boat at Port Douglas, a few meters underwater, not looking at pristine reefs, but instead at a wasteland. I had imagined that I would see a flourishing rainbow of corals and fish, but the part of the reef that I was diving on looked almost as if a bulldozer had driven right over the top of it. This part of the Great Barrier Reef had been reduced to mere rubble. I couldn't believe it. I was expecting to find a wonderland streaming with life and color, not a lone cuttlefish in a ghost land. Was this really the famous Great Barrier Reef I had always dreamed of?

Once out of the water, I quickly learned some of the causes for the reef's demise, including climate change. When I hit the shore, my interest had been piqued, and what was happening to our atmosphere was no longer an abstract concept but a harsh reality reshaping life on land.

It was the beginning of a journey for me. I had heard about climate change, but like most people at the time, my understanding was mixed up in confused, semi-factual conversations about ozone and CFCs and other scientific terms. It was big, but I didn't know how big, and I hadn't had anything but a passing interest until now.

All that seemed long ago as I took Phil's advice and took some deep breaths, soaking it all in. That night, millions of people from all walks of life in Sydney were sharing a moment of hope and action. Yet, perhaps ironically, Earth Hour was born out of frustration. A growing frustration with the mainstream public's lack of engagement in the fight against climate change.

Among my colleagues there was a realization that fear, anger, and protest—the traditional approach of climate campaigners—wasn't motivating people any longer but alienating the great majority. And yet we were dealing with an issue that, if you really wanted to be serious about solutions, would have to involve everybody—citizens, business, schoolchildren—the whole lot. This may seem obvious now, but at the time it was a radical discussion. It was almost as if we had forgotten the 60 percent in the middle and were only talking to the 20 percent that agreed with us. Bang in the middle was the vast majority, a slumbering giant of public opinion that environmental campaigns were ignoring.

We realized we had to think more street party than street protest. We had to bring communities together, not against each other. We had to find leaders in business, sports, music, and community groups across the world, and they needed to be from all walks of life. And I knew that we needed to reach far beyond the green movement if we were to effect any real change.

The conversation had started less than a year ago in May 2006 at a breakfast at the Hilton Hotel. I had gathered together a small group of creative minds from WWF and advertising company Leo Burnett to discuss the dilemma that faced us. We were all throwing ideas around, but it wasn't until my WWF colleague Liz Potter spoke that the vision of Earth Hour began. It had been the buzz in our circles for weeks; somebody just needed to say it.

During an oil fuel crisis in Thailand, the government had asked people to turn off their lights to save energy. It was a simple idea, but powerful. And we began to wonder, would something like that work in Sydney? The reaction at the table was mixed. Some said yes. Others were doubtful, saying it would never work. One said outright that we should prepare for failure. But the guys from Leo Burnett loved the idea, and I could see their creative minds going into overdrive.

I believed, personally, that we could do it, but the challenge would be to find the right partners and convince them to help us. The idea of a lights-out event may not have been new, but making it actually work on such a grand scale was. No one had done this before. I mean, where do you start? How do you make the lights go off in a city? Who do you need to help you? Who are the heroes? Would people do it at all? Were we delusional?

For the time being we labeled the project "The Big Flick" and then set out to try and make it happen. Before I knew it, a meeting had been arranged for me with Fairfax Media. And that's how I met Phil. Phil was the group editor at Fairfax, one of Australia's largest media organizations, and was keen to help. Before I knew it, we were at Coast restaurant in Darling Harbour, discussing climate change, the Big Flick, and a partnership with Fairfax. Tall, bald, and straight to the point, Phil was a newspaper man through and through. Later, I'd learn that he was a true believer in the power and responsibility of a newspaper in the community that it served, something that would make him a prime mover behind the campaign.

A few rounds of Crown Lager later and the conversation was flowing. Armed with a draft of the Intergovernmental Panel on Climate Change report, I showed a graph that displayed the consequences of a small rise in temperature on the Great Barrier Reef. I wanted to make a very clear link between the need for action and the size of the issue. But it turned out that Phil was better informed on climate change than I had expected. He had already registered that this had the potential to be a major political issue for the incumbent government and, more important, for the society that Fairfax served. I took confidence from the fact that almost immediately he was talking "how to," not "whether or not to." Having Fairfax on board was a real success because it meant that we had two of Sydney's major newspapers involved, the *Sydney Morning Herald* and the *Sun Herald,* giving us a level of influence that would open many more doors and reach a mass audience. We now had what we believed would be the key to open this door.

The Leo Burnett team soon did away with the Big Flick title and converted it from sounding like a crappy commercial radio station competition to something far more inspiring. Todd Sampson, our leading person at Leo Burnett and one of the best creative minds I had come across, presented the new name and logo. It was a simple and beautiful piece of art —the planet as a sixty, representing sixty minutes. He said we would call it Earth Hour. Capturing the desire of people in Sydney—and perhaps, one day, beyond Sydney—to spend an hour reflecting on the state of the planet. I loved it immediately. It captured the energy, scope, and focus of what we were trying to do.

With Fairfax and Leo Burnett behind us, we soon secured the political support of the mayor of Sydney, Clover Moore, and the then premier of New South Wales, Morris Iemma. This was important step because the government controlled all of the emergency services and owned lots of the buildings in the city, so without their support, any attempt to get the lights out would be nothing but a pipe dream.

By February, we had formed a hodgepodge team of volunteers, and everyone was pulling favors all over the city, asking for advice and assistance wherever we could get it. Within a week of us announcing the campaign, one hundred corporations had signed up. But what was much more amazing than that was the groundswell of public support. We were meeting extraordinary people from all walks of life—male strippers and clergymen, top chefs and fish-and–chips diner owners. Everybody seemed to want to be part of Earth Hour. Each week, our team gathered around the boardroom table and discussed problems. And each week, we saw our progress, as we ticked off another iconic building in the city that had agreed to participate. For an idea that some had said would never work, the momentum felt impossible at times. But there we were, beating all odds.

However, I knew it was one thing to agree to participate, but the real question was a logistic one: how do you actually get the lights to go off in the enormous buildings where the lights were left on all night? We discovered a world of unknown heroes—facilities managers. A facilities manager at the Intercontinental Hotel mobilized his friends across the hotel industry to get the hotels in Sydney to come on board. We were soon humbled by the knowledge that many people had been trying to get the message through on energy conservation for years, and Earth Hour was simply giving them the platform from which to work.

Climate change had gone from a "green" issue to an economic and social concern. Whereas before climate change had been, to many, an issue of little concern, now it was becoming mainstream.

We started to get a sense that everyone did actually care. The response that we were getting from CEOs, sports clubs, and schools was that most people were concerned about climate change but the issue was so big that they felt powerless and therefore unable to do anything about it. The message we kept hearing was, "I'm just one person. What can I do?" In some ways, I felt powerless myself. Crossing my fingers and hoping that on the night of Earth Hour people would mobilize and act as one. But I knew only time would tell.

After months of busy organizing, suddenly the day was here. On the morning of Earth Hour, I decided I'd go for a head clean by taking a dip in the ocean at Bronte Beach. I dived in, trying to dispel the growing sense of anxiety gnawing away at my stomach. I knew that we had done everything we could, but now that it was supposed to be happening, I wasn't all that confident that it was going to work. I got out of the water, feeling not much less anxious than before, only to realize that my car keys were in my pocket and were now thoroughly drenched. This was just what I needed, I thought, as I left my car there and dialed a cab, hoping that this wasn't a sign of disasters to come.

That afternoon, after doing a television interview for which I needed a lot more takes than usual, I got into a taxi and headed for the office. Making small talk on the ride there, the cab driver asked me what I was doing over the weekend. When I told him I was coordinating Earth Hour, he launched into an expletive-rich, aggressive rant about how totally stupid it was, how climate change was a joke, and how we were wasting our time. Ordinarily, comments like these would have been water off a duck's back, but today nerves were getting the better of me. When I got to the office, I found that the lights were still on. And I thought to myself, if we couldn't get the lights off at WWF, how on earth was the whole city going to do it? For the first time, I really started to feel the pressure.

With two hours to go, I got a call. "Hi there, it's Phil here. Just been getting a coffee . . . there's Earth Hour logos everywhere, and I'm hearing people at the tables talking about doing Earth Hour. How's everything going at your end?" Phil's timing had been perfect, giving me a greatly needed boost in confidence. If people were talking about doing Earth Hour in the coffee shops, then perhaps this was going to work after all.

The final few hours were a blur of television interviews and meeting and greeting guests at our small event at Circular Quay on Sydney Harbour. And then it was time, 7:30 PM I took a deep breath in those final few moments as time seemed to stand still.

And then I watched the city skyline as, building by building, logo by logo, one by one, the lights went out. The bridge went dark. The Sydney Opera House flickered off. Within what seemed to me like a particularly long minute, all of the major buildings in Sydney had switched off . . . except one. I swore under my breath. What had happened at the Stamford? Were they doing this on purpose to make their own logo stand out in the darkness as a bit of free advertising? Several people in the crowd pulled out their phones and started searching for the phone number of the hotel. Then a second later, to my profound relief and the collective cheers of the crowd, its lights went off too. I felt a friendly hand on my shoulder, and there was Phil.

That night, March 31, 2007, 2.2 million people, more than half the population of Sydney, took part in Earth Hour. The story went around the globe. This was an action that had happened with virtually no money, enormous amounts of free advertising, and volunteers. It had succeeded in Sydney because of the determination, efforts, and time of many, many people, previously unrelated but now united in one powerful symbolic act for an issue that affects us all.

The next day, the world's media was calling us. They wanted to know if we were going global, if Sydney was just the beginning. Buoyed by the success of Earth Hour in its first year, I truly believed the campaign would take off around the world.

Three weeks later, the first to sign up after Sydney wasn't another Australian city but Toronto, Canada—on the other side of the planet. Within months, we had cities in thirty-three countries lining up to take part in Earth Hour 2008. And the debate had changed. *An Inconvenient Truth* and the *Stern Review* had elevated climate change from a "green" issue to an economic and social concern. Whereas before climate change had been, to many, an issue of little concern, now it was becoming mainstream.

One billion people participated in Earth Hour across the world, nearly one-sixth of our world's population. There could have been no greater signal that the mandate for change was there.

The world was moving on, and Earth Hour had to move with it. The growth of the campaign in such a short time had been incredible. Yet we were still running Earth Hour on a miniscule budget, with a very small team in Australia of only six people and a dog, and we didn't have the funding to change that. This was rapidly becoming a global event, not just an Australian one, and we needed to find a way to grow without needing more resources.

Fortuitously, a global communications revolution was happening at the same time—social media. Facebook, YouTube, Flickr—you name it—social media was becoming the critical means by which people were talking to each other about what was going on with the world. We had built Earth Hour to be open to anyone. We didn't own it. Everybody did. We just provided the basic resources: from examples of how to approach your local mayor and available posters to put up to guidelines on how to run an event and, of course, ideas on how to reduce your footprint. In essence, the whole project was "open source," a very unusual approach in any organization at the time, as the brand is open to everyone and can be used by any interested party as long as it is within the spirit of the campaign.

The parallel rapid growth of social media enabled Earth Hour to grow at an unprecedented rate, without central bureaucracy getting in the way and without the need for a lot of resources. And in 2009, Earth Hour became viral. With the amazing efforts of some inspirational people within WWF, Earth Hour happened in more than four thousand cities, in eighty-eight countries around the world. It reached well over a billion people, and we knew that hundreds of millions had participated in the global concerts.

This 2009 Earth Hour had an even bigger purpose, to build itself as a global mandate for action on climate change, in time for the Copenhagen Climate Summit, as a way of reminding and inspiring our national leaders across the globe to finally address our planet's crisis. Nine months before the Copenhagen Climate Conference, one billion people participated across the world, nearly one-sixth of our world's population. There could have been no greater signal that the mandate for change was there.

In the aftermath of Copenhagen, I realized that trying to corral that many countries into one agreement is not necessarily the best way of achieving success. The power is not solely with global leaders but far more so with our city governments, business leaders, community leaders, and, most important, with individuals.

Yet in many ways, as we headed closer to Copenhagen, it dawned on me that we had put an awful lot of trust in our leaders, many of whom were convinced that a deal would happen. But what if it didn't? Would everyone lose faith? Would Earth Hour have been a waste of time?

Believing that people would still have hope, no matter what the outcome at Copenhagen, WWF staff in Denmark and the Earth Hour team in Sydney had organized a one-city Earth Hour in Copenhagen on December 16, 2009. But disappointment soon fell upon us. Maybe it was naïve hope that so many years of rhetoric would be met with action. Yet the bubble was quickly burst.

Exhausted, miserable, and going on empty, I boarded the plane back to Australia.

It took me a little while to realize, with the benefit of retrospect and a some quality time in Australia's outback, that some good did come out of Copenhagen. For the first time, 118 world leaders had met specifically to talk about climate change. It was agreed across all countries to endeavor to keep emissions low enough to keep temperature increases below two degrees Celsius (3.6 Fahrenheit degrees). And in the aftermath of Copenhagen, I realized that trying to corral that many countries into one agreement is not necessarily the best way of achieving success. Just like back in 2007, when Earth Hour started, the power is not solely with global leaders but far more so with our city governments, business leaders, community leaders, and, most important, with individuals. It was in the movement we had helped build. This knowledge helped me remain hopeful that we could still finish what we started.

Predictably, in the wake of Copenhagen, the minority climate skeptics smelled blood. For a few crazy weeks, it seemed as if the basic argument to deal with emissions was under threat. I wondered if this would undermine peoples' interest in Earth Hour 2010, which was only three short months away. Had public perceptions of the problem gone backward? Had all the media stories on skeptic arguments begun to affect peoples' views on the peer-reviewed science? Many in the environmental world seemed to think it was having an influence. It seemed to me that Copenhagen had created a sense of panic among campaigners. No one seemed sure what to do next. For me and my team, while I had some concerns, this only increased our determination to make Earth Hour 2010 happen on an even greater scale.

We set to work, and before we knew it, Earth Hour 2010 was here. Just before heading to the office on the night, I stood on the balcony at home holding my four-month-old son, Solo, while my wife, Tammie, took a photograph. He was wearing his WWF Earth Hour t-shirt. I felt calm and under control, a far cry from the extreme anxiety of this same night three years earlier. By then I knew that at least 129 countries and territories around the globe would be taking part in Earth Hour in the next twenty-six hours, up from eighty-eight the year before. Earth Hour would be bigger than ever. In spite of the failure of Copenhagen—or perhaps because of it—Earth Hour's reach had grown. I gave my small son a hug, then walked out the door to watch the world switch off its lights.

———————

Andy Ridley is the executive director of Earth Hour, the annual global climate change campaign by the World Wildlife Fund. He is currently organizing Earth Hour 2011 and is continuing to work toward a sustainable future for his son, Solo, and future generations.

WIETSE VAN DER WERF

▶ Twenty-seven ▶ Netherlands ▶ Art Activist

Evolving Activism at the G8

Lack of joy should be taken seriously, especially among so-called responsible people furthering a good cause.

—ARNE NAESS

I PUT ON MY SHOES AND REACH for my bag. As I open the front door, the cold England air blows in my face. Doing up the buttons on my coat, I walk down the steps and find my way to the bus stop. Looking up at the clear, star-filled sky, I consider that in a few months, the world's most powerful economic leaders will be holding their annual summit in Scotland. They will meet behind closed doors, and the details of their conversations will be kept secret from the public, despite the daunting reality that their decisions directly affect our lives. With Africa's debt to Western nations growing and escalating climate crisis, many are calling on the Group of Eight to take responsibility for the outcomes of their policies. In the silence of the night, I wonder if that day will ever come. My thoughts are interrupted by the squeaky brakes of a double-decker bus. I step inside and nod at the driver.

"Single, please. Cheers, mate."

As the bus makes its way toward the city, I envision the rich politicians sitting down for exclusive dinners in extravagant hotels, wearing top hats and cleaning their whiskers. I find myself excited about the prospect of going to Scotland and dream of running through the Highlands and making life difficult for the delegates attending the summit. I want to send a message: We are going to raise hell unless something changes. The G8 represents the destruction caused by the free market economy and the raping of the world's resources. I'm ashamed to live in a so-called civilized society, where people's only cares revolve around sports, soaps, and never-ending celebrity gossip. Isn't anyone paying attention to the reality of what is happening to our planet? I get off the bus and follow a stream of people heading out for a night on the town.

Crossing the road, my eye catches a display outside an art gallery. I feel drawn to it, and among a small group of people, I can see two women dressed in all white distributing what appear to be copied banknotes.

"We're asking people to write on this money what they would do if the world economy was in their hands," one girl says.

With pen and paper in hand, I consider the question at hand. Other notes, already written on, are pinned to their white dresses, making such proclamations as:

"I would make sure everyone has a home to live in."

"Take from the rich, give to the poor."

"Double taxes for the corporations and free tea for everyone else."

Some of the suggestions make me laugh. Others make obvious the painful reality of our current global economic climate, the inequitable way in which our resources are divided, or how the current economy has turned the world upside down. I scribble something about justice and abolishing money on my fake banknote and pin it to the dress. I consider what a fun and clever way this is to engage people with an issue. Instead of handing out leaflets with facts and figures, this approach requires people to question themselves, arrive at an answer, and exchange their ideas with others. While I had been involved in activism and political protest for years, I had never considered art in my activism work. I began speaking with the girls. One of them remarked: "It's really empowering to give people a pen in the street and ask them to write about their feeling on an issue. It makes them think for themselves. When they pin their note onto our dresses, they read other peoples', and in the dialogue that follows, they enrich their knowledge about the subject."

I let the women know how impressed I am by this "conversation," exchange contact details, and head off.

While I had been excited by the girls' activist style, my thoughts about how to incorporate this style into my own protests were fleeting. Then, by chance, I ran into the girls again, and we arranged to meet. While sipping tea in a local café a few days later, we discussed the upcoming G8 summit and the idea behind their performance style. It was inspiring to see people getting active on issues that lay close to their hearts and in small yet creative ways.

After our second meeting, I decided to stay in contact with these women and learn to engage my activism with art. Up until this time, I had been involved in activism for a while and was a little set in my ways on how to go about making things happen. For *real* action to be effective, I thought, there needed to be mass mobilization, intense organization, and a *"we're not gonna take it"* attitude. This time, when working with these art activists, the strategy was completely different.

Every single style of activism has its own unique purpose, yet it is the collaboration of these movements working together that can inspire global change.

We decided to go with a geisha theme and gather a group to protest the G8 summit in Edinburgh. Our hope was that geisha outfits, decorated with G8 policies, would deliver a powerful message while remaining peaceful enough to thwart off inevitable altercations with the police. This wasn't a passive protest; there were no meetings or information sessions. There were no forms to fill out or donations to make. This was something low-key, attention grabbing, and easy for people to participate in. Very soon, we began to see our initiative was something much larger than costumes and dresses walking around the G8 protests. You could see that people who had little interest in traditional methods of activism were suddenly becoming involved, talking about the issues, and learning what's at stake. We began to hold costume-making workshops, and before we knew it, more than twenty of us were dressed as beautiful geishas and on our way to Edinburgh.

Once in Edinburgh, I split off from my geisha friends and went to work on what I had previously committed to do, to produce alternative coverage with an independent media group during the protests. Much of my days were spent in an office, and soon I wished to be on the frontline too. I started to question my form of traditional activism. Activism should be inspiring and fun, and although my ways of doing things had shown me to be successful, I wondered how I could branch out and make creativity more a part of my life.

I find myself excited about the prospect of going to Scotland and dream of running through the Highlands and making life difficult for the delegates attending the summit. I want to send a message: we are going to raise hell unless something changes.

It all came together during the G8 protest. On the big day of action, there was mass protest from all directions, descending upon the hotel where the world leaders were meeting. The geishas walked in protest from the east, a large group of clowns were coming from the west, cyclists were arriving from the north, and yet another group of dedicated citizens were coming from the south. I watched as the groups formed lines and rallied around in protest. Each individual group, with their own unique style of activism, moving toward each other, finally reaching a collective focal point and successfully stopping the delegates from entering into discussion for most of the day. In this moment, I realized that every single style of activism has its own unique purpose, yet it is the collaboration of these movements working together that can inspire global change.

After the protest, the geisha team and I regrouped in Nottingham, exhausted and inspired, to share our experiences. It was the first experience with civil disobedience or direct action for most of them. There were stories of police aggression and brutality but also creativity and fun times at the protest camp. I listened intently:

"Well, we decided on a really soft approach because we were feeling quite fearful of what could happen," claimed one group member.

"It was such a powerful image when we stood there as a line of geishas, opposite the police, who were looking scary and terrifying defending the weapons of mass destruction," said another about an action at a nuclear submarine base.

"Yeah, with those people in the lock-ons, we just slid between them and the police, keeping the blockaders safe. It was calmness and madness all at the same time," a third offered.

I was elated and filled with a sense of pride that this group of young artists were excitedly discussing taking collective action against a major global financial institution that was partly responsible for the problems facing our planet today. In the weeks that followed, our goal was to become a collective that offers support to campaign and action groups by adding creative elements to their protests. Not long after that, we became known as the Mischief Makers.

We focused on street performances, costume making, puppets, and banners. We actively encouraged recycling, cycling, and living a vegan, cruelty-free lifestyle. We joined a protest demanding rights for migrant workers. We decorated our bikes with flags and streamers to join a critical mass of cycle activists. This type of activism made me uncomfortable at first, as I was used to traditional ways of protesting and direct action. I endured a steep learning curve. Yet, with each action, I began to see the benefits of this different approach. There is power in the creative, whether it's dressing up in costumes or performance art. By acting in uncommon ways, it makes passersby stop, take notice, and question what you're doing. Often, it sparks a conversation. And dialogue is where change really begins.

Inspired by the concept of "think globally, act locally," we wanted to contribute to large-scale global issues by doing what we could to improve our own community. Most of our work was with local groups and campaigns in our hometown of Nottingham, but it wasn't long until a significant opportunity emerged—an application lodged by a waste company to expand an incinerator facility in the city. The incinerator originally was built in the 1960s, was already outdated, and had repeatedly been cited for breaching its emission quotas. Expanding the facility meant more waste would be imported from nearby counties, and as a result, more emissions would be belched up into the air and dispersed. Needless to say, the expansion proposal didn't go down very well with nearby residents and environmental groups.

I knew that Nottingham had one of the worst recycling rates in the UK. Going for a walk on garbage collection day, anyone could see the cans, bottles, and paper just sitting in the trash bins. Our city was burning an abundance of waste that could be recycled and reused. It was time to take action to ensure that the expansion would be denied and the local waste situation improved.

We helped the local group Nottingham Against Incineration and Landfill (NAIL) organize a public meeting to raise awareness in the community. I was thrilled to see the community coming together in big numbers to stand up against their city, with families uniting and children learning about the effects of the incinerator on their environment. We had a variety of creative strategies for the campaign. We dropped huge banners across streets in the area most affected by the incinerator and held a protest rally at the town hall. We organized two community festivals called Rubbish Day Out, where we invited families from the neighborhoods to create arts and crafts from waste and recycled materials. The days were filled with live music, performances, and wondrous costumes. They were a huge success, and soon we had captured the attention of local councilors.

Within a few months, we had enabled the campaign to go from small to impossible to ignore. One of our main purposes was to encourage an understanding about what was happening to the city's waste. It was thrilling to watch members of the community learn and participate. I felt that I was a part of something really remarkable.

There is power in the creative, whether it's dressing up in costumes or performance art. By acting in uncommon ways, it makes passersby stop, take notice, and question what you're doing. Often, it sparks a conversation. And dialogue is where change really begins.

However, despite our best efforts and various court procedures, the incinerator expansion was eventually approved. Even though this is a devastating blow when you've worked on something for so long, it is important to reflect on the positive outcomes of the campaign. Besides raising consciousness about waste and recycling within our community, we had fun. Having fun and enjoying yourself is vital to activism. It can be hard to see results straightaway, and at times this can be quite disheartening. Using art activism can be a welcome relief from the soulful weariness that comes from traditional forms of change making.

I have spent quite a long time trying to discover good ways to engage people and inspire them to get active. The Mischief Makers seemed to have found one of the solutions. We built a bridge between the heavy political and inaccessible academic approach and those who are uninformed or perhaps uninspired. Whatever we do and wherever we go, we always make sure to create an open, accessible, and friendly environment to allow for all people to participate. It is much easier for people to draw their own conclusions and develop new ways of behaving when they don't feel judged or preached at. Just as crucial, we never pretend to have all the answers. We listen and talk, sharing our ideas and experiences.

My work with the Mischief Makers has shown me that being creative as an activist is an effective, fun, and inspiring way to raise awareness and encourage people to change. We might not have done anything that spectacular, but it all added up. We were just a bunch of friends who cared enough to fight together on issues we found important. In doing so, we learned to creatively communicate our ideas and beliefs in and beyond the activist community and inspire each other and the people around us. That, if anything, is worthwhile.

Since his time with the Mischief Makers, Wietse van der Werf has now turned his attention to protecting marine wildlife with an organization he co-founded called The Black Fish. When not campaigning, he writes for various newspapers and magazines about conservation issues. The Mischief Makers collective continues to spread the spirit of art activism inside the movement and out.

JO-ANNE MCARTHUR

▸ Thirty-three   ▸ Canada   ▸ Photographer

PHOTO BY JO-ANNE MCARTHUR

Through the Lens of Compassion: Capturing an End to Bullfighting

Humankind has not woven the web of life. We are but one thread within it.

—CHIEF SEATTLE

"WHY DO YOU WANT TO BECOME A MATADOR?" I asked the young boy who was no older than six years of age.

"Because I love bulls," he said.

I was jarred by the response but kept a cool demeanor. He waved his red *muleta* and acted out an imaginary scene between man and bull. I crouched so we'd be equal in stature while I took dozens of photographs. He was one of many children training at a bullfighting school off a dusty highway, just a few hours' drive from Madrid, Spain. It was hard to understand his disconnect between love and murder, but then again it's something I often see as an animal advocate.

I was working with two activists, Juan and Christina, who had called the school in advance to ask if we could visit. We agreed on a story ahead of time: I was a photojournalist from Canada, doing a story on the culture of bullfighting and they were my driver and interpreter. Technically speaking, ours was not such a tall tale. When I am doing this kind of investigative work, I like to keep the deception to a minimum; the more lies, the easier it is to blow your cover.

With our motives for the shoot in check, the unsuspecting director of the bullfighting school agreed to have me spend the evening documenting the bullfighting classes. As our car pulled up to the school gates, the director walked to our car through billows of dust and warmly extended his hand. We all walked up a hill to the arena, where matadors-in-training practiced their postures, stances and the final act of plunging a sword between the shoulder blades of the bull. The recipient of these blows, in this case, was a bale of hay placed on a wheelbarrow with a plastic bull's head to represent the target.

I like people. I try not to judge them. By extension, I don't like lying to and deceiving them. My motives for doing so, however, outweigh the deception. In this case, I am working to expose the cruelty of *la corrida,* the Spanish bullfighting, with my photographs. They will become part of my long-term photo documentary about our uses and abuses of animals worldwide, called *We Animals.* It has become my life's work, a combination of my skills, my activism and my passion. In the weeks following the bullfighting school shoot, I'll put myself through danger and stress undercover while bearing witness to the slaughter of dozens of bulls at the Spanish bullfighting festivals - purely for the entertainment of humans.

BACK AT THE BULLFIGHTING SCHOOL, men of all ages train while I work, and I go mostly unnoticed as I take their photographs. In another section of the arena, very young children are being trained and it's them that interest me the most, so I turn the camera in their direction. Most children have an innate love for animals, so it fascinates me that they are training to be their killers. When the boy tells me he wants to be a matador because he loves bulls, I am once again jarred by the disparity in humans' understanding of animals. By definition, a Matador kills bulls for sport, money and fame. I'm reminded of their commodification and our disregard, or complete lack of understanding that animals have their own intrinsic values.

As I shoot their training, I politely ask questions through my interpreter, Juan. I feel comfortable asking absolutely anything because I'm in the role of journalist and, as far as they know, I am a newbie to their culture and to *la corrida.* Amidst more benign questions, I ask about the bulls as well. They inform me that the bulls are bred by the thousands all over Spain, and graze happily in pastures their entire lives; they are the most respected animal, being Spain's national animal and symbol; their deaths are clean, instantaneous and noble; they are bred not to suffer; and adrenalin during a fight keeps them from feeling any pain. The information gathered during these lucrative talks are building blocks for my photo project.

I believe that most of us are not intentionally cruel, that our misguided intentions are fuelled by a lack of knowledge, or hunger, or need in general, whether perceived or legitimate.

Though I am passionate about my work as an animal rights photographer, I don't look forward to the upcoming shoots at the *ferias,* which are the bullfighting festivals. A lot of time has to be spent emotionally fortifying myself against what I am about to bear witness. Emotional stress aside, there are imminent hurdles that must be jumped before I can successfully document the events to come. At first, I need initial access to the events by attaining a media pass. From there, and over the course of the *feria*, I have to gain the trust of the staff, security guards and the matadors themselves. Finally, I have to keep my mouth shut at all times when it comes to my motives for the photo story. Should I say the wrong thing, or even let a look of disgust shadow my eyes when a bull is being slaughtered while people wave their white flags in celebration, I can be ousted as a dissenter, at which point my job and safety can both quickly be put in jeopardy. Most importantly, if my work or health is compromised, if I fail in my mission to expose cruelty to animals, it is the animals who will continue to pay with their lives, not me.

IT IS LATE AUGUST, THE END OF THE SEASON of *ferias* in Spain. Over the next ten days I'll be jumping from one bullfight to the next. I hate witnessing these gruesome events but it's my responsibility to shed light on the issue through the way I know best. Superficially, the world knows what a bullfight looks like: a *torero* (a bull), an arena, bright colors, cheering fans. What most don't know, however, is the brutality of the event, the manner in which the animals are treated, and what happens to the bulls once they are stabbed and dragged away.

The bullfighting story is an excellent example of the macho and male-dominated industries I must often infiltrate in order to get my work done. On one hand, this might seem to pose an increased danger. I usually work alone, which means it's just me amidst a large group of men who have made careers out of dominating others. However, I use these situations to my advantage. A group of macho men like nothing more than a singular woman new upon their turf, a woman who smiles and asks a lot of friendly questions. People love talking about themselves. Asking them about their lives, goals, work and their "brave" endeavors is an excellent deflector to my mission, and allows me to take photos of my surroundings while we walk and talk.

On day one of my three-day mission at one particular *feria*, gaining trust was a bit of a mission. I was gazed upon with suspicion and then turned away. I stood my ground, though, and stuck to my story. I refused to be refused. After much inquisition on their part, I was given my media pass and escorted to my place in the media box, crowded with other photographers elbowing for space, and told to stay there. I explained that the project was more about the people than the actual fight, but they didn't budge on their decision. That was okay; I used that evening to document the actual fights and the crowd.

There is always an extreme sort of loneliness that sets in when I'm documenting this kind of brutal event. I've experienced this deep melancholy at the countless rodeos and circuses I've documented. The abuse and murder of animals for the sole purpose of our entertainment confounds and offends me, and it seems that in those moments of cheering crowds and celebration, I'm an island. In those moments, I feel a deep disconnect from humanity and an even deeper sorrow for the animals at the event. My soul screams silently while I continue my work, and I know that this internal screaming has damaged me permanently. While working, I can't allow myself an outlet for the pain. Superficial professionalism at all costs. The outlet is the post-production work, when I get to show and publish the photos of the atrocities I have witnessed. The outlet and the healing happen when people who see my photos are moved to react, respond and change their habits that support the exploitation of animals.

The following evening, day two at the *feria*, I decide on a different approach. With media pass around my neck, a big smile and flattering clothing, I confidently bypassed the security guards while waving to the men I'd met the previous evening, who were on the other side of the security barrier. The guards assumed that was ok. From there, I smiled and shook everyone's hand and chatted easily. Everyone around assumed I was meant to be there because this was the image I was projecting. If the people in charge doubted it, they didn't question, or they assumed someone else in authority had sanctioned it. As for the flattering clothing I wore that evening, consisting of a skirt and open-necked top, I'm sorry to say that this is also an easy and useful tactic when doing my activist work in a male-dominated industry. Small distractions such as these open doors.

From there I wandered into the area where they slaughtered the bulls after they had been brought down by the matador's sword. I walked around, looking genuinely fascinated, all the while seemingly taking idle photographs of people and details. Instead of fleeing when I was being watched, I'd walk towards that person, introduce myself and ask them to tell me about their job at the arena. In this manner, I got photographs of the slaughterhouse, where the animals sometimes start to be dismembered before they've even taken their last breaths. I was reminded that humans can be evil incarnate. During the bullfights that evening, I walked confidently around the arena, taking photos from all angles. It felt great to be getting the photos I wanted. The emotional side effects of bearing witness, however, are carving themselves into my body in the way of an increasingly furrowed brow, wrinkles, grey hair and an often sick stomach!

By day three, most of the staff recognized me. I had free reign of the arena as well as the areas where the bulls were kept, where the butchering and post-*corrida* parties happened. I had one last hurdle, though, which was gaining entry to the sacred chamber where *mataderos* prepare their body and their *traje de luces*, the traditional bullfighting clothing, for the fights ahead. The entrance was guarded by security. I decided to use the "just walk through with confidence" trick, smiling at the guard as I walked by, but he stopped me. Only select few were allowed entry, mostly politicians and perhaps one high-ranking cameraperson. At this point my choices were bribery or begging. I chose the latter. With the sweetest expression I could muster, I pleaded that he'd be doing me a huge favor, that these photos would be so great for the success of my story and I promised to spend only five minutes and I'd be extremely discreet. I was lucky; he capitulated easily. The five minutes turned into ninety. When he periodically came in to check on things, I would throw him a flirtatious wink and he would respond with a smile and leave me to my photography.

I've blown my cover on a few occasions. While doing investigative work for the organization Zoocheck, the only way to get the photograph I needed of a polar bear kept in a backyard was to trespass. I was caught, but talked my way off the property and escaped the scene before the police arrived. The same thing happened while doing a story in South East Asia about bear bile farming. Luckily, my "dumb tourist" act bought me enough time to leave the property.

The abuse and murder of animals for the sole purpose of our entertainment confounds and offends me, and it seems that in those moments of cheering crowds and celebration, I'm an island.

Again, I don't like lying and I dislike the fear factor of being discovered as an activist and investigator, then suffering the potentially dangerous consequences. I believe that most of us are not intentionally cruel, that our misguided intentions are fuelled by a lack of knowledge, or hunger, or need in general, whether perceived or legitimate. In countries where resources are scarce, the needs of the family will always precede the rights of animals. Until money and food can no longer be made from their bodies, pelts, bile, and skills as workers and entertainers, and until speciesism is abolished, they will be used.

I take these calculated risks for my activist work so that I can change people's hearts and minds about our treatment of animals. The images I make aren't usually grotesque, like so many of the images we see on activist pamphlets. I'm not saying these aren't effective; they helped make an activist of me, after all. But my photos aim for something subtler, a less conspicuous message. Images that make the viewer go deeper, ask questions, take notice, rather than turn away in horror or reacting with compassionate fatigue.

On my final day of this *feria*, I'm at my wit's end. As the last bull is dragged off to the *matadero,* paralyzed by a severed spine but still alive, I take photos of the party that is underway around him. The partygoers descend the stairwells *en masse* and fill the streets for a night of festivities while the bull takes his last breath. That familiar solitude and loneliness has set itself in my bones, but my solace is that the photos of these horrific events will be seen, published, examined, discussed, and shared. The images I've captured ask the viewer a question. My job is done if the images are evocative and compassionate enough to make people provide the answers. Only then can there be understanding, accountability and change.

———

Jo-Anne McArthur continues to shoot at bullfights in Spain as well as factory farms and circuses to expose the hidden cruelties of animals around the world. As her We Animals project expands, she attempts to further animal rights by collaborating with various animal organizations, such as Zoocheck and the Jane Goodall Institute. For years to come, she plans to assist activists, animals and campaigns alike to help build compassion in this world.

PHOTO BY KAROL ORZECHOWSK

TANYA FIELDS

▶ Twenty-nine ▶ United States ▶ Urban Farmer

The Little Urban Farm
that Could

They can cut all the flowers, but they cannot stop the coming of spring.

—*PABLO NERUDA*

IT WAS HOT, THAT STICKY, HEAVY, BOOGIE DOWN BRONX HOT, and, as usual I was agitated. I was sweating a lot, which wasn't unusual given the fact I had gained about twenty-five pounds (11.3 kilograms) of baby fat. I kept telling myself I was going to work it off. I was going to get up early and go running. But as a single mom of two small children and few jobs in sight to support them, that was merely a pipe dream. Not to mention between April and September, my community smelled like a toilet on the account of the New York Organic Fertilizer Company, which didn't inspire much morning jogging. But I am getting ahead of myself.

On this sticky April afternoon, I was enrolling my eldest daughter in kindergarten at a local charter school, and as usual I felt this burning in the pit of my belly. This burning was an actual, physical burning. I was tired. I was finally graduating with my bachelor's after five years at a local city college. During those five years, I was hustling, doing any job I could find. I worked at Starbucks, slinging overpriced coffee. I worked as a receptionist at a small literary firm. I bartended and waitressed. I suffered the indignity of standing in the welfare line. I had faced possible eviction and had to siphon electricity from my neighbors to do my term papers, as my own lights had been turned out. I was miserable and left with feelings of failure and invalidation. I felt angry, I *was* angry—that was the burning in my belly. I struggled for more than five years to get this piece of paper, and nobody seemed to give a shit. There were no lofty jobs on the horizon and no piece of the American Dream for me. What was worse, I was watching the world unfold into political turmoil, and I felt tired and helpless about it all. I felt as if I couldn't do anything about it. To try to solve my own situation, I inquired about internship programs and was told that they didn't recruit from my school. My school wasn't good enough. I heard I wasn't good enough. In so many ways, I was being told that the most I could hope to achieve in this life was to be an assistant to a CEO. Well, that just wasn't good enough for me.

I was on the way home after enrolling my daughter as this internal narrative played over and over in my mind, and this hot, sticky, stinky day felt no different on my body. In fact, I didn't even realize I was going the wrong way until I saw a sign reading MADRES EN MOVIMIENTO ("Mothers on the Move" in Spanish) posted above the doorway of a storefront. I knew I was nowhere I had been before. Yet I couldn't peel myself away to find more familiar ground. Instead, I stood there dumbfounded. I was a mother, I was on the move, and here was a group of activist women doing something of that sort with some sort of cause right here in the hood. I felt overwhelmed and flushed and afraid. If my first impression of this organization was correct, that people, that *women,* like me were taking action, then I was not alone. I could not pull myself away from standing there in the window, but I was not yet courageous enough to walk through the door. I stared at the material hastily taped to the outreach window. There were campaigns they had won, campaigns they were currently working on, services offered locally, and referrals. I read one aloud: "Tired of that stinky smell in your neighborhood..." but just then an imposing black Puerto Rican woman interrupted me.

"Can I help you?" she asked. Well, actually it was more like a solicitation.

"I dunno, I was just trying to see what ya'll do here."

"Then why you standing there? Come inside." She turned around before I could accept or decline the invitation.

Only now, almost five years later, do I realize it was never an invitation. It was a command. She told me later she knew she "had" me. I stood at that window too long. The question really was, Would I be courageous enough to act on my feelings? Would I attempt to tame that burning in my belly? She was Wanda Salaman, the executive director of Mothers on the Move. She introduced me to Thomas Assefa, the environmental justice organizer. Finally, I knew I wasn't crazy. There was this distinct connection between the environment—or rather lack of sustainability—and poverty. Thomas explained what that stinky smell was. It was from a private facility called New York Organic Fertilizer Company. It treated 70 percent of the city's municipal waste, and it sat smack-dab in my community. Around the corner from that was one of the city's municipal water treatment facilities. I would come to learn that my community had eighteen open-air transfer stations and several power plants. All this within fewer than two miles (3.2 kilometers) of each other, all in one community.

> *Environmentalism has to be presented in a way that is relevant to the people of the community. It is certainly hard to think about climate change, deforestation, and Styrofoam cups if you can't pay the light bill or are facing eviction. If you tie these immediate needs in to the everyday lives of people, if you help present them as relevant and illustrate how the lack of attention to them has facilitated the -isms they are currently facing, you will be surprised how many of those people become "environmentalists."*

They had me at hello. I threw myself into my volunteer work with them. I made myself available. I believed in the cause of environmental justice for community justice; it became my life and even helped to save my sanity. I was happier than I had been in a long time. I discovered a sense of validation that I was not getting anywhere else in my life outside of being a mother. For once, I felt as if I could fulfill my potential and that the things I was good at could finally be used for something meaningful.

Mothers on the Move (otherwise known as MOM) quickly identified and used my talents. I learned to speak to the press, write press releases, run an effective campaign, knock on doors, and canvass, and I received a crash course in the history of environmental justice. I had quickly become visible on a local level, and that once-agitated stereotype of the angry black woman had become self-assured and confident. The young lady who was encouraged to keep quiet in the corporate sector, in less than six months time, had spoken out publicly, ended up on the cover of the local community newspaper, and been quoted in the *New York Times*. I worked with MOM for three years, and in that time I started to feel confident that I had a different but just as effective way to make the change in the community. It was also during this time that I became pregnant with my third child, a son. While unexpected, I felt more confident than ever to raise this child. I had a paying job and finally decided to make the leap to start my own nonprofit, the BLK ProjeK. I was starting to feel validated and that my work, even my existence, was meaningful.

> *The answer was right in my face: Every day, for seven years, I looked at a half-acre plot of underutilized land owned by the New York City Department of Parks and Recreation called the Fox Playground.*

Through my work in my own nonprofit, I started to make some serious connections between poverty, environment, and health. I started to think back to my days in the welfare office, surrounded by disempowered poor women of color, many of them in failing health and overweight. I, like them, had food stamps, and I remembered only being able to afford low-quality, nonorganic products and overprocessed food in my local grocery store. I also remembered that there was only one grocery store in the immediate area and not much food access. This epiphany wasn't anything profound; others had already made the connection. There was a ton of material out there speaking to these connections, but I still felt there was something missing about solving it. Then, I went back to that place in my life, a place I still begrudgingly end up on occasion. The place where I was nearly thirty pounds (13.6 kilograms) heavier, sweating after walking a few blocks; the place where I felt disempowered and lonely. I thought of that feeling of helplessness and how the food traditions passed down to me were steeped in oppression and assimilation. I also remembered my inability to find culturally relevant food that was also affordable and fresh. Then I thought of how messages in the media and mainstream society somehow made me feel as if I had done something wrong for being poor. Add political and social subjugation, and you have all the ingredients for an unhealthy community.

What was the solution? Damn sure not a Whole Foods or Garden of Eden. They're merely health stores for privileged culture. While I am sure that they are wonderful places, they are not places that speak to my community and would only serve to help catalyze gentrification. What we needed was to get back to our roots, reanalyze our connection to the land, and wrest control of what we put in our bodies—and women needed to be at the forefront of that. Three out of five households in poor and working-class neighborhoods are lead by women. Historically, women have been the gatekeepers in single-parent and dual-parent households of what gets ingested. Women hold the majority of food-related service-sector jobs; coincidentally, most of those said jobs are some of the lowest paying.

As I became more knowledgeable through my work with Mothers on the Move, and as I became known as a community resource, I felt empowered. It became easier for me to put better things in my mouth and in my home, and I wanted the spaces in my neighborhood to reflect how I felt about myself. It was this empowerment that facilitated behavior change and made me want to pursue policy change that would help build a healthy, more sustainable Earth. Hot damn! I was onto something.

I knew all the things that were wrong, but I needed to find the things that were right. I started to volunteer with a local community farm in Port Morris and discovered that urban agriculture could be a powerful tool for community development, particularly for youth. I was reading Vandana Shiva and exploring eco-feminism. I was certain that it could be for women like me as well. In terms of creating alternate food systems that could subsidize the rising food costs and its impact on women, I knew low-income communities of color practicing urban agriculture was an important and significant tenet to add to it all.

At that point, I started looking around. The answer was right in my face: Every day, for seven years, I looked at a half-acre plot of underutilized land owned by the New York City Department of Parks and Recreation called the Fox Playground. The only use it had at that time was as a dumping ground for dogs. Most times, the grass and weeds would get to more than three feet (0.9 meter) high. You could often find garbage strewn around the perimeter. I knew there were plans to renovate this park, and they were short by about one million dollars. I saw this as an opportunity. I wanted to turn this half acre into an urban farm, a safe place that would not only nurture the soil and grow food but also nurture the soul and grow relationships. This place would be a place of liberation. It would be called the Libertad Urban Farm and I was swelling with pride. In my mind, neglected land + community organizing = piece of cake. But that was all before I became introduced to the bureaucracy of the New York City Parks Department.

What we needed was to get back to our roots, reanalyze our connection to the land, and wrest control of what we put in our bodies.

PHOTO BY FLONIA TELEGRAFI

In the meantime, I did my homework; I read articles and books on urban farming and community gardening. I asked what one did if they wanted to orchestrate a local farming coup. I knew there had to be some science behind it. But the more I learned, the more I realized that there wasn't; you just did it. That was the point, to make a splash, to empower through sheer brashness, but I also wanted to be careful. My community has its fair share of cynicism and apathy. We have long gotten used to being used and exploited and having promises that were never fulfilled. I did not want to create a project that would ultimately end up being torn down by the Parks Department. I would organize guerilla farming, but I would simultaneously engage the Parks Department to get permission to make the farm permanent. I would seek them out to be a viable community partner.

It was spring of 2008, and I was definitely feeling like the little engine that could, and we were chugging along quite nicely. Within a month, donors had donated a boatload of trowels, shovels, hoes, and rakes. My friend Dwaine, who worked in agriculture, and I broke the lock to the plot of land in Fox Playground and started to plant. Stepping into that lot, we felt invincible, we felt bold . . . and, well, we felt a little bit scared. But a rag-tag team of revolving volunteers supported us. With Dwaine's expertise, we planted hydrangeas, marigolds, butterfly bush, mint, and sunflowers.

PHOTO BY FLONIA TELEGRAFI

People across the street in the senior building helped, little kids playing in the nearby playground helped, and even the winos that sat outside the lot with maltas and dominoes helped. If the dogs tore down our makeshift gate, the very next day someone from the community would put it back up. If the plants needed watering, the winos would do so without being asked, and we often found little girls running through Fox Playground with marigold flowers in their hair. We felt the support from the community, and it was the lifeblood of the project. All materials that were not donated were funded directly from my pocket, and with three kids and a fourth on the way, it was difficult, but the passion and enthusiasm from the community motivated me to keep going.

Every hot day that Dwaine and I were out there, our attitude and passion became contagious. Some of the residents who were unaware of our activities would stop and ask what we were doing, and my being out seemed to make them feel encouraged. Quite a few passersby would even stop and ask if they could help, and they were most certainly welcomed. I was heavily pregnant at the time, and this was no easy task for me. In fact, many of my peers expressed disbelief and admiration for my dedication. But I felt as if I didn't have a choice. I could not let something like being eight months pregnant stop the momentum of this project. When people would spark up conversation about me being pregnant and farming, I always saw this as an opportunity to talk about how urban agriculture can be used as a social benefit, an effective community development tool, or a means to food sovereignty, as well as an opportunity for environmental education.

I once spoke with some students at the University of Vermont, a mostly white, liberal, progressive school in Burlington. One well-meaning and enthusiastic student during the question-and-answer period asked me, "How do we get people in your community to care about the environment?" Too often I have heard environmental activists ponder over or outright ask me the question of how to get people of color, primarily low-income people, to care about the environment, as if somehow they weren't part of this world in peril. My answer is always that it wasn't that they were apathetic toward the environment, but that environmentalism has to be presented in a way that is relevant to the people of the community. It is certainly hard to think about climate change, deforestation, and Styrofoam cups if you can't pay the light bill or are facing eviction. I have been on that end of the stick, and I would have scoffed at the time at air quality and soil remediation if it had been brought up in conversation. But if you tie these immediate needs in to the everyday lives of people, if you help present them as relevant and illustrate how the lack of attention to them has facilitated the -isms they are currently facing, you will be surprised how many of those people become "environmentalists."

Dwaine and I shared information with the community on how farming on brownfields and lots in the area could provide soil remediation and improved air quality. We also talked to many parents whose children suffered from asthma, which is not surprising, since there are approximately twelve thousand diesel truck trips a day through our community to the food distribution center. With those parents, we discussed how a project like ours, if replicated, could help offset much of the carbon dioxide that was emitted through the burning of fossil fuels in our community, how green spaces like this would not only feed the community but also filter the air, cleaning it of some of the particle matter that hindered their children from breathing easier.

It just seemed like good sense to us and to the residents of the community to eat good and breathe good. We were passionate about sustainable agriculture and about setting it up to be an ecosystem. This type of farming would help clean water and reduce rainwater runoff by not only absorbing it but also capturing it and using it to feed the plants and crops. This project would reduce waste through composting and by capturing the "waste" from the compost and using it to heat the greenhouse. We even discussed the possibility of farming fish and using the waste of the fish to nourish the soil. The environmental benefits of a sustainable farm are lengthy, and we shared this knowledge in abundance, while also making sure to be receptive to the wisdom of many of the elders in the community who came with a deep tie to the land. A tie they brought with them from their previous country or state.

However, our enthusiasm was not shared by all. Some residents felt that the space was better used as a dumping ground for dog crap; some felt urban agriculture was a conundrum and that a city was no place for growing food. Local environmental organizations expressed concern that the environmental hazards were too risky for growing food. Even a community member said to us, "This community don't need no farm, the people just gone tear it up." But probably the biggest critic of them all was Bronx borough commissioner Hector Aponte. At one point in a meeting facilitated by Councilwoman Arroyo, he became combative and explicitly stated to me: "As long as I am the Bronx borough commissioner, there will not be any food growing on park lawns, not at St. Mary's, not at Van Cortlandt, and not at Fox Playground!"

Hmph, I guess he told me. I was put off to say the least; I was also appalled at how public officials who have absolutely no investment in the communities they oversee can be so quick to exclude the larger community from the decision-making process. Even with all that said, I was still not prepared for what the Parks Department had in store, which was to ultimately shut me out of the park and try to stop the momentum of this project altogether.

I felt a sense of panic, as if someone had hit me in the gut and I couldn't breathe. For a week, there was this knot in the pit of my stomach, and when they tore up my plants, I stood across the street and cried.

I rang everyone, from the Parks Department commissioner to the Bronx borough president, pleading with them to help me with Aponte's tyranny. I kept getting the same old story: "Your project sounds great, and while I may not necessarily agree with Commissioner Aponte, it's his backyard, so hey . . ." I was all but beat down. But then we decided to fight back, fight back with a block party. We held the Libertad Urban Farm Family Fun Block Party in late September, and man, it was slamming. The day was warm but not too hot, and I had woken up that morning feeling inspired and determined.

People were buzzing around, our promotional posters still present. Our DJ was setting up and our band all the way from Boston was tuning up. There was chicken and fresh corn on the cob on the grill, and the smell wafted all the way down for blocks. Rap music played in the background while kids and women got down on yoga mats in downward dog position. Seniors volunteered from 745 Fox Street helped to sign people in and hand out free donated veggies. All those detractors who said low-income folks didn't care about the Earth should have seen the crowd taking the workshops on urban agriculture and forestry that day. Every elected official was present or represented, and much to my surprise, we even got a call from the outreach coordinator of New York state Senator Chuck Schumer's office. I was flying high—my big mouth, Dwaine's expertise, and our combined dedication had us on the right path—but the high was short-lived.

The Monday following the block party, I received a call from the Parks Department informing me that they were suddenly ready to renovate. After six months of telling everyone involved in the park that they didn't know when they would have the money to break ground, suddenly they got sure. He was nice enough to tell me I could go retrieve our raised beds and plants, but where the hell was I going to put them? I lived in a tiny one-bedroom apartment. We hoped our guerilla farming and community organizing would push the Parks Department to legitimize the farm and integrate it into the existing plans. Instead, it only propelled them forward to appease a few restless community members and stop the Libertad Urban Farm.

I felt a sense of panic, as if someone had hit me in the gut and I couldn't breathe. For a week, there was this knot in the pit of my stomach, and when they tore up my plants, I stood across the street and cried. It truly felt as if someone had stolen something special from me personally and, more important, from my community. In a week, we lost everything we had worked so hard for. Community members stopped me and expressed sorrow that our project wasn't going to happen. But I explained that just because it won't happen at the Fox Playground doesn't mean it won't happen.

In our hood and much of the Bronx, there are still many lots that need remediating. Urban farms are ripe for the growing, and we will build them together as a community. I have kept the concept of the Libertad Urban Farm alive, we hold monthly community meetings where we get feedback from community members, and we are currently in the process of engaging a private landowner to grant us a lease on our next location. I remember that nothing worth having comes easy, and there are pioneers who have struggled longer and harder and watched their dreams and the dreams of their people come to fruition.

In May 2010, we engaged in an act of civil disobedience on Memorial Day, breaking into a neglected lot and cleaning it up. We planted sunflowers, and within a week, unlike the sunflowers at the previous site, they started to bloom quickly and resiliently. In a matter of three weeks, they were tall and proud just like my community. Their brilliant yellow and sunshiney figures give me faith and hope that our little urban farm would grow and blossom just the same.

And as the guerilla garden grows, I've come to realize that we the people have every right to manifest what we want to see in our world, and no stinking bureaucrat can stop the will of the people, especially when there is food involved.

¡Viva la Libertad!

PHOTO BY FLONIA TELEGRAFI

Tanya Fields is the executive director and founder of the BLK ProjeK, a nonprofit that empowers women through urban agriculture, civic engagement, and holistic health. She is still an active member of Madres en Movimiento and is working diligently to find a permanent home for the Libertad Urban Farm. Currently, Tanya is successfully running a yoga program for underprivileged women and a farm share, bringing healthy, affordable produce to the hood.

SUSIE WHEELDON

▶ Thirty   ▶ Britain   ▶ Cycling Crusader

PHOTO BY SUSIE WHEELDON

The SolarCycle Diaries

Act as if what you do makes a difference. It does.

—WILLIAM JAMES

THE SNOW BURNED AND WHIPPED AGAINST my face as I pedaled my bicycle on, my gears and brakes freezing in the chilly climate of central China
during a freak snowstorm. My temples pounded painfully from a severe
headache brought on by the cold. My cycling partner and I continued our
slow, arduous journey to the next stop with our heads down, our motivation buckling under the heavy snow. Regretfully, we declined ride after ride
from concerned passersby, determined to reach our cycling goal of one
hundred miles (160.9 kilometers) a day, until a minivan pulled up in front
of us and I stopped. That was a mistake. I put one foot down briefly to tell
them through chattering teeth that we weren't crazy for cycling in such
weather—we were actually just crazy for cycling around the world.

Unbeknownst to me at the time was that the foot I had set down was getting covered in ice and snow along with the pedal. So as I watched the warm,
safe glow of the minivan drive off in the distance, I tried to get my foot back
on the pedal. I tried again and again to no avail. My toes were frostbitten, and
I was at the end of my rope with only one option—pedaling the rest of the
way with just one foot. We were halfway through our round-the-world cycle
promoting solar power, and instead of basking in sunshine, were caught in
the worst blizzards China had seen in fifty years.

What had I gotten myself into? This wasn't the first or last time I would
think this in my life. Three years ago, I was in a desert, running in the Marathon des Sables held in the Moroccan Sahara, blasting my '80s rock music in

the sweltering heat. It struck me while preparing for my run that the sun is a free power source that anyone could use. The desert would be the perfect place to try out my new Solio charger, a universal solar charger for my mp3 player. Needless to say, it was a hit among the other marathoners and the beginning of my personal love affair with solar energy.

More energy falls on the world's deserts in six hours than its population consumes in a year. Knowing this, we continue in our pursuit to promote this incredible store of potential energy.

Upon returning home to London, I immediately started investigating a way to combine my passion for adventure with promoting a solar energy solution to climate change. For me, being an activist and making change didn't have to involve protests and petitions, because those weren't my strengths. It was thrilling instead to think about spreading awareness of solar energy in new ways while also staying true to myself.

At a friend's wedding, I approached Jamie Vining, my soon-to-be cycling partner, about doing an adventure with me, and he immediately jumped onboard. Iain Henderson, a childhood friend, was an investment banker at the time looking for a career change; within ten minutes of our initial conversation, he too was on the team. Though Iain would later leave the expedition, they both would become the most fantastic traveling companions I could have ever asked for. Calm, driven, and always quick to make light of any difficult situation.

Planning the journey, our team at first researched a solar-powered rickshaw, since these are now operating in India, but that turned out to be too cumbersome. Eventually, through a series of twists and turns, the plans evolved into a straight cycling idea, but in the form of a cycling adventure that would take us around the world. A friend soon put us in touch with G24 Innovations, who had constructed flexible solar panels and offered to incorporate them onto our bike panniers.

But we didn't want only our expedition to use solar energy; we wanted to highlight its potential to everyone we passed globally. We teamed up with

SolarAid, the UK's first solar energy charity for the developing world. SolarAid trains local people in impoverished areas of eastern Africa to install solar systems in schools, clinics, and community centers. These provide access not only to clean renewable energy but also to employment and development opportunities vital in these regions.

To make this all possible, sponsorship was key to our trip. Marketing teams from Nokia, G24 Innovations, and Solar Century helped us spread the word about our adventure and cause. Highlighting the potential of solar power was more important to me than actually completing the trip itself. I did question whether or not corporate sponsorship was in some way "selling out," but much of what we were promoting, such as massive commercial power stations, will only be achieved with support from big companies and organizations. I believe that these kinds of organizations will have to be involved with efforts to mitigate climate change. I only hope that their involvement in projects like ours encourages them to become ever more sustainable themselves.

In preparation for the ride, I took a bike maintenance course, went on test runs, and found sponsors. As things grew, it all just began to spiral until we were being waved off by the mayor from city hall in London. It was European Union Solar Day and a fitting date to begin "The SolarCycle," a twelve-thousand-mile (19,312.1-kilometer) cycle around the world. We set off with the latest flexible solar panels sewn onto our packs and Nokia phones with tracking devices, allowing us to update our blogs and websites from the road. We had to pack as little as possible, carrying only a lightweight tent and sleeping bag, bike maintenance items, a couple of toiletries, and a select few pieces of clothing.

Our first trek was to voyage through Europe down to the vast North African Sahara desert. Cycling through the desolate expanse turned out to be one of the most exhilarating and terrifying challenges of the trip. We pushed onward, pedaling in oppressive heat. Sweat poured from my skin, burning my eyes and blinding me along with the relentless glare of the sun. With nothing to block the wind, it mercilessly whipped us with sand, stinging any exposed bits of skin. Dead camels littered the road ahead—a chilling reminder of nature's power and our potential fate.

On one desert section, the ride took a turn for the worst. Only too late did we realize that we had run out of water. My heart caught in my chest as I realized we wouldn't make it to our destination. As the adrenaline coursed through my body, I resisted every urge to panic. Studying the map, we saw a potential settlement to the right, a few miles ahead. Deciding to take a risk, we deviated from the road using every bit of energy we had left to push our laden bikes through sand dunes covering the disused track. Luckily, we found an abandoned village with a few workmen who were able to show us a well. They told us the water was safe to drink, so we pushed aside our usual caution in our desperation and gulped it down unpurified. Sadly, our stomachs didn't find it as easy to hold down as theirs did, but it did get us out of immediate danger.

Despite the stupidity of cycling through the Sahara in the summer, we had decided to do so in order to highlight the importance and potential of solar power in Africa. A continent that struggles with adequate power supply in all its countries, yet its deserts could provide an unlimited amount of energy. According to Desertec, an organization that researches solar power's potential throughout the world's deserts, more energy falls on the world's deserts in six hours than its population consumes in a year. Knowing this, we continued on in our pursuit to promote this incredible store of potential energy.

Our journey would take us through Africa, the Middle East, Asia, and the United States until we would come full circle back to my homeland of the UK. We cycled through searing hot deserts and over snowcapped mountain ranges. Our ride was not short of challenges—from running out of water mid-desert (twice) to encountering the plague in Libya, snowstorms in China, and impossible heights on the Tibetan plateau.

But there was also breathtaking beauty, both manmade and natural. We passed many of the most magnificent monuments in the world: ancient Roman coliseums, the Pyramids of Giza, and the Great Wall of China. Even more awe-inspiring though was the beauty and force of nature. Traveling through a western Texas terrain void of people, I had a surreal moment when I noticed there no sources of unnatural light, just sunsets that coated the whole sky with stunningly vibrant hues of red, gold, and purple. Cycling on my bike, with the ever-changing landscape, I knew that anything was possible.

Everywhere we went, we spread awareness of the potential of solar energy by meeting with politicians, giving talks, and getting media coverage. It was heartening to be so well received by people in every corner of the globe. Gainesville, Florida, even had a solar cycling week scheduled around our arrival with cycling and solar events taking place all over their university. It was inspiring to meet people in countries so far away from the UK and where we had started, absorbing and incorporating our message. Each and every encounter reminded me of the potential we all have to help build a positive future.

Much of what we were promoting will only be achieved with support from big companies and organizations. I believe that these kinds of organizations will have to be involved with efforts to mitigate climate change. I only hope that their involvement in projects like ours encourages them to become ever more sustainable themselves.

But in that moment in central China, the irony of cycling to promote solar energy and getting caught in a snowstorm was not lost on me, or my frost-bitten toes. Long after night had fallen, we reached a town and saw the lights of a small hotel. Chilled to the bone, we lugged our muddy packs inside the hotel and took a room. With visions of a hot bubble bath dancing in my head, we boiled water in a kettle just as the power went out due to the storm. Leaving us with no heat, hot water, or luck. We were so close to the end, but my spirit was so low that night that I briefly considered just packing it all in and heading home.

The following morning we spent four hours chipping the ice off our bikes and made it to Shanghai at long last. I ventured out to buy shoes while my teammates warmed up, and there I was in a Shanghai market with frostbitten, swollen feet and feeling as blue as my toes, when I saw the one item I knew I needed at that moment to lift my spirits. A pair of red stilettos.

Yes, that's right. I wanted to feel like a woman, and I missed not being covered in sweat and grime from the road. I needed this little bit of normalcy to remind me that this was only a brief moment of misery in what would turn out to be an incredible life experience. I rammed my aching feet into those heels that night in Shanghai and celebrated with Jamie without a second thought about the past week of cycling in snow hell.

Upon arriving home, we were met by a huge crowd of our biggest fans at Stansted, just outside of London. Namely, members of our immediate families, waving banners and holding welcome home helium balloons. We had a great evening catching up, and were fed more than it should have been physically possible. Waking up the next morning for our final pedal to the finish line, we opened the curtains to see a flake of snow fall. For the last time, we donned our thermal gear, layered up, and set out on the last leg back to city hall.

In the end, we made a video of our journey that was aired in the House of Commons. Partly because of the awareness we brought to solar energy, a feed-in tariff program was initiated in early 2010, providing cost-effective means for the solar industry to flourish in the United Kingdom. Our expedition supported the Desertec program, which has begun a solar industry in North Africa and the Middle East. We also raised ten thousand dollars for SolarAid to help build further solar energy projects in the developing world. And while my global trek may have ended, the journey of alternative energy is only beginning.

Susie Wheeldon is currently writing a book about her cycling adventure, any proceeds of which will go to support SolarAid. She plans to continue to save the planet through adventure, with trips in motion for 2012. Meanwhile, the solar industry in the UK is growing after the feed-in tariff program was introduced.

PHOTO BY SUSIE WHEELDON

HANNAH FRASER

▶ Twenty-nine ▶ Australia ▶ Mermaid

A Mermaid's Fight

Another world is not only possible, she is on her way. On a quiet day, I can hear her breathing.

—ARUNDHATI ROY

IT DIDN'T HIT ME UNTIL AFTER THE massacre came to an end.

It was the first moment of calm after the storm; the shock started to set in, and my hands began to shake. We tumbled out of the getaway van, and I stood out on a rocky cliff, looking out to the windswept ocean. My heart sank as I grappled with the understanding that the dolphins I had been swimming with less than an hour ago were being systematically slaughtered. At that very moment, they were probably drowning in their own blood. Emotion overcame me. I was frustrated and helpless. It was the way in which they were being killed, a casual brutality that struck me with a chill far colder than the icy waters of Taiji Bay in which I had just been swimming.

I thought to myself, How could we as a species be capable of acts of such cruelty? How could these fishermen blindly sacrifice their own humanity on the points of their spears?

I started to weep.

My fellow activists crowded around, comforting me. We all took a moment to comprehend the loss. I gazed into the faces of these brave souls, their eyes haunted, swimming in the torment of what they had just witnessed; however, I felt reinvigorated by the knowledge that my friends had put their lives on the line for animals that could not speak for themselves. My faith in humanity might survive after all, but only because of people like these.

I was left wondering how to comprehend the contrasts of the human species. Are we really so polarized between good and evil? Or are we all just doing the best we can with the knowledge we have? And then, is knowledge the key that will end the unnecessary slaughter of life, like what I had experienced in Taiji?

The annual dolphin slaughter carried out at Taiji Bay (otherwise known as the Cove) in southern Japan certainly challenged the way I thought about the world and humanity. These murders have been ongoing for many years, and despite the vigilant efforts of activists such as Ric O'Barry—the original *Flipper* trainer and longtime dolphin activist—the killing remains protected by the Japanese government. Why? So we can touch a dolphin's nose and watch them do tricks for us in marine parks. But in our pursuit to get closer to these wild animals, we are slaughtering them.

I have seen the underwater world change before my very eyes in my short lifetime. It's easy to ignore what we can't see, but there is a beautiful world beyond our own, a world beneath the waves that is critically out of balance because of us. I fear that if it dies, we all die.

The "lucky" ones caught in Taiji Bay are captured and kept in captivity for the remainders of their lives. For wild dolphins, their newfound cage can lead to severe psychological and mental disorders and, in some cases, suicide. The rest of the dolphins captured, those not pretty enough to entertain us, are hacked into pieces and sold as mercury-poisoned meats. Twenty thousand such dolphins find this fate annually in Japan.

Fighting for cetaceans has been my life's purpose. Not so that I can dictate to another culture and people how they should live their lives, but because I have wanted justice for the oceans for as long as I can remember.

I have always felt connected to the oceans. When I was nine years old, I fashioned my first mermaid tail so that I could experience life under the sea. Despite living near the desert, hours from the ocean, I happily swam for hours in our pool, telling stories of how I had traveled to the bottom of the sea and met all the ocean creatures. As I grew up, my passion turned into a career as a professional mermaid, a performance artist that swims and looks like a mermaid. I have been featured in films, photo shoots, music videos, and advertising for my work.

I learned how to free dive, diving to the depths of the ocean with only the oxygen in my lungs, and created my own specially designed mermaid monofin tail that gave me the speed, agility, and courage to swim in the ocean. I swam with whales, dolphins, seals, turtles, and even great white sharks. Through these techniques, I gained access to the underwater world in a way most humans never have, as if I was part of this world myself, not just an alien tourist. I witnessed the intelligence of these marine creatures up close and interacted with them as if I were one of them.

After years of work and practice, my dedication to being a mermaid finally gave me the opportunity to swim with humpback whales in the South Pacific. As I swam alongside, the curiosity of a baby whale brought me closer to a cetacean than I had ever been. It was continually looking at me in the eye and playfully swimming around me. I could hear the deep bass notes of its mother singing. The vibrations ripped through me like a blasting speaker, rumbling my ribcage. It was cold, dark and difficult to see, but any fear melted rapidly away when these leviathans glided effortlessly around me, taking care to avoid buffeting me with their massive tails while they looked closer. It felt like my cells had been rearranged by the sound of their song, and I was touched by the realization that despite my kind killing theirs for centuries, these intelligent beings still chose to swim and play with me.

So my connection to the oceans has been nothing short of a lifelong love affair. But traveling to all corners the world with my mermaid performance, I have seen the underwater world change before my very eyes in my short lifetime. It's easy to ignore what we can't see, but there is a beautiful world beyond our own, a world beneath the waves that is critically out of balance because of us. I fear that if it dies, we all die.

I decided to speak up and be a voice for the oceans. I attended several meetings of the International Whaling Commission to share what I had seen, and ironically, the only suffocating moment in my ocean life was here. The IWC's corruption, political posturing, and out-of-touch decision making was monstrous. They only had the interest of a few pocketbooks in mind, not of the cetaceans they were supposed to protect. I decided then it was time to take action.

In 2004, my then husband, professional surfer David Rastovich, my good friend artist Howie Cook, and I gathered a group of like-minded activists, surfers, actors, filmmakers, and musicians who cared deeply for the ocean. We formed a nonprofit organization called Surfers for Cetaceans, and we had a goal to mobilize against the capture and killing of dolphins and whales.

Dolphin killing remains protected by the Japanese government. Why? So we can touch a dolphin's nose and watch them do tricks for us in marine parks. But in our pursuit to get closer to these wild animals, we are slaughtering them.

Three years later, we would get our chance. Led by David, more than forty of us convened in Osaka, Japan for an ambitious action—in some ways, mission impossible. People had flown from around the globe with little information and almost no knowledge of what they were about to do, due to the need for keeping an element of surprise in our action. All they knew was that we were going to try to stop the Taiji dolphin hunt and that there would be great risks to do it.

We joined forces with the Oceanic Preservation Society film crew who had been filming the dolphin slaughters for two years while remaining completely undercover in Japan. But we weren't as lucky in keeping our operation covert. After arriving in Japan, we learned that the Taiji fishermen had somehow heard of our plans to hold an action, and rumors of violence against us were being filtered back to us via our Japanese contacts.

Four of us decided to make the long drive to Taiji to speak personally with the locals and clear any confusions about our protest. We professed our intents to hold a peaceful protest but were met with great resistance. Some of the locals felt that we were attacking their cultural heritage, and they were concerned that our actions would portray them negatively to the international community. Up until then, the world at large knew very little about the dolphin slaughters, and to the outsider, Taiji was just another quaint fishing village in Japan.

The picturesque seaside town of Taiji is surrounded by majestic green mountains and stunning bays. Large, bright murals, filled with happy images of dolphins and whales, welcome visitors to the town. At first glance, it appears that this is a community that reveres and loves these animals. Even the killing bay looks like nothing more than a stunning postcard destination. Except for the odd dolphin burger restaurant, one would never know the darker side of Taiji. It's not Taiji Bay that is dark; it's what happens there, and that's what we were aiming to stop.

On the day of the planned action, October 28, 2007, I was so nervous I couldn't eat, and I felt my stomach turning into knots. We had all been up since before dawn with anticipation, coordinating our action. It was a nerve-wracking drive to Taiji; forty of us hiding in the back of three vans, the drivers wearing surgical flu masks to cover their Western faces.

After four tense hours, we reached the beach unobstructed, thinking our ruse was successful. But seeing the empty bay with not a killing in sight, we realized that the fishermen had anticipated our arrival and halted the dolphin kills out of fear of being filmed.

Even though the fishermen had hidden their crimes from our cameras, we still paddled out into the middle of the cove on our surfboards, holding hands in a traditional surfer's ceremony circle, mourning the lives lost. I cringed as I imagined this beautiful bay full of the blood of dying dolphins. In my mermaid tail, I dove down to the bottom of the bay and held onto the slippery rocks, letting the current sway me back and forth in the cold silence. In my meditation, I became acutely aware of the violence that had been perpetrated in this seemingly peaceful arena. I could sense the death around me despite the bay's seemingly peaceful façade that day.

Coming up for air, I looked back on the beach, and saw a group of fishermen were gathering, and the police had arrived. The film crews on land were confronted as they tried to gather footage of the ceremony. We paddled back in, despairing with the thought that all our planning and sacrifices had been for nothing. I took off my tail and walked out of the frigid water and tried to leave, but the police stopped us. They began interrogating us while we were still shivering and cold, and the fishermen looked on with piercing anger but their bodies showed restraint.

We were eventually allowed to leave and arrived back at the hotel exhausted and defeated. We had filmed our ceremony, and although any day without a dolphin dying is a victory, we knew that in the big picture, it wasn't a victory at all. We had accomplished nothing until we could show the world what was really going on at the Cove. Withdrawing to our own rooms, I contemplated that we may have lost our only chance.

I was heading to bed, feeling like the whole world was doomed, when we received a call. It was from one of our insiders in Taiji, informing us that the fishermen had gone out immediately after our departure and captured over forty dolphins in the Cove. "The next slaughter would begin at sunrise," he said.

This was it. We had our second chance.

This was what we had traveled across the world to achieve, a peaceful but strong protest face-to-face with the fishermen and the bloodshed that would capture the brutality of the annual kills. But it wasn't going to be how we had all imagined it. It was impossible to mobilize our entire crew of over forty people and get back down to the bay without being seen. So it was decided that we would just send a core team, professional surfers David Rastovich and Karina Petroni, actresses Hayden Panetierre and Isabel Lucas, writer Peter Heller, and me. And before my hair was dry from the last swim, we were heading down for another dive.

It was before dawn, and we knew we would soon be in the frontlines against armed fishermen making their kills. It was understood that this mission carried far higher consequences. If the police caught us interfering this time, we would be arrested and possibly jailed for years. So we took precautions, taping Ziploc bags containing passports and lawyer contacts under our wet suits. Hiding in the van for hours, under blankets, waiting for the right moment to make our move.

Once the moment was right, we charged out onto the beach, grabbing surfboards and frantically paddling into the cold sea. Through a mixture of exhaustion and adrenaline, I remained fearless. The water we waded through was stained red. We could see the trapped dolphins swimming in the blood of their slaughtered family frantically trying to escape their netted prison. It scared me to see this, but I just told myself to keep going.

The film crew was positioned in high-tech camouflage gear around the different points of the bay to capture the massacre, while a mini helicopter strapped with a camera flew overhead to capture an aerial view of the confrontation. We were now "officially" interfering with the fishermen's operations and could be arrested at any time as we swam out to the nets. It was a net that crossed the bay, trapping the dolphins and dividing us from them. Just beyond the net we could see the dead bodies of half of the dolphin pod, scattered across a hidden beach, while the rest of the captive dolphins were meters away in the water, screaming.

We formed our circle and held hands, each one of us with a burning desire to cut nets and fight with the fishermen for these dolphins' lives. However, our mission was to stop this butchery forever, and to do this we had to stick to our commitment of a peaceful protest. I knew we couldn't save these select few; rescuing them was impossible. But not cutting those nets was the hardest things I have ever had to do. A dolphin looked me straight in the eye, pushing against the nets and squealing in terror. At that moment, it was the most important creature in the world to me, and I felt I was failing it, as if I were somehow indirectly killing it.

Before I could have second thoughts about cutting the nets, fishermen sped over to us in a small boat and began screaming in Japanese. Remaining silent and keeping our places on our surfboards, we brought our hands together in prayer to show that we meant only peace. In response, they backed their boat propellers toward us, trying to frighten us with their spinning blades.

I realized in that second that we had underestimated their anger, but none of us expected this violence. Fishermen began hitting us with large poles. I was astonished they were physically attacking us for such a peaceful protest. They were treating us just like the dolphins, and for a second, I thought they might even kill me.

I tried to calm myself down and stay on my board. I thought back to my time in the Pacific, swimming fearlessly with the whales regardless of the consequence. I meditated and tried to stay strong and sustain the fishermen's beating, despite the injuries.

The physical pain brought the plight of the dolphins even more into perspective, and our group began to weep with sadness for the slaughter, as we knew it would happen once we left. We had carefully planned to be in the water for only five minutes to avoid violent confrontation and arrest, but we didn't care anymore. Twenty minutes later, we were still in the water past our strict deadline.

More fishing boats raced toward us, and the fishermen were becoming ruthless and unpredictable. As the threat of a serious beating amplified, we decided we had to head back to shore before one of us became a casualty.

Hayden Panettiere was the first to reach the beach. She was overcome with grief and exhaustion, falling to the sand, crying. I scooped her up in my arms, and we ran back to the van where the film crew was holding off the fishermen. Dripping wet, shivering, and shaking, we threw ourselves into the already moving van as it sped down the road. We hid under blankets in the back as we passed the police cars, sirens blaring. If we had stayed in the water just one more minute, we would have been hauled off to a small-town prison.

Once we thought we were safe, we stopped on a beachside cliff top for a short interview with a foreign news crew. Turning away from the camera, I looked out to sea, feeling a heavy weight on my soul. The enormity of the brutality I had just witnessed overwhelmed me. I wept as though I was experiencing the loss of a friend. I was, several of them. It may be difficult to comprehend why I care so much for these creatures. I can only respond by reminding you of the intense joy I have experienced in the wild, experiences that were life altering for me, and understanding that gave me a sense of purpose in this world. I have been shown that the sentient, peaceful, intelligent creatures that surround us should have the same rights as us to live in this world. These things are worth fighting for.

On our way back to Osaka, we were stopped at the Wakayama Precinct border by dozens of police officers with paddy wagons. My heart fell into my stomach. I thought to myself, "This is it . . . time to face the music."

Claustrophobia began to sink in at the idea of being enclosed in a cell. And panic for the first time in this journey poured into my soul.

We were all made to exit our vehicles. Our passports were checked, video and photos were taken of us, and for hours we endured repeated questions about the protest. To our amazement, we were allowed to leave. We speculated that these police were from another prefecture and were not convinced that we had broken the law, nor could they decide what to charge us with.

Returning to our hotel in Osaka, we packed to leave in a mad dash; protecting the video footage was our top priority. Reports came in that heavy-handed Yakuza gangsters had been visiting surf shops along the whole coast, threatening violence if surf locals didn't give up our location and details. It was definitely time to get out of there, I thought.

At Tokyo Airport, I was afraid I would be flagged and arrested on sight. We had heard that our information and photos were being circulated to relevant authorities, as the Taiji police were intent on arresting us before we left the country. Despite my fears, I walked on my plane without incident, and after the exhausting journey, landed back in my home country of Australia.

I have been shown that the sentient, peaceful, intelligent creatures that surround us should have the same rights as us to live in this world. These things are worth fighting for.

Thinking back to it all now, in many ways, I believe our campaign was a success. After our action, there was an explosion of international media on the dolphin slaughter. BBC, CNN, and *Entertainment Tonight* and many more newspapers and magazines around the world ran stories on the protest. The media attention helped expose the truth that dolphin and whale meat is highly toxic and unsuitable for consumption. As a result, many local schools and supermarkets in Japan removed all dolphin meat from their shelves. The film crew that worked with us, the Oceanic Preservation Society, showcased their documentary *The Cove*, which took the world by storm and received an

Academy Award in 2010. It has even showcased in Japan, helping to educate the people about what their government and corporations are doing.

A few years ago, nobody knew what was happening inside the Cove. Today, the dolphin slaughter is being drastically reduced in Taiji, and international pressure continues to put an end to it. The fight to educate the Japanese consumers has even been taken up by some local citizens and politicians in Taiji, who have been campaigning against the distribution of the mercury-poisoned dolphin meat.

For me, being involved in the action was empowering. It makes me realize that one crazy idea, conceived by a few ocean-loving individuals, can gain enough momentum to make a ripple of change in this world.

PHOTO BY DAVID WARTH

Hannah Fraser continues her work as a mermaid performer, using her unique link to the ocean to inspire and educate people on the importance of marine life. Meanwhile, the film The Cove *has won an Oscar for Best Documentary and is raising awareness globally about the realities of Taiji. As for the dolphins, the battle continues. Activists held back the hunt in 2010, but despite great efforts, dolphins are still being slaughtered and need our help.*

KEVIN OCHIENG

▶ Twenty-three ▶ Kenya ▶ Leader

A Fire in Kenya

Youth are uniquely equipped to change the world because they dream.
They choose not to accept what is, but to imagine what might be.

—DESMOND TUTU

KENYA IS BURNING. PEOPLE HAVEN'T BEEN ABLE to grow their crops for the last two seasons, and the food stores are all dried up. They're hungry, and they're angry. They swept into Nairobi and Mombasa two weeks ago and began rioting. There are so many of them the government lost control. The police are powerless. In the countryside, the scorched earth can't even produce a single green shoot. And when the rains do come, they're so violent that the topsoil is washed away, and people cower in their houses in fear. I see Kenya, I see my country, ruined by climate change.

It was late November in 2009. I'm awoken suddenly by the cry of a young child. The clock beside the bed says it's 3 AM, and I sleepily look around the unfamiliar room. It takes me a few seconds to realize that I'm in Nairobi, far from home, and today is going to be one of the biggest days of my life. My host's four-year-old boy walks barefoot into the room and right up to my bed. He is staring at me and crying.

"I am scared, Kevin," he cried. He was having a nightmare of a burning house, and his scream was what awoke me. But my mind was heavy with the big day to come. After months of planning, this was our moment. The media was now daring us, the politicians were guarded, and civil society was eager to witness what the young people of Kenya could accomplish in the battle against global warming. All systems were a go.

Five thousand young people from across the country were preparing to travel to Mount Kenya and stage a symbolic protest against climate change.

I was one of them, and I was helping lead the event. Yesterday, I had traveled to Nairobi, the capital city of Kenya, from my home in the far coastal areas to help stage the event. For I knew that this protest had the potential to make history.

There is a feeling among most that nothing we do here is going to make a difference on the world stage. Even if Kenya went 100 percent sustainable tomorrow, it wouldn't save us from global warming. We needed to get the big Western governments on board, and that wasn't going to be easy— especially for a bunch of kids from Africa.

I did not have much time to prepare. I grabbed a cup of Kenyan tea and caught up with the news. The international media was filled with conflicts in Somalia and the economic crisis in the United States. The local media was occupied with the story of a draught-stricken village. Everywhere I looked, the world was on the brink. One of our greatest challenges had been to try to get our story out to the world, because most mainstream media in the country did not think our story was juicy enough to be worth telling. If it was not politics, or some disaster somewhere, it wasn't a story. But after months of pleas and negotiations, we had convinced a local broadcaster to send a camera team. Now we just had to give them something worth filming.

It was set to be an event of a lifetime. A flash mob of Kenyan youth would gather at the base of our biggest mountain, Mount Kenya. The mob would hold hands around the mountain as a protest against the melting ice on its top and the threat climate change has brought to our source of life. A small group, me included, would then scale the mountain and unfurl a banner on live television with a message to the world leaders set to meet at the Copenhagen Climate Conference. I had no small task. I was in charge of everything.

The stakes were high. Police violence was a definite possibility, and maybe once it was all done, no one would know because the media might decide not to cover it. But if it worked, it might just be the final push needed to forge an international consensus on battling climate change.

The idea for the Mount Kenya action was born in early 2009. Sitting around the office, my classmates and I were reading the paper and drinking tea as usual when I came across an article that argued that the Copenhagen summit was a waste of time. This kind of talk makes me cross. It's not a question of whether anything is going to happen; it's a question of what will happen if we don't do something. I asked a friend whether he thought the meeting was going to bear any fruit. He told me he had no idea what the leaders were going to do in Copenhagen. It struck me that his reaction would have passed as normal if he was not a student of environmental science. But unfortunately, he was. If someone like him already felt defeated, then we had lots of work to do.

It's not a question of whether anything is going to happen; it's a question of what will happen if we don't do something.

As for me, I had already been engaged in climate change advocacy for five years. At twenty-three, I was supposed to be making quick money and looking for a wife for the short life ahead. At least that's what my mother often told me. "Stop running up and down playing music to the deaf creatures embodied in politicians," she would say. She thought that it was a waste of time trying to save a planet designed to perish. A desperate waste of time.

She would go on to tell me of how my peers were doing well professionally and settling down, some already upgrading to their fifth car. I never paid her much attention. But she did have a point. I was in a third world country after all, and everyone was running after the few resources remaining. And this hardly inspired much activism. To make it worse, there is a feeling among most that nothing we do here is going to make a difference on the world stage. Even if Kenya went 100 percent sustainable tomorrow, it wouldn't save us from global warming. We needed to get the big Western governments on board, and that wasn't going to be easy—especially for a bunch of kids from Africa.

This is the thought that kept me moving the morning of the action. Despite my rude awakening, I was out of the house within minutes and on my way to Parliament Square where we were to all gather for our "Green Mile" departure. Green Mile was the name we gave to the environmentally friendly travel we were to stage to and from our destination. Two local companies had partnered with us to facilitate the Green Mile travel. One company was offering five buses. The other was offering fuel made from recycled vegetable oil that would otherwise have been drained into municipal drainage systems by five-star hotels.

It was a chilly morning. We left at 5 AM, armed with two writers for the local press. They were young enough to understand what we were fighting for. Our destination was Nyeri, a calm town at the foot of Mount Kenya, a four-hour bus ride from Nairobi. A couple of minutes before 9 AM, we joined a group of about five thousand young faces in Nyeri. It was a very emotional moment for me. Mobilizing five thousand young people may have seemed like a normal task in a developed country where young people have a clear view of the skyline in life. In a developing country like Kenya, most youth are disenfranchised with life and don't give a hoot about advocacy. They're too worried about getting one of the all-too-rare jobs available to young people and making sure they'll have enough money to start a family. Abstract issues like climate change seem like a problem for another day, once your basics have already been covered.

We had been working for months to break through this apathy. Here in Africa, it's all about creating networks. Community groups are strong, and if you can get a group on board, you will instantly have hundreds of members on board as well. It's far better than trying to convince people one by one. What's more, almost everyone belongs to a church or a football club, a mosque or a choir. So we reached out to all kinds of groups; we met with their leaders, and they spread our message about the urgency of fighting climate change in a way that was suitable to each group. We didn't have lots of money, but we did have numbers. And that is our strength. Across Africa, we've seen time and time again that he who mobilizes the biggest number of people carries the day.

They don't have to be hardcore activists, just people who support you, regardless of whether they really understand why or not. Numbers get the media's attention. Numbers get the government's attention. We're not asking people to do much. Just come out and show support. It's a way of saying something without speaking, without having to know it all, without having to be a radical.

In Nyeri, we gathered at a stadium and had a session with the local leaders who were kind enough to give us the go-ahead for the flash mob. Even the member of Parliament for the region was present. This was highly unusual. More often than not, we felt like freedom of expression was just a piece of write-up in the Kenyan Constitution and not a reality for most Kenyans. Not with tear gas canisters and gunshots flying every time in any kind of protest.

I had seen it firsthand during Kenya's 2007 presidential elections when protests in the streets were violently repressed by police. I was an electoral officer, and accusations that the vote was rigged turned into mass marches in the streets. You could feel the tension. People were willing to sacrifice their lives for political gain. The government had a police force that was capable of deadly tactics. It was a vicious cycle, and one with an inevitable result: 1,200 people killed and some 350,000 displaced.

But we were hoping that we had taken all the right precautions to avoid any violence. We had met with the local authorities, and our location was perfect for the event. Mount Kenya is on national parkland and administered by the Kenya Wildlife Service, who were enthusiastic and supportive of us. So instead of having to face menacing police, we would be accompanied by friendly wildlife officers.

So we gathered peacefully at the stadium, all five thousand of us. I stood up on the stage and addressed the gathering, telling them how important this action was. "We have a moment to make a case for Africa," I said. "We have a moment to right the wrongs causing climate change. This is our moment," I shouted. I was not the best orator by any standard, but with the crowd's cheers, I knew this movement we were making for ourselves was coming alive. It was an unforgettable time. Africans taking ownership of an international issue wasn't just symbolic—it was a declaration of our importance. I hoped that this would mean that African voices would be heard on an international stage. When I finished, people were excited, and we rushed out of the stadium ready to take part in something historic.

Mount Kenya is the second-largest mountain in Africa, and going around it was not child's play. We realized how naïve our idea, or rather my idea, of holding hands around the mountain was. There were places that were impassable and others that had wild animals. So we went for the next best option. We gathered around the mountain as best we could, not necessarily holding hands. Then the five of us leading the protest, including myself, started hiking up the mountain.

Our chosen location was significant. Community members of the largest ethnic group in Kenya, the Kikuyu, believe they originated from Mount Kenya. So by climbing it, we were returning to our roots. As we walked up, the rest of the five thousand young people, representing the future of our country, stood around the base in silence. Their silence demonstrated the gravity of the problem: we were being muted internationally, but our very livelihoods are what are at stake. Yet, though we were keeping silent, we weren't just going to stand by and watch it happen. We had a message to deliver through our banner, and we hoped that this message would make it out to Kenyans across the country, to Africans across the continent, and to people around the world.

The climb was hard; the cold was biting. I was in decent shape, but I didn't feel like it at the time. Early into the hike, my feet were already sore, and my legs ached. I wanted to give up along the way, but remembered the cry of my host's four-year-old son: "I am scared, Kevin." With climate change, the entire Earth would be burning, not just the little house in his dream. I had to do this.

We walked in single file, and while we started out purposefully, energized by the gathered group at the base, all conversation died out, and we each entered into our own heads, battling our own demons, asking ourselves, Is this going to work? Is anyone going to care?

The forest was thick, and it closed in around the rocky path. The strong sun was blocked out by the trees. We were trying to move forward, battling through the branches, but we couldn't see our way. We knew that we had to make it, and we kept pushing uphill, but we didn't know exactly how we were going to get there or how long it would take. It was like the battle against climate change itself. We have an idea of what a carbon-neutral future looks like, and we know what direction we have to move in to get there, but we don't exactly know how long it will take or how it will end up working.

We have an idea of what a carbon-neutral future looks like, and we know what direction we have to move in to get there, but we don't exactly know how long it will take or how it will end up working.

It took us six hours to climb to the top of the mountain. Everyone else was still bravely keeping the silence in respect for the endangered mountain. The whole drama was being transmitted live to the nation on television. As the forest finally gave way and the blue sky opened up in front of us, my friend Grace ran ahead with a burst of energy she had been holding back during the climb. At the rocky summit, we could see for vast distances in every direction. It felt like the center of the world. It was at this moment that we unfurled our banner and unveiled the message: SAVE THE WORLD, SAVE AFRICA, SAVE MOUNT KENYA: WE NEED A DEAL.

"It's too wordy," one of our team members said. "We won't be able to pass the message well enough." I argued that we needed to capture both the global and the local aspect in the messaging. The message was simple. All we needed was a large enough banner. The one we ended up using was one hundred feet (30.5 meters) long and sixteen feet (4.9 meters) wide. I think the message was visible enough. And later, when we saw it on the news, we knew that people agreed.

We left the banner at the summit, held up with poles we had brought with us. I turned around before entering back into the forest for one last look at the banner. It fluttered in the distance. What had seemed so big when we were painting it and building it now seemed so small, dwarfed by the majestic mountain and swallowed up by the endless sky. We had done what we set out to do, but now it seemed like such a small gesture in the face of the daunting worldwide crisis of climate change.

The climb down was exhausting. The five of us had been used to a lot of physical training, but the exercise was nevertheless tiring, and at times we had to stop, rest, and have some food. By 6:30 PM, we had reached the base and gathered with the rest of the participants. But they weren't the only ones at the base of the mountain.

The prime minister had sent a representative to congratulate us for our bold gesture, and he strode forward from the cheering crowd, promising us that he would take our message to the rest of the world. The media was now listening. The camera flashes popped as I shook his hand. Now that the prime minister had taken interest in us, we were a story. He announced that the prime minister had personally reserved hotel rooms for us so that we would be well rested for tomorrow, when we would set on our Green Mile journey back to Nairobi.

The next day my friend Lawrence cried out, "I'm tired," as we climbed aboard the bus. He was part of our team and had put in countless sleepless nights planning for the event. "But it was worth it," I added to break the silence that was beginning to give me the feeling that my colleagues felt we were stretching ourselves too thin. "Someone had to do it," I added. I was happy when I saw the smiles beginning to form on their tired faces.

The sky was blue that day. The bus ride back to Nairobi was unusually long. I took a nap, and when I woke, we were winding our way into the capital city. The trees looked greener and the air smelled fresh. There was a beauty about the world again. The media was waiting for us. We had a press conference, and the room was packed full with journalists from far and wide. We had been noticed. I was nervous, but this is what we wanted. Now that we had the media's attention, it was time to use it.

I left for the Copenhagen Climate Summit the next day with the four colleagues who had hiked with me, carrying photographs and videos of our action to show the world leaders. We felt that there was plenty of media hype around our action. With a handful of lessons and experiences, we had hope that a better future was feasible. The world is what we make of it after all. You could see this hope playing on my face and the faces of the many young people I had helped inspire. But in Copenhagen, I came up against the harsh realities of geopolitics. We had succeeded in getting some attention in Kenya, but out in the bigger world, no one had ever heard of us. What's worse, the message the prime minister gave us at the base of the mountain was not the message he and other African leaders were giving the world at the climate summit.

Despite the fact that my continent, our continent, was going to be hit especially hard with climate change, our leaders weren't taking the problem seriously. This was clear in Copenhagen. On a major international debate moderated by BBC *HARDtalk*'s Stephen Sackur, other countries had sent their presidents and prime ministers to talk, but the only African representative in attendance was South Africa's environment minister. It was an embarrassment. It was as if Africa wasn't taking climate change seriously, and the world wasn't taking Africa seriously. She seemed outgunned. I was sitting in the audience with Kenyan Nobel Peace Laureate Wangari Maathai and wondered why she wasn't up there. At least she would have had something to say. But she was not invited to speak, and as I later spoke to the head of G77 and China, there was a sense that Africa was being deliberately muted on the world stage.

I soon came to learn about an offer leaders from developed countries made to developing countries, some token sum to heal the wounds caused by climate change. A type of climate financing that would give African nations the monetary means to adapt to a predominately Western-caused catastrophe. The discussion of a ten-billion-dollar annual climate fund for developing nations may have sounded great to many. It did have the African leaders, with smiling faces from the news, wining and dining their counterparts. But the stark reality is it will cost one hundred billion dollars a year for developing nations to adapt to climate change, according to the World Bank, a far cry from what we were being offered. But instead of maintaining a voice for African nations in the negotiations, we were quiet afterward, selling our future away for a small piece of a the political and monetary pie. It infuriated me to the bones but showed me that politics was mightier than environmental realities, no matter how bad that reality was.

Then, after two years of talks and so much preparation, President Obama showed up on the last day of the conference. He went into a room with the presidents of China and India and some other countries, and within minutes they had produced a document supposedly forging some sort of "international consensus." But if anything, it really showed who's calling the shots, only a few select rich developed countries. I was left with a feeling of powerlessness, so were we all. Of course, Obama's roots are in my country, Kenya. What happened in Copenhagen really showed how the world is such a small community, yet a community against itself.

The summit left a feeling with us all that only the powerful countries make decisions. It brought into focus how the politics in the world work. There's a lot of talk, but only influences count. I believe developing countries can have a role in changing this pattern. Africans can lead the way, but I'm afraid we're not doing it yet.

Since Copenhagen's failure, I haven't given up the fight; if anything I'm fighting even harder to making African voices heard. I'm organizing and building networks, as this is what we need the most right now. It's about building these networks between Kenyans, between Africans, and between people from around the world if this movement is to truly be global, to truly be effective, and to truly make the change we need. Because I've seen that you don't need lots of money to change things. It's money, in fact, that's holding change up. What you need is people, groups of people, to get together and make a stand. It's the only way.

As for that four-year-old boy, I spoke with him many times after. The dream of a burning house still plagued him from time to time. But the dream started to change as the fire began to dwindle. The fire became intimidated and backed down as more and more people sprinkled water on its core. Soon those people became a mammoth crowd and the water like a rainfall. And he too, the little boy, joined the crowd, taking down the fire until it was no more.

Kevin Ochieng is currently serving as youth advisor to the United Nations Environment Programme. When not working for UNEP, he is working within his own organization called Earthfest, a youth network across Africa that is encouraging an environmental movement through education, local actions, and promoting green jobs.

WILL POTTER

▶ Twenty-nine ▶ United States ▶ Journalist

Eco-Terrorism 101

If you've got a blacklist, I want to be on it.

—*BILLY BRAGG*

IT STARTED WITH A KNOCK ON THE DOOR. Someone had pounded three times. I turned the knob without looking through the peephole. It must be the landlord, I thought. He had gotten into the habit of arriving unannounced with prospective tenants to show our apartment, one of the freshly renovated studios in a seventy-something-year-old building in Chicago. Before I had opened the door, though, I knew it was not Steve the Landlord. Our dogs were barking. Wildly. The dogs, Mindy and Peter, were snarling, and they never snarled, they never growled. I opened the door anyway.

The guys behind it—gruff-looking early-thirties guys with manicured goatees, navy suits, ties with outdated geometric patterns, scuffed black shoes, broad shoulders, hardjaw lines, wholesome haircuts, and eyes looking for fights—were just naturally FBI agents. I didn't even need to see the badges.

I just said I was in a hurry, that I had to get ready for work, and then I started to close the door. The good cop—well, I will call him the good cop, only because he looked less eager to kick my ass—put his left palm on the gray steel door, firmly enough to put pressure but not firmly enough to make any noise. I could either come downstairs, he said, or they could make a visit to my place of work, the *Chicago Tribune*.

Dogs barked. Panic. I was not afraid of them, but I was afraid of a spectacle in the newsroom. I relented and then closed the door to get ready.

"What's going on?" my girlfriend at the time, Kamber, asked from the futon, half asleep.

"It's the FBI," I said matter-of-factly, as if it had been Steve the Landlord.

A few minutes later, we crammed into the freight elevator, Good Cop, Bad Cop, and me. The elevator ground to a halt, the latticework steel door creaked open, and we walked through the dark hallway to the alley. It was a gloriously sunny Chicago summer day, but the sunlight could not overcome the condominium towers of steel and glass, could not swim through the cracks in the walls, and so I stepped into an alley shrouded in gray.

In college, I had learned about government operations like the Counter Intelligence Program (COINTELPRO), and the FBI's history of harassing and intimidating political activists. False names, phone taps, bugs, and infiltration were used in attempts to disrupt groups like the Black Panthers, American Indian Movement, and Students for a Democratic Society. I had learned from books, professors, and *Law & Order* episodes that if approached by the FBI, for any reason, you should never talk. Nothing good can come of it.

Both Good Cop and Bad Cop had heard that line before. The shorter, "nicer" cop started talking anyway.

"Look, we just want to talk to you," he said. "We want you to help us out. We can make all this go away."

WORKING LONG HOURS ON THE METRO DESK at the *Chicago Tribune*, covering shooting after shooting, murder after murder, had turned me into the type of reporter I never wanted to become. I felt detached, apathetic, and cynical. Just before the visit from the FBI, I wrote in my journal, "I'm tired of writing meaningless stories, I'm tired of going to sleep at night feeling like I left the world the same way I saw it in the morning."

After only a few months at the *Tribune*, I had already built a spectacular wall of emotional detachment. It felt as if it were made of broken bottles and concrete chunks, sharp and gray. I thought I would never survive this beat, unless I found some way to keep a toehold on my humanity. So I decided to go leafleting.

When I worked at the *Texas Observer*, I wrote a story about an animal rights activist who was prohibited from protesting fur stores as a condition of her sentence for nonviolent civil disobedience. In my research of other draconian legal attacks on activists, I also learned about Stop Huntingdon Animal Cruelty, an international campaign that had formed for the sole purpose of closing the notorious animal-testing lab Huntingdon Life Sciences.

Five undercover investigations had exposed animal welfare violations in the lab. I remember sitting in the *Texas Observer* office, downloading a clip of undercover video filmed inside of Huntingdon. It showed animal experimenters with beagle puppies. The puppies' veins were too small, and one of the experimenters could not insert a needle. He grew frustrated. He shook the dog and then suddenly punched the puppy in the face, hard enough to knock a grown man down. I will never forget that dog's punctuating wails.

I became obsessed with finding out why I would be targeted as a terrorist for nothing more than leafleting. The focus of my life would shift to investigating how animal rights and environmental activists had become, according to the FBI, the "number one domestic terrorism threat."

When I decided I wanted to do something positive to balance out the futility I felt at the *Tribune*, I decided to leaflet about Huntingdon. One month prior to FBI agents knocking on my door, Kamber and I met six local activists at the A-Zone (or Autonomous Zone) in Chicago, which was part independent bookstore and part rabble-rouser gathering place. It offered titles on topics including the Zapatistas, herbal medicine, and bicycle repair, and it smelled like punk rock.

From there, we caravanned to a suburb north of Chicago and the home of a corporate executive with Marsh, Inc., an insurance company for Huntingdon. Once out of the van, I hung leaflets on front doors, urging their Marsh neighbor to cease doing business with Huntingdon Life Sciences. The fliers made no suggestions of violence or property destruction, they made no threats. Instead, they spelled out what went on in the lab, how Marsh is connected, and why readers should ask their neighbor to use his power wisely.

After about twenty minutes of leafleting, police arrived. They radioed back and forth with their headquarters, trying to decide what to do. Then they handcuffed us.

AFTER THE FBI AGENTS FOLLOWED ME OUT of the apartment building and into the alley, Bad Cop started needling. He asked if I knew the type of people involved in the campaign to close Huntingdon. He said they were "extremists."

"I can tell you're a good guy," he said. "You have a lot going for you." He said he could tell by the way I dressed, where I lived. "You don't want this to mess up your life, kid. We need your help."

He told me I could help them by providing more information about the other defendants and other animal rights groups. I had two days to decide. He gave me a scrap of paper with his phone number, written on it underneath his name, Chris.

"If we don't hear from you by the first trial date," he said, "I'll put you on the domestic terrorist list."

Wait, what? I felt as if I was staring blankly ahead, but my eyes must have shown fear.

"Now I have your attention, huh?" he said.

Put me on a terrorist list for leafleting?

"Look," Chris said, "after 9/11, we have a lot more authority now to get things done and get down to business. We can make your life very difficult for you. You work at a newspaper? I can make it so you never work at a newspaper again."

I replied that people who write letters, who leaflet, are not the same people who break the law. As I walked away, I crumpled his phone number and tossed it in a nearby dumpster, and just before I left the shadows and could reach the sunlight, Chris said, "Have a good day at work at the Metro Desk."

Say hello to your editor, Susan Keaton. And tell Kamber we'll come see her later."

I wish I could say the visit did not affect me. But the history nerd in me could not help but think about all the times when the government had targeted political activists. I could not help but think about the deportation of Emma Goldman and the relentless spying and harassment of the Rev. Dr. Martin Luther King Jr. I thought of the White Rose, a group of students my age who covertly printed and distributed anti-Nazi leaflets and, when caught, when interrogated and tortured, refused to show fear. They were beheaded. I had always hoped, as we all do after reading stories like this, that if I were ever put in a similar position, I would not flinch.

But I was afraid. Even though I never considered, even for a moment, becoming an informant, I could not stop thinking about how I was on a domestic terrorist list. I was convinced my journalism career was over. Even worse, I was convinced these FBI agents would somehow pass the word to my parents, who would be so disappointed in me, and to my little sister, who would stop looking up to me. These thoughts burrowed somewhere deep behind my eyes and, no matter how irrational they sound, I began to see them as truth.

I did not know it then, but this experience would mark the beginning of both a personal and political journey. After the initial fear subsided, I became obsessed with finding out *why* I would be targeted as a terrorist for nothing more than leafleting. The focus of my life would shift to investigating how animal rights and environmental activists had become, according to the FBI, the "number one domestic terrorism threat."

———

IN HINDSIGHT, THE PATH FROM THAT FBI visit to my current life seems completely straight and natural. In reality, I spent years straddling fences, cautiously poised between "unbiased" reporting and advocacy journalism, between my career and the passions I have labeled side projects.

I made some small efforts to climb down. I left an "unbiased" newspaper job covering politics in Washington, DC, to use my writing for very biased purposes at the American Civil Liberties Union, ghostwriting op-eds and speeches on the Patriot Act and government surveillance. At night, I continued researching and writing about activists being labeled terrorists. Through my work at the ACLU, and my freelance reporting, the true scope of the attacks on political activists came into focus.

The environmental movement, like all social movements, has a wide range of elements. There are people who leaflet and write letters. And there are underground groups like the Earth Liberation Front, which have vandalized SUVs, burned ski resorts, and destroyed genetically engineered crops. Even at their most extreme, none of these tactics have injured a single human being. Not one.

Meanwhile, the Department of Homeland Security does not list right wing terrorists on a list of national security threats, and the FBI omits right wing attacks in its annual terrorism reports. Those groups have been responsible for the Oklahoma City bombing, the Olympic Park bombing in Atlanta, violence against doctors, and admittedly creating weapons of mass destruction.

Through my reporting, I learned that environmental and animal rights activists are being labeled terrorists not because of violence, but because of their beliefs. Corporations and the politicians who represent them have waged a coordinated campaign to push their political agenda.

They have sent out press releases accusing mainstream organizations like the Sierra Club, PETA, and Greenpeace of supporting "eco-terrorism." The children's movie *Hoot* has been dubbed "soft-core eco-terrorism for kids." *American Idol* star Carrie Underwood was smeared as supporting terrorists when she encouraged her fans to support the Humane Society.

Examples like this would be funny if they had not worked their way into the top levels of government. In 2006, politicians proposed "eco-terrorism" legislation similar to bills that had been introduced at the state level for years. Because of my reporting, colleagues at the ACLU recommended that I testify at a hearing by the House Judiciary Committee. Leading Democrats on that committee agreed. Suddenly, the fears that I thought I had overcome began to crawl back into my head.

If I challenged this legislation, the Animal Enterprise Terrorism Act, would I be smeared as an "animal rights terrorist"? Would FBI agents fulfill their promises from years ago and tell members of Congress that I am on a domestic terrorist list? Would the representative from Wisconsin turn to me and ask, "Mr. Potter, are you now, or have you ever been, a vegetarian?"

The historian Howard Zinn always advised his students, "You can't be neutral on a moving train." The committee staff explicitly told me that Democratic leadership supported this bill; I was to speak about my reporting but not challenge the legislation. Meanwhile, corporations and industry groups wanted nothing more than for their bill to proceed unchallenged. The train was moving, I thought, whether anyone liked it or not.

I decided I would not be a token gesture of dissent in their spectacle of democracy. Rather than propose modest tweaks to the bill, I testified that lawmakers must reject it in its entirety. I said that scarce terrorism resources should not be exploited to protect corporate interests. In my testimony, I compared the "eco-terrorist" legislation and scare mongering to one of the darkest periods of U.S. history, the communist witch hunts of the Red Scare.

Scarce terrorism resources should not be exploited to protect corporate interests. In my testimony, I compared the "eco-terrorist" legislation and scare mongering to one of the darkest periods of U.S. history, the communist witch hunts of the Red Scare.

As I awaited questions from members of Congress and braced myself for the reaction from the Democrats who invited me, I looked down at my notes and at my hands. It struck me that they were perfectly still. It was an empowering feeling, to have my words and my actions completely in line with my beliefs. Never in my life had I felt so calm.

Immediately after the hearing, I began calling activist groups and urged them to notify their members about the legislation. I began to write regularly for a website I created, *GreenIsTheNewRed.com*. And I began speaking at law schools, conferences, churches, potlucks, punk rock shows—anywhere I could to raise awareness about the law and help stop it.

Months later, the law was rushed through the House of Representatives with only six members of Congress in the room. Most lawmakers were breaking ground for a new memorial honoring Martin Luther King Jr. when legislation was being passed that labeled King's tactics—including nonviolent civil disobedience—as terrorism.

It was a major defeat, and for the corporations who supported the Animal Enterprise Terrorism Act, it was only the beginning. Since then, similar legislation has been introduced in many other states.

In Utah, a lawmaker said legislation is needed to target people like Tim DeChristopher, the University of Utah student who disrupted an oil and gas auction by bidding on parcels of land. In Tennessee, Rep. Frank Niceley argued before the general assembly for eco-terrorism legislation, saying, "Eco-terrorists are left wing eco-greenies. It's a different type of terrorism. They don't have Osama bin Laden leadin' them."

So how have these "eco-terrorism" laws been used? In California, four activists were arrested under the Animal Enterprise Terrorism Act for protesting animal experimentation outside of the experimenter's home. Their indictment lists that they chanted, protested, made fliers, and wrote slogans on the ground in children's sidewalk chalk. As I write this, they are awaiting trial.

For those who have been convicted as "terrorists," the label follows them from the courtroom into prison. For example, Daniel McGowan was arrested in 2005 for his role in two arsons by the Earth Liberation Front. He targeted genetic engineering and a timber company that logged old-growth forests. In a court hearing, the lead prosecutor called the Earth Liberation Front a terrorist organization and compared the property destruction of McGowan and his codefendants to the violence of the Ku Klux Klan.

McGowan pleaded guilty to his charges and was sentenced to prison as a terrorist. He is now incarcerated in a secretive prison facility on U.S. soil, called a Communications Management Unit (CMU). He was transferred there without notice and without opportunity for appeal.

The CMUs radically restrict prisoner communications with the outside world to levels that rival, or exceed, the most restrictive facilities in the country, including the Supermax ADX-Florence. Inmates and guards at the CMUs call them "Little Guantanamo." They have also been described as prisons for "second-tier" terrorists.

According to the Bureau of Prisons, these inmates "do not rise to the same degree of potential risk to national security" as other terrorism inmates. Most prisoners are Muslim, and the secretive prisons have also housed Andrew Stepanian, an animal rights activist convicted of "animal enterprise terrorism" charges.

Through interviews with attorneys, family members, and a current prisoner, it is clear that these units have been created not for violent and dangerous "terrorists," but for political cases the government would like to keep secret.

———

MY EXPERIENCE WITH THE FBI PALES IN comparison to what many activists have endured, both during this "Green Scare" and in other eras of government repression. I have not been threatened with prison time, terrorism enhancement penalties, or anything like that. However, my experience has prompted the stark realization that the overly broad use of the word *terrorism* affects many more people than those who set foot in a courtroom.

Few activists will be visited by the FBI, even fewer will be arrested. The real purpose of all this—the FBI visits, the public relations campaigns, the legislation—is to instill fear and make everyday people afraid of speaking up for their beliefs. The scare mongering has had what attorneys call a chilling effect: it has made everyday people feel as if they must choose between their activism and being labeled a terrorist, and that is not a choice anyone should have to make.

It can be unsettling and frightening to learn how far the government has gone to attack political activists, and sometimes I wonder if spreading this information simply makes more people afraid. But time and again, in dozens of venues, from the New York City Bar Association to anarchist bookstores, I have seen an incredible thing happen when people learn about these issues and then turn to their neighbors. Their conversations are never about how they are afraid; they are about how they are angry and want to take action.

The best way to handle the fear these scare tactics create, I learned, is to confront it head on. "Never turn your back on fear," Hunter S. Thompson wrote. "It should always be in front of you, like a thing that might have to be killed."

THE LEAFLETING CASE IN CHICAGO WAS EVENTUALLY dismissed, and we decided to move back to Texas. Kamber and I packed our few belongings and prepared for the journey home. I dreaded moving day. Not because of any attachment to the city, but because I did not want to walk downstairs, through the marble lobby with its Corinthian columns and Victorian couches, and enter Steve the Landlord's office to turn in our keys. He knew, I thought. He must.

The building was old, but secure. The FBI agents did not kick down any doors when they visited our apartment. They flashed badges and were escorted inside. They probably told Steve that Kamber and I were suspected terrorists, and that this was a national security matter that needed urgent attention. Perhaps they showed him my photo, film noir style. Would he even buzz me into his office? I wondered. Would he ask me to slide the keys under the door, to keep me at a safe distance? Would he refuse to return my security deposit, because there was a "no terrorist" clause in the fine print of the lease?

I opened his door and walked up to his desk as he spoke with a couple of young, beautiful prospective tenants. I tried to silently slip the keys across the desk, but they jangled like jailer's keys, and the sound of metal on wood echoed up into the vaulted ceiling. I turned, exhaled, and walked away. He called after me when I was almost to the doorway. Here it comes, I thought. Steve the Landlord is going to say how disappointed he is in both of us. How he is going to take custody of the dogs because they should not live with such terrorist scum.

"Hey, Will," he said. I turned to face him. "Give 'em hell."

Will Potter is an award-winning independent journalist based in Washington, DC. He frequently lectures at universities and law schools and writes for both mainstream and independent media outlets. He has just released his first book, Green Is the New Red, *from City Lights Books.*

JOSHUA KAHN RUSSELL

▶ Twenty-six ▶ United States ▶ Mobilizer

Joshua Kahn Russell (right) with Vandana Shiva.
PHOTO BY MATT STERN

We Shut Them Down: Ending Coal at the Capitol Power Plant

Each generation must, out of relative obscurity, discover its mission, betray it or fulfill it.

—FRANTZ FANON

THERE WERE THOUSANDS OF US. The snow was four and a half inches (11.4 centimeters) deep and it was nineteen degrees Fahrenheit (minus 7.2 degrees Celsius) outside. We could already hear the Fox News commentators and their usual absurdities: "A global warming protest in the snow? Maybe this climate change stuff isn't real after all." But by the end of the day, even Fox gave positive coverage to the largest civil disobedience to solve the climate crisis in U.S. history.

On March 2, 2009, around four thousand people came to the Capitol Power Plant in Washington, DC, a coal plant that powers the Capitol building. More than two thousand of them risked arrest in a sit-in. The vast majority had never been to a demonstration of any kind before, let alone engaged in a form of nonviolent direct action. People from communities most directly impacted by coal's life cycle—from Navajo reservations in the Southwest to Appalachian towns in the Southeast—led the march. With vibrant, multicolored flags depicting windmills, people planting gardens, waves crashing, and captions like community, security, change, and power, we sat-in to blockade five entrances to the power plant that literally fuels Congress. We called the whole thing the Capitol Climate Action. I was a lead organizer. And I was exhausted.

We had been organizing for ten months. Watching the idea grow and take a life of its own was almost like raising a child—complete with snotty temper tantrums and sleepless nights among the awe of bringing a light into this world. And the action scenario was actually pretty simple.

When I flip on my light switch, it's like a trigger, blowing up a mountain thousands of miles away. My stomach still hurts when I think about how my convenience comes from the pain of communities like these. I will never have to cry over my child poisoned from resource extraction. But others will. We have a word to describe the act of flipping that light switch: privilege.

The belching smokestacks just two blocks from the Capitol building made a fitting target for a national flash point. They symbolize the stranglehold that the dirty fossil fuel industry—and coal industry in particular—has on our government, economy, and future. Democrats on the Hill had spent nearly three decades trying to get the plant off coal, only to be blocked by coal-state legislators in their own party. Speaker of the House Nancy Pelosi had made feel-good statements about cleaning up Washington before, but we had yet to see any action. She enters our story later though. But here's the point: burning coal is the single biggest contributor to global warming. We won't be able to solve the climate crisis without breaking its hold.

———

THE ACTION CONVERSATION STARTED in the summer of 2008 while walking down a dirt road. The road's brown dust arced around boundless fields and dense Virginia trees. It fed into an encampment of tents interspersed with banners and slogans like "Leave it in the ground!" hand-stitched in cloth. The ridge of trees sheltered makeshift clearings intended for workshops and strategy sessions and opened like a mouth into a wooded area with even more tents hiding in the underbrush. The Southeast Convergence for Climate Action brought together activists from across the region and was coordinated by a grassroots network called Rising Tide. I went as part of a facilitation team to run trainings.

We spent our nights listening to panels of retired union coal miners, talking about their thirty-year struggle to protect their families from a reckless and parasitic industry. Their communities were impoverished. Their tap water was so contaminated with heavy metals that it ran orange. That's what happens when you blow tops off entire mountain ranges in order to feed America's fossil fuel addiction. And almost nobody paid attention to their struggle—they were poor after all.

Their families were on the frontline. I considered how when I flip on my light switch, it's like a trigger, blowing up a mountain thousands of miles away. My stomach still hurts when I think about how my convenience comes from the pain of communities like these. I will never have to cry over my child poisoned from resource extraction. But others will. We have a word to describe the act of flipping that light switch: *privilege.*

Burning coal is the single biggest contributor to global warming. We won't be able to solve the climate crisis without breaking its hold.

At that camp, we heard grandmothers tell of their lifetimes of activism. I found myself captivated by stories told by aging antinuclear activists. Wrinkled faces were lit up around a campfire as the shared tales of the historic occupation of the Seabrook nuclear facility, an action that helped shift and inspire a mass movement and resulted in a de facto moratorium on new nuclear power plants.

We all agreed: our generation needed our Seabrook.

Rising Tide had made arrangements for a Navajo activist named Enei Begaye to come from across the country to speak. I drove to pick her up from the airport. On our way back, we rolled across the Virginia hills and spent hours talking about our work. Enei told me about one of the biggest strip-mining companies in the country, Peabody Coal. "Our people have maintained a lifestyle that is in line with Mother Earth and the caretaking of all things, well before 1492." Peabody's operations were devastating Black Mesa in a Native reservation in Arizona. But her community was resisting. She chuckled, "Indigenous communities have been green way before it was hip."

Black Mesa is a sacred mountain. Many families on the reservation do not have running water or electricity. Yet the company steals 3.3 millions of gallons of pristine fresh water to mix it into a coal slurry so it can be shipped to provide power to cities in my state of California. Enei's face hardened.

"The Indian wars are not over. We are still fighting to protect our lands and territories." We talked about colonization most of the way home. I thought more about my light switch.

The next day, Enei sat before a hundred activists and declared,

> We are all connected through the bloodlines of energy. Through the grid lines of power plants. And in realizing our interconnectedness, we need to unlearn the individualism we're taught in this country. We need to relearn the responsibility of community.

She was right. The light-switch flippers are inextricably bound to those who live in places where resources are stolen. I was caught in that web, just like everyone else. But I have dedicated my life to transforming it.

That night, after facilitating back-to-back trainings, a few friends and I sat down to chat about the big picture. The mosquitoes were biting. I had spent the day talking myself hoarse to young activists about the organizing lessons of Ella Baker, an unsung civil rights heroine who helped build the Student Nonviolent Coordinating Committee, a black-led civil rights group helping register Southern black voters in the early 1960s. I had become obsessed with her methods of building mass movements. *Mass,* as I had learned from Ella, meant *millions.* Our task was daunting. I swatted a mosquito and scratched my skin till I bled.

A friend named Matt mentioned an idea that had been on the backburner, something activist Bill McKibben had proposed to him a year earlier—a small civil disobedience at the Capitol coal plant. The idea was inspired by images of civil rights protestors half a century earlier, dressed in suits, prefiguring the world they wanted to see by sitting-in and integrating in the lunch counters.

One key piece of Ella Baker's organizing was moving beyond inspiring a committed core of righteous do-gooders, to a mass-action model. Unlike mass actions some of us had been a part of, we didn't want to mobilize just activists, but also lots of people who had never done activism before. We picked the Capitol Power Plant as our target. We called it a generational act of civil disobedience.

———

BILL MCKIBBEN WAS ENTHUSIASTIC ABOUT THE WAY the idea had evolved. With Bill as a key spokesperson who could connect to large groups of passive allies and light-switch flippers, we proceeded to build a coalition of national groups.

That's where the challenges started.

Three months later, we had about sixty groups endorsing the action. We tried to collaborate with another coalition called Energy Action. I had been on Energy Action's steering committee at the time, but we were mired from the start in coalition challenges. It was time for another conference call. The debate was the same: representative after representative voiced their support for the action. And then one or two people would "block" the proposal. I had a certain ritual for these calls by now. I sat on the floor in the corner of my office so that I could repeatedly bang my head into the wall. I tore my hair out, literally. We were running out of time. I thought about Ella Baker's slow work of building consensus among people with different perspectives. Despite coalition differences, we had gotten more than 120 groups to endorse, and we reached the point where we needed to launch. I emailed Bill. He wrote the call-out letter with poet Wendell Berry. It went public. They opened with this:

> There are moments in a nation's—and a planet's—history when it may be necessary for some to break the law in order to bear witness to an evil, bring it to wider attention, and push for its correction. We think such a time has arrived, and we are writing to say that we hope some of you will join us in Washington, DC, on Monday, March 2 in order to take part in a civil act of civil disobedience outside a coal-fired power plant near Capitol Hill.

And then the floodgates burst.

Dr. James Hansen, the NASA climatologist who first publicly articulated the phenomenon of global warming, endorsed our action and did a public service announcement. So did Susan Sarandon and other celebrities. Former mayor of Salt Lake City Rocky Anderson called to say he wanted to get involved. Soon we had an ever-expanding list of scientists, celebrities, politicians, and other "legitimizers."

The action was viral. Endorsements were flooding in from organizations across the political spectrum. There were calls between rabbis, pastors, and preachers about a faith-based march contingent. Will.I.Am, Goapele, Michael Franti, and other famous musicians endorsed. Racial and economic justice groups, public health organizations, and green businesses wanted to sign up to be part of our action. We trained more than two thousand people in nonviolence. Hundreds of first-time activists were getting trained daily. The action was showing up on Internet message boards, Twitter, Facebook, blogs, and across the web. Guerilla wheat paste, graffiti, and stencils promoting the action began to appear in iconic places across the country. People were registering to participate on our website daily. None of this was magic—it was the result of slow work of dozens of people in our organizing core. Volunteers were phone banking, making hundreds of calls to recruit people. We held teleconference mass meetings where hundreds could call in and get updates. And I got to facilitate them.

There was no turning back now.

The action had become its own organic being. We struggled to keep it all together. The twice-weekly conference calls between convening organizations, various working groups, and action teams were barreling forward. We had lined up interviews with our major spokespeople, and they started to appear in national papers. Capitol Climate Action was a beautiful beast that we were racing to keep up with and shape.

IT WAS A COUPLE WEEKS UNTIL THE BIG DAY. We were in Washington, DC. The slush sloshed. The ice cracked. We could see our breath in the cold. Gales of wind cracked our faces as we emerged from the subway, across the lawn in front of the Capitol building. Five other organizers and I trudged down the tundra that had become downtown Washington, DC. The Capitol dome looked almost majestic as it offered itself to the rays of sun peeking through the clouds. It was short-lived. A haze of emissions pumping out of the smoke-stacks would soon obscure its view. That was the image we wanted plastered on newspapers across the country.

We looped around the coal plant and measured out each entrance. Come the day, we didn't want anyone to get in or out. We needed to clarify how many people were required to block each gate. Which march routes were the most visually compelling, so a camera can see the Capitol building, the marchers, *and* the smokestack. What would be the most fun; marching in circles is simply boring. And what would be tactically effective, so that each team could deploy at each gate while secure with a crowd of people around them.

This was our third time scouting the area. Everything needed to be per-fect. There would be grandmothers and children at the action. All the orga-nizers felt a responsibility on our shoulders to make sure it was a safe and well-coordinated event for all.

By the time we were back at the subway, there was a small huddle of beefy cops. They were there for us. Actually, we had planned a meeting with them. I wasn't our police negotiator. But one approached me, asking, "So you're going to have a few people down here to protest the plant, eh? You don't have a permit."

"Actually, a few thousand are coming."

"You're definitely going to need a permit."

"We're not getting one."

Meanwhile, another organizer was hanging out back at the coal plant. It was the shift change. We had met with the union who supported the work-ers at the plant, to clarify that we had no problems with them. We supported workers. The union was supportive of our action, but we needed to make sure that there wouldn't be a conflict on the day of. So we leafleted during the shift changes. Gone are the days when we'll allow the media to frame our issues as "environment vs. jobs." We wanted a *just transition* to good, sustainable jobs for all.

ONE WEEK LEFT. I WOKE UP TO NELL GREENBERG'S frantic typing. Nell is a communications genius and had been conspiring about the Capitol Climate Action from the beginning. "Joshjoshjosh!" she called to me in a blur of fingers slamming on keys. "You'll never guess what just happened!" Nancy Pelosi had just made a proclamation on Capitol Hill. They were going to phase coal out of the power plant.

We were caught between moments of shock and the compulsion to react as fast as possible. Did we win? What did it mean?

We had been talking to Pelosi for a while, and she had not been pleased with our action. The Capitol plant had been a bit of a black eye for a well-intentioned set of eco-initiatives. She didn't want us to shine a light on the Democratic Congress's inaction.

We called up people like Bill. We called up our frontline allies and consulted with the community group that had been fighting that plant. "How could we march on a plant with a demand that had already been met?" we asked. "Let's turn the action into a victory party in the streets," Bill suggested.

"Pelosi is trying to take the wind out of our sails . . ." Nell interjected. The Capitol plant was indeed switching away from coal . . . to natural gas. We knew that this action was supposed to be a flash point for a larger commentary on coal—it wasn't about this specific plant as much as about an entire industry. And while natural gas is an improvement, climate justice activists across the country were opposing natural gas pipelines and the community devastation they cause. "A victory party would be premature," I finished. By now, Nell and I were completing each other's sentences.

But Pelosi did give us the gift of validation. We put out a press release stating our intention to continue the protest—that this proves the efficacy of grassroots people power—and we're gonna keep pushing. The *New York Times* and a number of other national papers picked up the story. The announcement had put our action into the spotlight. It underscored the careful dance between radical activists and the mainstream—how bold demands create more space for what is "politically possible" in Washington. It proved to those who would disparage civil disobedience that our tactics *work*.

We were rolling.

———————

T MINUS FOUR DAYS.

I navigated a labyrinth of several hundred flags being painted bright green, yellow, blue, and red. We had converted a warehouse space into an art factory. Art is beautiful, but ours was also functional. The different-colored flags were set up to designate different "blocs" in the march. Each set of colors would have a mass of people behind it, deployed at different times down the march route, and occupying a different entrance. It was just one way we were able to direct and organize mass action in a fluid and clear way.

The hum of sewing machines stitching fabric together competed with hip-hop and reggae. Butts were shaking in tune with spray cans shaking. Stencils with POWER, COMMUNITY, CHANGE, and JUSTICE were churned out faster than we could hang them to dry. Young people with circular saws cut hundreds of bamboo shafts, while others strung cloth across them. Banners were painted. POWER PAST COAL placards were stained.

German playwright Bertolt Brecht once said, "Art is not a mirror to reflect reality, it is a hammer with which to shape it." By making all our art ourselves, we were reshaping new clean energy economies.

While we strung together our protest signs, organizers were meeting down the hall to plan out the direction they'd offer participants. At this point, hundreds of people were pulling all-nighters to make the action possible.

Finally, it was the big weekend.

We converted a second warehouse into a Capitol Climate Action convergence space. The broken beams, dusty walls, cracked bricks, and holes in the floor seemed fitting. It hosted more art parties and continuous nonviolence trainings all weekend. The Ruckus Society brought a crew of trainers of color to teach civil disobedience to hundreds of white students. They joked about their role, "We're here to put some chocolate chips on this cookie!" Race was front and center in a lot of conversations about how we would build a new world together. Legions of light-switch flippers were beginning to understand their role in our power lines of relations. I wished to myself that we had the time and space to go deeper with people about movement strategy and making change. I was proud of our nonviolence training factory but nervous that it was too much of a surface introduction. "The real victory for this action," I told a friend, "is whether or not all these people go back home and roll up their sleeves and do community organizing." I decided to say the same thing to kick off our first mass meeting that night.

Nearly four hundred packed into our dusty warehouse. The walls were coated in cracking brick and giant colorful banners. Pressing the megaphone to my lips I shouted, "Who here is from the *Northeast?*" Cheers thundered across the room. "What about the *Southwest?*" "*Yeahhh!*" activists boomed. As I called out each section of the country, the noise was deafening. Everyone was in tha house. Part infosession and part pep rally, that meeting brought a catharsis that reminded me why those endless hours of organizing were worth it. Crews of youth from Oakland taught everyone chants. Mass-action veterans and elders like Lisa Fithian broke down the plan, with giant maps papering the walls. We were organized. Later that night, youth from across the country danced and celebrated the birth of a new era.

THEN IT WAS THE BIG DAY. Energy Action Coalition had a rally in front of the Capitol building, mobilizing some thousands of youth. I was encouraged by their turnout. The so-called apathetic youth didn't exist here that day. When their rally was over, we had teams in place to direct people three blocks away to our convergence spot.

May and Will from *350.org* helped set up the sound system. Like bees buzzing around a hive, friends were setting up the banners and flags. I spotted my childhood hero Dr. Vandana Shiva. Her snuggly embrace made me feel like an old friend. It was our first time meeting in person, though we had spoken many times about us kicking off the rally together. Dr. Shiva's work had inspired me for years. I was giddy.

"Are you ready to start?" I asked.

"Let's do it." She smiled.

The bullhorn was back on my lips. In kicking off the rally, I think I said something cheesy about how the warmth of our bodies and action were going to heat up the cold day. After a few minutes of leading some chants, we suddenly found ourselves surrounded by thousands of people, already moving in unison. Dr. Shiva took the mic.

Vandana talked about the Global Justice Movement confronting the World Trade Organization ten years earlier in Seattle, grounding us in the streams of movement that swirled around us, helping us stand on the shoulders of organizers before us.

Dr. Shiva has a presence that is calm and grounded but loud. She didn't yell into the microphone as much as hummed,

> Your protest, your rally, your action today is definitely the signal to the world that the rule of injustice and the rule of oxymorons is over. We will tell the governments of the world, don't hide behind each other! We will challenge their false solutions, we have the real stuff. And we are gonna build it!

In handing me back the bullhorn, I felt as if she was passing the torch. I was humbled. "Let's go!" I shouted, and we were off.

It was like clockwork. Action teams deployed to each gate, locking them down. I thought about the brave crews of activists who were blockading the back gates, out of the view of the cameras and all the fanfare. Less concerned with the spectacle of it all, they were there to do a job. Many affiliated with Rising Tide, they wanted to lock down the back, to ensure that the Indigenous groups and Appalachians could lead the march and be in the spotlight. Solidarity. A Piikani and Dené Native named Gitz Crazyboy yelled into the bullhorn with an Indigenous contingent. He had come down from northern Canada to talk about how tar sands oil extraction was industrial genocide killing Indigenous communities and their way of life. As he talked about the cancer rates in his community, I looked at the army marching behind him and smiled.

We had a full program. And the clock was ticking—if we didn't surround our sound stage with people quick, the police were going to overwhelm us and tow it away.

I stepped on stage to emcee our main event. The sea of people swallowed the power plant in front of me. Insulated with cheering bodies, we had claimed our space. The cops couldn't move our stage now.

The Internet was streaming with real-time photos of beautiful images of young people blocking gates with banners reading CLOSED: FOR CLIMATE JUSTICE! Red, yellow, green, and blue banners swept around the DC streets like estuaries forming a river of endless faces yelling and singing.

I had to find some way to keep energy up and keep rolling through our tight program that featured hip-hop artists, scientists, politicians, community members, and folk singers. It was a blur. Amid the constant legal updates being barked over our radios, hot chocolate and blankets being distributed to participants, and speakers, we needed to keep people informed of the changing level of risk. Police negotiators were trying to make sure that those who were risking arrest were in the right places and that everyone was safe. I led chants and helped move us through our barrage of speakers. Bobby Kennedy Jr., Eleanor Holmes Norton, Dr. James Hansen, Gus Speth. The list went on. Then Enei took the mic.

"We're not environmentalists! We're here because our people are dying." She was so precise with her analysis the seas of people in front of her were captivated. Without a doubt, the stories from the frontline community members, like Enei, energized the masses of people who sat-in for hours upon hours—all day in the cold. Nobody was getting in or out of that plant.

Then Bill addressed the crowd, "I've waited twenty years to see what the global warming movement was gonna look like, and boy does it look beautiful!" He motioned to the power plant that was now swarmed. "One down, six hundred more to go!"

The day was wearing on. We had reached the end of our speakers list. And we got word from our police negotiator that the cops had no intention of arresting anyone today. And we didn't have any other cards up our sleeves. We had already achieved our goal—the plant was shut down for the day. But we were all worried that it would feel like an anticlimax.

Even in the eleventh hour, even after we won, we were still debating the exit strategy. We could have escalated. "What about scaling the fences?" someone suggested. Anyone trying to enter the actual facility would definitely get arrested. I smiled at the thought of Dr. Hansen climbing over barbed wire. Wasn't gonna happen. And the more radical activists who would be gung ho for such an endeavor would take the spotlight off of the frontline folks and spokespeople.

We needed to end on a high note. I got the go-ahead from the team and stepped onto the stage.

"Well, I've got some good news, and I've got some better news . . . " I joked. Cheers erupted. "The good news is that we shut them down. Operations have stopped. We've won!" When the yelling died down, I continued, "And the better news is that they didn't even need to arrest us for it to happen!" It was my somewhat ungraceful attempt at a reframe. People were too excited to care much. "Let's see a show of hands of who has shut down a coal-fired power plant before today?" One or two people put their hands in the air, a bit confused. "And who is now gonna go home after today and do it *again, and again, and again?*" The thunder had returned.

The crowd marched back up the street, singing. The action was over. Mostly.

A few stragglers were unimpressed. They wanted to stay locked down till the bitter end. "We were promised that there would be arrests. This isn't a real civil disobedience, this was a choreographed photo op." They had a point. We did much more hand-holding with this action than I had ever seen in any other mass mobilization. It was part of the terrain with the goal of engaging so many new folks. I still think we made the right choice in the end.

———————

THE CAPITOL CLIMATE ACTION HOPED TO CHANGE the national conversation on climate. Within a single media cycle, we had positive pieces about a mass climate action in the Associated Press, *Time Magazine,* CNN, *USA Today, New York Times, Democracy Now!,* the *Nation,* and a host of others. The action generated more than seven hundred media stories.

In doing so, we wanted to open a doorway into the movement for lots of new people and legitimize nonviolent direct action as a tactic. The breadth of endorsing organizations is one indicator of success. More than a hundred groups publicly endorsed the action, ranging from public health organizations, religious groups, and clean energy businesses to grassroots environmental networks, labor groups, and racial justice organizations.

I feel proud of how the Capitol Climate Action served to supercharge the anticoal movement in the United States. Just three days after our action, there was another civil disobedience action at Coal River Mountain in West Virginia. Six days later, there was a mass action in Belgium blockading European Union Finance Ministers, with more than 350 arrests, citing our Capital action as a big inspiration for their recruitment. On March 14, there was an action in Knoxville protesting the Tennessee Valley Authority around a recent coal ash sludge spill. The same day, eighty activists inspired by our action marched in Palm Springs, California, as part of the Power Past Coal campaign. Three inspired actions happened that week in Massachusetts. Decentralized

PHOTO BY KIMIA GHOMES

actions targeting coal happened across the continent on April 1. A month later, there was a mass action called the Cliffside Climate Action in North Carolina to stop Duke Energy's proposed coal plant.

And that's just the beginning. Our generation is entering a profound time of transition and crisis. That much is certain. But the future is unwritten. Our work together will determine whether or not there will be justice for people and the planet.

———

Joshua Kahn Russell currently works with the Ruckus Society training a wide variety of groups and networks in nonviolent direct action. The battle against coal in the United States has made some positive headway in recent years with new enforcement by the Environmental Protection Agency. But there is still a long and bumpy road ahead in the battle to end the fossil fuel madness.

CONCLUSION

ONE DAY SOON, WE WILL STAND at the edge of a cliff, toes dangling, as the earth begins to collapse beneath our feet and we look to the depths into which we will fall. We know already we are being pushed to the very limits. In many ways, it's not our fault; we've been pushed here by generations addicted to the idea of *progress*, no matter what the costs, and who trained us as toddlers to swallow its extravagance whole. But now we must take responsibility, responsibility for things that aren't even our fault. Yes, it's unfair. Yes, it's an injustice. But we have two choices now: survival or suicide. It's just that simple.

The time is now to become our own eco-warriors. Not praise the ones out there or fantasize about our own internal eco-warrior. Instead, let's cross the lines, choose our tactics, and dive nose-first into the chaos.

The good news is there is a movement, some would even say a revolution, as the stories in this book testify. It's not a reincarnation of the 1970s environmental movement, but an entirely new movement of its own. It's as diverse in its tactics as it is in its voices. It's as global as global warming is. And it's surging in the so-called apathetic youth of the 21st century. Why? Because it comes down to that very question of survival. It's not the survival of future generations, as we've been told, but our own—and we know it. So we have to fight, fight for our lives.

But we won't be able to do it alone. As much as the stories in this book are of individuals who fought, they are also of groups of individuals who fought the battle with them. The reality is heroes don't win the revolutions. It is ordinary people doing the extraordinary. And it takes all of us to battle for the changes that need to be made. Gandhi himself was not victorious alone but because of the people that stood beside him. Therefore, we cannot go at this alone either. The wheels of change turn because of groups of individuals and because of the masses, not ever because of one—despite what we like to tell ourselves.

Thus, for our movement to be victorious, we must seek past individual pursuits and past our own egos, desiring something greater than ourselves. Only when we sacrifice to be part of a greater collective and for a greater cause can we begin to connect with one another and with this revolution. But bridging ourselves will probably be the biggest test of our time. For we all may have varying issues, missions and tactics—our diversity, after all, is one of our strengths—but we must unify ourselves on some level, otherwise we are weak and divided. In the age of climate change, we have that possibility. But just as we may have an opportunity within our own revolution to unify, we must create the same opportunity outside the revolution. We cannot engage only with the millions who are a part of this movement already; we must engage also with the billions who aren't, bridging ourselves with the many who are unaware the battle we face even exists.

Only then can a truly global movement exist, not just local or national contingents. Only then can autonomous individuals network to be part of a collective with others. Only then can we begin to build a system based on more than selfish *progress*. Only then can the fire of this revolution become a phenomenon. And only then can we keep life, as we know it, alive.

Until then, a few select politicians, a few select elite, a few select individuals on the top of the power pyramid hold a tyranny over us. Let's make no qualms about it, they will slice the wrists of this world open and bury us alive in our own grave for the pursuit of short-term gains. And as we all come dangerously close to the edge, this is our moment, perhaps our last, to fight.

The time is now to become our own eco-warriors. Not praise the ones out there or fantasize about our own internal eco-warrior. Instead, let's cross the lines, choose our tactics, and dive nose-first into the chaos. Coming out finding ourselves nearer to the world we are aching for. For only when we take up the battle is there ever truly a fighting chance for that world.

This is *our* chance.

This is *our* moment.

This is *it*.

—*EMILY HUNTER*

ECO-WARRIOR RESOURCES

For more of *The Next Eco-Warriors*, visit us:

www.NextEcoWarriors.com

If you want to learn more about how you can become an eco-warrior, these websites will teach, connect, and inspire the beginning of your own story.

ACTIVIST NETWORKS

Changents
www.Changents.com

Ecological Internet
www.EcologicalInternet.org

Independent Media Center
www.IndyMedia.org

It's Getting Hot in Here
www.ItsGettingHotinHere.org

Riseup
www.Riseup.net

GROUPS AND MOVEMENTS

350.org
www.350.org

African Youth Initiative on Climate Change
www.ayicc.net

Beyond Pesticides
www.BeyondPesticides.org

The Black Fish
www.TheBlackFish.org

Black Mesa Water Coalition
www.BlackMesaWaterCoalition.org

The BLK ProjeK
www.TheBLKprojeK.wordpress.com

Earth Hour
www.EarthHour.org

Global GreenGrants Fund
www.GreenGrants.org

Green Is the New Red
www.GreenIsTheNewRed.com

Greenpeace International
www.Greenpeace.org

Huon Valley Environment Centre
www.huon.org

Indigenous Environment Network
www.IENearth.org

The Mischief Makers
www.MischiefMakers.org.uk

POWERleap
www.powerleap.net

The Ruckus Society
www.ruckus.org

Save Japan Dolphins
www.SaveJapanDolphins.org

Sea Shepherd Conservation
Society
www.SeaShepherd.org

Sharkwater the Movie
www.Sharkwater.com

The SolarCycle Diaries
www.TheSolarCycleDiaries.com

Surfers for Cetaceans
www.S4Cglobal.org

SurvivaBall
www.SurvivaBall.com

Tasmania's Southern
Forests
www.stillwildstillthreatened.org

We Animals
www.weanimals.org

World Wildlife Fund
www.WWF.org

The Yes Men
www.TheYesMen.org

Zoocheck
www.zoocheck.org

ECO-WARRIORS IN THIS BOOK

Hannah Fraser
www.hannahfraser.com

Emily Hunter
www.emilyhunter.ca

Ben Powless
www.flickr.com/photos/powless

Joshua Khan Russell
http://joshuakahnrussell.wordpress.com

TO OUR READERS

Conari Press, an imprint of Red Wheel/Weiser, publishes books on topics ranging from spirituality, personal growth, and relationships to women's issues, parenting, and social issues. Our mission is to publish quality books that will make a difference in people's lives—how we feel about ourselves and how we relate to one another. We value integrity, compassion, and receptivity, both in the books we publish and in the way we do business.

Our readers are our most important resources, and we value your input, suggestions, and ideas about what you would like to see published. Please feel free to contact us, to request our latest book catalog, or to be added to our mailing list.

Conari Press
An imprint of Red Wheel/Weiser, LLC
500 Third Street, Suite 230
San Francisco, CA 94107
www.redwheelweiser.com